Dress Codes

Dress Codes

Meanings and Messages in American Culture

Ruth P. Rubinstein

Fashion Institute of Technology, SUNY

Westview Press
Boulder • San Francisco • Oxford

Published in 1995 in the United States of America by Westview Press, Inc., 5500 Central Avenue, Boulder, Colorado 80301-2877, and in the United Kingdom by Westview Press, 36 Lonsdale Road, Summertown, Oxford OX2 7EW

Library of Congress Cataloging-in-Publication Data
Rubinstein, Ruth P.
  Dress codes : meanings and messages in American culture / Ruth P. Rubinstein.
    p.   cm.
  Includes bibliographical references (p.   ) and index.
  ISBN 0-8133-2282-0 (hard) — ISBN 0-8133-2283-9 (pbk.)
    1. Costume—United States—Social aspects.   2. Costume—United States—History.   3. Body, Human—Social aspects—United States.
  I. Title.
  GT605.R835   1995
  391'.00973—dc20   94-32808
                                                                                         CIP

Printed and bound in the United States of America

The paper used in this publication meets the requirements of the American National Standard for Permanence of Paper for Printed Library Materials Z39.48-1984.

10   9   8   7   6   5   4   3

To the memory of my parents,
Eliezer Peles and Sara Calderon Peles

Contents

Part 3: Clothing Signs and Social Imperatives

Part 4: Clothing Symbols and Cultural Values

Part 5: Publicspeak

Acknowledgments

Writing this book has been a challenge and a pleasure in part because it depended on the contributions of others. The support I received for my graduate education from the National Institute for Mental Health and the seminars I attended offered by the National Endowment for the Humanities have demonstrated the importance of investing in human capital. Professors Hildegard Peplau of Rutgers, The State University of New Jersey; Jan de Vries of the University of California at Berkeley; and Robert Wohl of the University of California at Los Angeles helped me acquire the theoretical sensitivity needed for the task at hand.

I owe thanks to Professor Robert Perinbenayagam of Hunter College for providing me with a summary of Gregory P. Stone's dissertation and giving me his moral support throughout the many years it took to complete this project. A former Stone student, he intuitively understood the kind of synthesis I sought to achieve.

I am also grateful to my colleagues at the Fashion Institute of Technology (FIT), members of the art history, political science, and economics disciplines. They patiently withstood years of incessant questioning in their particular specialties: Webster Boodey, Robert Cahn, George Dorsch, Larry Homolka, Jackie Lakah, Katherine Michaelsen, Justin O'Connor, Ernest Poole, and Charles Opincar. The staff of the FIT library provided constant support. This book demonstrates that interdisciplinary discourse is beneficial to students and faculty alike.

The grant of a sabbatical leave in fall 1993 made it possible for me to complete this project sooner rather than later. To the FIT administration and the United College Employees of FIT I extend my thanks.

Edith Sancroft, Acting Dean of Liberal Arts, also supported this enterprise. As a professor of dance she contributed to my understanding of the body and its use in social constructs for particular reasons and purposes. In addition, she made it possible for Jerry Gaschen, her assistant, to help me with faxes and other communications. Social Science Chairperson Barry Karp deserves particular thanks for encouraging me to submit my first formal paper (encapsulated in Chapter 2) for presentation at a psychology of fashion conference at New York University. I am grateful to the late Gladys Marcus, Dean of Liberal Arts at FIT, who first suggested that I teach a course on clothing and society at a time when I knew much about society but little about clothing. Students in my classes over the past ten years have had to shift their thinking away from fashion media hype to clarify ideas and make sense of actual observations. We have all gained in the process.

Loretta Lawrence Keane, Patrick D. Hennessey, and Beverly Douglas of the College Relations Division at FIT have also supported my work. By referring reporters and their questions to me they have helped me stay informed of popular interests and current concerns. At Westview Press my thanks go to Gordon Massman, editor of the Cultural Studies Series, who recognized the merit of my manuscript and coordinated the review process; in addition, I wish to thank Jane Raese, the book's production editor, and Beverly LeSuer, copy editor, who contributed immeasurably to the clarity of the text. Finally, personal thanks go to Ann and Karl Rodman of Camp Thoreau, New York.

Ruth P. Rubinstein

Part One:
Introduction

1

Dress in
Societal Discourse

MOST SOCIAL SCIENTISTS take it for granted that an individual's clothing expresses meaning. They accept the old saw that "a picture is worth a thousand words" and generally concede that dress and ornament are elements in a communication system. They recognize that a person's attire can indicate either conformity or resistance to socially defined expectations for behavior. Yet, few scholars have attempted to explain the meaning and relevance of clothing systematically. They often mistake it for *fashion* (a period's desired appearance), whereas *clothing* refers to established patterns of dress. As a result, neither clothing images nor the rules that govern their use have been adequately identified or explicated.

Writing on the changes that occurred in the early part of the nineteenth century in London and Paris, Richard Sennett (1974) pointed out that standardized modes of dress offered a protective "cover-up" at a time when the distinction between private space and public space first emerged. When one lived and worked among strangers rather than family members, there was a need to protect one's self and one's inner feelings. Wearing the expected mode of dress enabled individuals to move easily among the various spheres of social life. "Appearance was a cover for the real individual hiding within," observed Sennett. Clothing, as Sennett saw it, provided a buffer between the public and the private self.[1]

For the American economist and social critic Thorstein Veblen ([1899] 1953), the desire to cover up a lower social origin underlay consumption patterns in the United States. He claimed that in American society there was a general tendency to buy more expensive clothing than one should. This practice applied, as well, to groups and institutions, which buy expensive products in an attempt "to cover up the ignoble, selfish motives, and goals."[2]

In his article "Fashion," Georg Simmel ([1904] 1957) observed that fashion, the latest desired appearance, allows for personal modification, enabling the individual to pursue competing desires for group identity and individual expression. There is no institution, "no law, no estate of life which can uniformly satisfy the opposing principles of uniformity and individuality better than fashion."[3] The self is also an audience, and clothing allows individuals to view themselves as social objects. By extricating the self from a setting or situation, the individual can scrutinize the image he or she presents in view of the social response that is desired. This separation and objectification, in turn, allows the individual to correct the image if necessary.[4]

In contrast to the social scientist, fiction writers typically imbue a specific image of clothing with meaning. Nineteenth-century novelists, such as Balzac, Flaubert, Proust, Dickens, and Trollope, wrote detailed descriptions of what their characters wore. For example, when Flaubert described Madame Bovary's initial appearance in the kitchen of her father's small farm, he wrote that she was wearing a blue merino wool dress with three flounces. The clothing carried the message that she was fun-loving, frivolous, fashion-conscious, and out of place. Playwrights also describe garments as a means of delineating a character. Today, no newspaper reporter would write a profile of someone without describing the person's style of dress. The implication is that a person's clothing somehow reflects his or her character.

Fashion historians usually discuss clothing in terms of style and the aesthetic tastes of a particular period or a particular group in society.[5] However, they pay little attention to clothing iconography. Examining fascist propaganda, Laura Malvano in *Fascismo e politica dell'immagine* (1988) demonstrated the relationship between politics and patterns of dress, style, and appearance. She analyzed the ways in which Mussolini successfully utilized visual images to encourage consensus among his followers, creating a "new organic whole" composed of people from all levels of society. To promote this ideal he commissioned artistic representations that combined images from the classical art of the past with those from traditional folk art. In that art, men assume the various postures of victory portrayed in ancient Roman times yet they hold familiar farm implements and are thus seen as agricultural victors. Through this appeal to a pride in a shared past, made visible in synthetic images, Mussolini gained support for his political program.[6]

Adolescents and young adults have long recognized the significance of clothing. To signal connectedness and to distinguish themselves from others, groups of young people adopt styles of dress that express their particular, distinct identity. In making clothing choices they demonstrate their awareness that a style or mode of appearance has meaning.[7]

The Notion of Public Memory

Visual images from the past and present form what French sociologist Maurice Halbwachs called public memory. They are a part of core culture, like time and space, and give shape to a child's orientation to social realities. Ideas, beliefs, and values—the basic constructs of collective life—are embodied in images. They contain the central system of rules of behavior and thought that controls much of what we do. The growing child is bombarded by these images and their shared public meaning. As Halbwachs explained, learning begins early in life and in a most informal way, but full understanding requires both biological maturity and social experience.[8]

Public memory includes depictions of people in carvings, sculpture, paintings, mosaics, stained glass windows, prints, and drawings in books. These im-

Public memory. Through the portrayal of royalty in fairy tales children are introduced to basic ideas of social class and power. (Illustration by Françoise, in Margaret E. Martignoni, ed. [1955] The Illustrated Treasury of Children's Literature *[New York: Grosset & Dunlap].)*

ages are concrete, tangible representations of "currents of collective thought" from the various historical periods. The clothing in these visual portrayals has been so closely associated with ideas that the clothing itself is seen as embodying them.[9]

Prior to the nineteenth century, the majority of the people represented in Western European art were therefore figures of political power, religious authority, or both. Their dependents—wives, mistresses, children, or servants—also sometimes appeared. As might be expected, their clothing and accessories came to be seen as a physical manifestation of the ideas, the institutions, and the power they held or controlled. The clothing worn by individuals in authority in a given society at a given time has provided visual information about their position and power.

Because many of these works of art have survived, they now form a part of the cumulative public memory. For example, the crowning of a new monarch often set off a round of new paintings depicting the new court. These visual images would be added to those of the previous monarchy. In some cases new rulers continued and elaborated on past traditions. In other instances the new leaders attempted to distinguish themselves by espousing new ideas and values, which led to new styles of painting and dress. However, these would not wholly replace the old and would eventually be added to the existing body of images of royalty. The result has been an expanding vocabulary of visual images. A group searching for a visual image to embody its ideas might create a new synthesis from among the elements represented in the storehouse of images. This novel synthe-

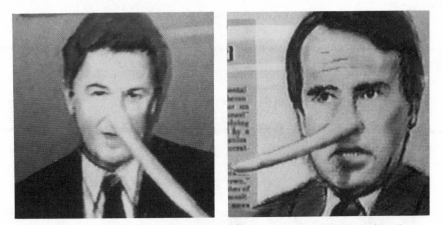

Public memory. Contemporary use of a nineteenth-century image from Pinocchio: *Jim Florio and Jim Courter portray each other as lying in the New Jersey gubernatorial race.* (New York Times, *October 16, 1989; reprinted by permission of NYT Pictures.*)

sis or pattern of appearance would, in turn, be added to the existing repository. In each instance the clothing, the accessories, and the style would be seen as embodying the ideas represented by those images.

Giacomo Balla's "Futurist Manifesto of Men's Clothing 1913," a proclamation that argued for a totally new approach to dress, attests to the powerful persistence in Western society of this storehouse of images and meanings. Leaders of the avant-garde Futurist movement sought to reject the images existing in public memory: the "pretty-pretty," "tight-fitting," "decadent," "unhygienic," "symmetrical," and "boring," the "gloomy" and "humiliating hypocritical custom of wearing mourning" (i.e., the black three-piece suit celebrated by Thomas Carlyle). The Futurists called for abolishing "sadness in dress" as well as "timidity," "harmony," and "good taste." In a world transformed by science and technology, observed Balla, "we must invent Futurist clothes, clothes that are happy and practical" and "spread good humour." Items of dress must have strong colors and dynamic designs, "triangles, cones, spirals, and circles," and come in a variety of styles to complement each mood. The cut must incorporate dynamic and asymmetrical lines. Above all, clothes must be made to last for only a short time to encourage industrial activity and "to provide constant and novel enjoyment for our bodies." The "consequent merry dazzle" produced by the clothes in the noisy streets "will mean that everything will sparkle like a glorious prism." With their noisy cries of rebellion the Futurists demonstrated a tacit awareness of the necessary connections between appearance, the self, and society.[10]

Clothing Semiotics

The first step toward a systematic understanding of clothing images and meanings in American society is to define the basic constructs of the communication discourse system. This step entails identifying the language and vocabulary of the images that give shape to contemporary discourse. All systems of communication consist of language and speech, with language providing a basic vocabulary and accepted rules of usage. It offers a structural framework within which an individual speaker can operate. As defined by Ferdinand de Saussure, language is a system of signs and symbols that exists prior to and outside its use by a given individual.[11]

When applied to clothing, the term "language" refers to the use of a particular vocabulary derived from the storehouse of images that support the structure of social interaction, the system of statuses and roles. Like words, clothing images become significant only when they are used in a specific social context. Images may function as signs that convey a single, relatively clear-cut meaning or as symbols that have multiple meanings and connotations or associations. Images are signifiers that carry meaning and value.[12] Seen from this perspective, the language of clothing can be analyzed, as sociologists Erving Goffman (1951) and Gregory P. Stone (1959, 1962) have suggested, in terms of signs and symbols.

Since our contemporary clothing vocabulary has been culled from the storehouse of images in Western history and supplemented by the "American experience," definition of the parameters of the language of clothing requires a study of the historical record (that is, the types of images, their origins, their purposes, and their permutations over time).

Style of Dress

Style of dress has significance beyond that of conveying information. The early-twentieth-century psychologist J. C. Flugel suggested that styles of dress and elements of appearance act to summon distinct feelings that enhance role performance. One's sense of importance is increased when "different parts of the whole, body and clothes, fuse into a unity." This style "expands the proper self." Flugel called this visual image *confluence* (see Figure 1.1).[13] A visual image in which a person's appearance is augmented by elements that extend the body's reach (for example, a guard carrying arms) increases the person's physical ability to control the environment. "The consciousness of our personal existence is prolonged" and the sense of power is enhanced when a walking stick is used or tools are carried.[14] Conversely, clothing that is too big, too tight-fitting, or too small, or that "refuses to become a part of an organic whole with the body," can "dwarf the body" and imbue the person with a sense of insignificance. Flugel called this image *contrast*.[15]

Clothing Signs

Attire that constitutes a clothing sign is characterized by (1) being task-oriented or instrumental; (2) having one primary meaning; and (3) being generally recognized as a sign by those who wear it. In many instances, formal code, promul-

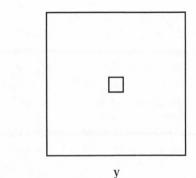

W = *The size of the person*

X = *Confluence: The mind fails to distinguish between the body and the clothes, "expanding the proper self."*

Y = *Contrast: Clothes that are too big or too small make the person seem smaller, imbuing the person with a sense of insignificance.*

FIGURE 1.1
Effects of "Contrast" and "Confluence"
Source: *J. C. Flugel (1966)* The Psychology of Clothes, *figure 4 (London: Hogarth Press. Originally published in 1930.)*

gated by those in authority, mandates the wearing of specific elements of dress in a particular pattern to signify social position and its distinct rights and responsibilities (for example, military or fire department uniforms). Those wearing such clothing arouse a set of expectations for behavior in both themselves and the audience.

Clothing signs make visible the structure and organization of interactions within a specific social context, as Carlyle pointed out with respect to the English justice system: "You see two individuals, one dressed in fine Red and the other in threadbare Blue; Red says to Blue: Be hanged and anatomized." The man dressed in red has the power to order the death of the other, a right signified by the red judicial robes. Such "visible emblems" are points of reference that give members of a society their bearing.[16]

Exercising authority, wielding power, differentiating the sexes, and arousing sexual interest are all facilitated by the employment of categories of clothing signs. Carlyle's example of a British judge wearing red judicial robes and the prisoner wearing threadbare blue portrays the category of clothing that conveys authority. A judge, moreover, is supported by men carrying implements capable of inflicting harm; they manifest the category of clothing that conveys the image of power.

Contemporary example of confluence. (1993 J. Press brochure.)

scaled up or
downsized,
jackets and
pants acquire a
new sense of
proportion

too big/
too small

Jumbo jeans and a shirt
balance the tiniest dou-
ble-breasted jacket.
Pants by Tag Rag, $60.
Jacket by Plein Sud by
Fayçal Amor, $699.
Shirt by Brooks Broth-
ers, $70. Sneakers by
Converse All Star, $35.
Hat by Whittall & Shon,
$120. Shady Character,
NYC suspenders.
Hair, these four pages,
by Serge Normant for
Oribe at Elizabeth Ar-
den; makeup by Bobbi
Brown for Frederic
Fekkai at Bergdorf
Goodman. For details,
stores, see SHOP.

205

Contemporary example of contrast. (Mademoiselle, *April 1993.)*

The social distinction between male and female is facilitated by another category of clothing sign—clothing that differentiates the sexes. Sex differences, as Stone (1962) noted, are forcefully regulated by the personal evaluation, social judgments, and expectations governing "appropriate" dress.[17] Male-female dress distinction is signified by the shapes, colors, and fabrics of clothing and by the two basic forms—skirts and pants. As M. Gottdiener (1977) observed, women in American society have been given a weaker social position than men, and the mere act of wearing women's clothes situates the person in a subordinate role, validating male dominance.[18]

The final category of clothing sign is seductive attire. Flugel observed that to feel sensual and to show an inclination toward sexual intercourse requires something more than sex-specific attire. The décolletage, for example, which was first worn toward the end of the Middle Ages, was expected to arouse sexual desire. The church fathers described seductive attire as that characterized by an interplay between covering the body and exposing it, achieved through the use of "transparencies and half concealments," color, and ornament.[19]

Clothing Symbols

In "Symbols of Class Status" (1951), Goffman observed that unlike clothing signs, which identify positions within a social institution and are governed by rules and regulations, few rules apply to the wearing of clothing symbols. The latter are items of dress that reflect the achievement of certain cultural values.[20] Wearing such attire does not indicate group membership. It is not required dress, and it does not arouse in the wearer or the audience expectations for role behavior. Goffman gave the example of the wearing of clothing associated with high socioeconomic class. The decision to wear such clothing is personal. It is worn in the hope of acquiring social prestige.

According to Thorstein Veblen, attire that reflects the achievement of cultural values, what the society considers good and desirable, enhances one's sense of social significance.[21] He called the elements of dress, ornament, and appearance that demonstrate such achievement status symbols.[22] Veblen used the style of dress worn by the European aristocracy to illustrate that freedom from physical labor, or leisure, reflected a basic cultural value. Members of the aristocracy wore clothing made of expensive fabrics fashioned in the latest style, thus indicating that they could not possibly toil in a field. Wearing this attire demonstrated not only wealth but also social superiority and entitlement.[23]

Through the centuries visual images have emerged as a way of proclaiming specific cultural values. The desirability of wealth, beauty, aesthetic awareness, freedom from physical labor, youthfulness, and health is conveyed in images embedded in public memory. Since clothing symbols reflect ideas about what is valued in a society at a particular time, their meaning is to some extent open to individual interpretation. Unlike clothing signs, the wearing of clothing symbols implies nothing about the individual's rights and obligations, nor is it a reliable predictor of behavior. Symbols may have more than one meaning, and values may have more than one manifestation. An accurate interpretation of a person's choice of a symbol—that is, a style, a color, or an ornament—requires an intimate understanding of the person and his or her history.

Individual Speech

Clothing "speech" can be defined as an individual's manipulation of the language of clothing to produce specific utterances characterized by personal intonation and style. A person's clothing speech reflects intrapsychic dynamics with few implications for society. It is analogous to talking to oneself. Consciously or unconsciously, an individual may choose clothing with a particular meaning. The choice might express a personal vision, mirror an emotional state, be idiosyncratic, or be important to the individual; yet it has no real social significance. As Stone (1962) noted, clothing speech reflects an individual's interpretation of a situation, attitude, and mood. Some people dress in dark-colored clothes when they are depressed. Others may purposely choose bright and cheerful colors to counteract feelings of depression. The choice and meaning are specific to the individual.[24]

Just as vocabulary choices often reflect a person's cultural background and upbringing, clothing speech reflects the individual's resources and the extent of his or her exposure to the elements of the language of clothing. The color red, for example, may be chosen by an individual because it is easy to see, or because a favorite aunt was known to prefer it, rather than for its association with passion. Analysis of clothing speech may be useful to persons concerned with an individual's psychic or intrapersonal dynamics.

Publicspeak

When a large number of individuals choose a style or element of dress that lies outside the established vocabulary of images, the choice is no longer individual speech but "publicspeak." Publicspeak reflects the sentiments of similar and dissimilar individuals and aggregates.[25]

Such dress may serve as a public announcement that the group has declined to accept the ideas or values of mainstream culture; their clothes indicate heresy. Moreover, such clothing may convey a message about a particular social condition, or a political or economic event. As such, the styles are a form of societal discourse.

Clothing *tie-signs*, clothing *tie-symbols*, and *contemporary fashion* are three categories of dress that reflect collective responses to the structure of interaction, events, or the inner necessities that animate social life. Because of the right to free speech and the tradition of individualism, the public memory may be searched for newly appropriate visual expression. In bypassing the established vocabulary and existing definitions, new associations are formed and new categories of behavior may be legitimated. Leather jackets, an element of dress worn by soldiers in the ancient past, for example, had suffered many centuries of neglect before being resurrected by the movies of the 1940s and the 1950s to signify toughness and gang membership. Again today, American youth have come to consider leather jackets a very desirable element of dress (except among animal rights activists).

Each category of appearance has its own set of authors, its own intended audience, and the capacity to equip the wearer to feel, think, and act in a different way.

Clothing Tie-Signs

Tie-signs refer to the attire of social subsets, such as Hare Krishnas or the Amish, that reject the Establishment's ideas, beliefs, and values in certain areas. Mem-

Clothing tie-sign. Guardian Angels, an organization founded in 1979 in New York City by Curtis Sliwa (center). A voluntary group with no formal authority, the members patrol city streets and trains. Their uniform consists of a red beret, a T-shirt with "Guardian Angels" insignia, and a red jacket. The insignia "I support the Guardian Angels" identifies those in training. (Reprinted by permission.)

bers of these groups develop a world of meaning separate from institutional so-cial arrangements. Their clothing ensembles are carefully conceived to set their behaviors apart from others and to reflect the group's distinct ideas, beliefs, and values.[26] The wearing of group-designated attire is required, distinguishing members from nonmembers. It conveys a single meaning while communicating norms of behavior, rights, and obligations.

Clothing Tie-Symbols

Just as there are clothing tie-signs, there are also clothing tie-symbols, elements of dress and styles of appearance that reflect an individual's fears, hopes, dreams, or desires. People wear tie-symbols to inform themselves and others of their rejection or support for political ideas or social agendas. For example, Spike Lee's black baseball cap with the mark "X" reflects his admiration for Malcolm X. T-shirts with political messages, such as "Save the Earth," are other examples of tie-symbols.[27] Madonna used her offscreen "cheeky" style in the

*Clothing tie-symbols. Ethnic associations in the 1988 U.S. presidential election: Bush's An-glo-style cowboy hat (left) versus the Mexican-style worn by Dukakis (right). (*New York Times Magazine, *October 30, 1988. Photo of Bush by Cynthia Johnson; photo of Dukakis © David Burnett.)*

film *Desperately Seeking Susan* (1985), and the yards of chain that she wore around her neck, the perfectly precise makeup, and the lacy lingerie became popular among many young American teenagers.

The wearing of tie-symbols is governed by personal choice. The meaning of the attire and the reason why someone elects to wear it are specific to the person. Some wear the attire because it reflects their beliefs. Others wear it to claim an association in order to obtain "social gains." Still others may appropriate such symbols because they like the look or the color. Hence, the meaning of a tie-symbol is often ambiguous.

Tie-symbols are similar to clothing symbols in that they imply little about the particular individual's rights and obligations; and like clothing symbols they are not reliable indicators of behavior. Nevertheless, tie-symbols are important be-cause they are an expression of grass-roots sentiments and are often the first step in the organization of a social movement and social change.

Contemporary Fashion

In his "shifting erogenous zones" theory of fashion, Flugel ([1930] 1966) observed that the purpose of fashion is to create sexual interest and that the phenomenon of fashion entails the shifting of focus from one part of the female anatomy to another.[28] Observing the fashion process in the 1960s, Herbert Blumer (1968, 1969) argued that a style becomes a fashion through the process of collective se-lection. As Blumer explained, a designer offers a large number of styles on the runway, but only a few of these, those emotionally most relevant, are chosen by buyers, magazine editors, and boutique owners to be offered to their clients.

When consumers reorder their choices, those styles become the fashion. Consumer relevance, not the designers, turns a style into a fashion.[29] Unlike clothing signs and clothing symbols, which tend to be somewhat stationary, fashion reflects the sociocultural dynamics of the moment at a more frenzied pace.

ﺒ   ﺒ   ﺒ

To conclude, in American society clothing is significant primarily in terms of the visual image it conveys. The contemporary vocabulary of clothing is based on the images found in the "repository" that has developed through the centuries in Western society, the public memory. These images are the primary constructs of social organization and interaction. They direct and inform social behavior. To quote Carlyle, "For neither in tailoring nor in legislating does man proceed by mere Accident, but the hand is ever guided by mysterious operations of the mind."[30]

Nineteenth-Century Theories of Clothing

PRIOR TO THE NINETEENTH CENTURY, learned discussions of clothing behavior focused on persons who dressed in fashionable attire that exceeded their social rank. Critics claimed that wearing the clothing of "one's betters" was an immoral act that would lead to dire consequences for the person, the economy, and even society.[1] In the nineteenth century, however, the discourse on clothing acquired a new dimension. The belief that all phenomena should be systematically examined encouraged scholars to ask questions about the very nature and significance of clothing. Such scholars as Thorstein Veblen ([1899] 1953) and Georg Simmel ([1904] 1957) distinguished fashion from everyday attire and focused on the socioeconomic advantage that accrued to individuals who wore fashionable attire.[2]

At the same time, a general interest in the origins of things led to scholarly discussions about the origin of clothing. Christian thinkers insisted that the interaction between Adam and Eve in the Garden of Eden made clothing basic to human nature. Medical scientists attributed the origin of clothing to the need to protect the biological integrity of the body and the need to survive in treacherous physical environments. Other scholars observed that although there are many societies in which the people are unclothed, there are no societies in which the people are unadorned; hence, the origin of clothing may lie in adornment.

Three theories regarding the origin of clothing emerged: the modesty theory, the protection theory, and the adornment theory. These theories and their critical reevaluation provide a context for a modern explication of the language of clothing.

The Modesty Theory

English costume historian James Laver pointed out that "until quite recently—less than a hundred years ago perhaps—it was almost universally agreed that the primal and fundamental reason for wearing clothes was modesty. ... For those who accepted the literal truth of the Genesis story, there was no question about it." Adam and Eve, having eaten of the fruit of the Tree of Knowledge, "knew that they were naked" and made themselves "aprons of leaves."[3]

Saint Augustine (A.D. 354–430) was the clearest of the early church fathers on the subject of covering the body. He explained that prior to the Fall, nakedness

The biblical origin of clothing. Adam and Eve cover their genitals in shame, having sinned in the Garden of Eden. Detail from the Sarcophagus of Junius Bassus, *ca. A.D. 355, Vatican Museums. (Photo courtesy of Alinari-Scala/Art Resource, New York.)*

was the natural state and neither sexual organs nor bodily functions were shameful. When Adam and Eve disobeyed God in the Garden of Eden, man became unable to control his lust, and lust became independent of man's will. All mankind became afflicted with the insubordination of the flesh.[4]

The injunction to cover the body initially applied to men only, according to Augustine, because only in men is sexual arousal obvious. Soon, however, women also had to cover their bodies. Their ability to seduce, church fathers argued, would lead men to stray from the spiritual.[5]

Suggesting that every society develops its own ideas of what is appropriate and that these ideas are associated with social identity and expected behavior, James Laver observed that modesty is a learned behavior and not instinctual, as the church fathers had claimed. Missionaries and other observers of "primitive" or nonliterate societies have told of people who walk around naked and seem to feel no shame, guilt, or any other ill effects. Australian aborigines, for example, are indifferent to their nakedness but are deeply embarrassed if seen eating. An Arab peasant woman caught in the fields without her veil will throw her skirt over her head, thereby exposing what to the Western mind "is a much more embarrassing part of her anatomy."[6]

In the desert and away from camp, Bushmen prefer to sleep in the warmth of the daytime sun. At night, they huddle close to the fire. (Photo courtesy of Constance Stuart.)

Moreover, Laver observed that the term "modesty" applies differently to each gender. Women's clothing is expected to cover the body to "dampen sexual allure," and women offend modesty by wearing sexually alluring attire. Conforming to the expectation of modesty entails concealing the body and denying sexual allure, encouraging sexual inhibition. Expectations for male appearance and behavior dictate that men must restrain the self. They must dress in a manner that fosters conformity with the public definition of maleness. Men offend modesty by "swagger," an attempt at self-aggrandizement.[7]

Christian thinkers and their injunction to modesty instituted two images and their associated meanings in Western society. The first image denies the body and is nonseductive. It signifies a social self directed toward obedience to church authority. The second, a style of dress that exposes the body or alludes to the body underneath, is seductive. (See Chapter 8.)

The Protection Theory

The need to keep warm in the bone-chilling dampness of Europe, as well as reports of expeditions that perished from exposure in the vast reaches of Canada and Antarctica, gave weight to the commonsense view that the origin of clothing lay in the need to maintain the physiological integrity of the body. Yet, observations by Charles Darwin and other travelers to "primitive" societies described people who walked around naked in harsh environments in which strong gales, heavy rains, and powerful winds were common.[8] In a report on the Yahgans of Tierra del Fuego (at the tip of South America), for example, Darwin noted that in inclement weather the Yahgans went about wearing nothing. At night they slept naked on the wet ground "coiled up like animals." When Darwin and some of his crew went ashore, they had to huddle around a fire and wrap themselves in blankets to keep warm. In contrast, a family of Fuegians, all naked, were some distance from the fire and yet perspiration streamed down their bodies.[9] Similarly, B. Spencer and F. J. Gillen described the ability of Australian aborigines to walk about without any body covering despite sharp changes in temperature.[10]

Medical researchers could not find any special biological differences between Europeans and Australian aborigines when they attempted to discover the secret of how to survive sharp changes in temperature without shelter or clothing. Their findings merely verified the observation. They thus concluded that people who lived on the continent of Europe in the remote past were probably just as able to endure the cold as the indigenous peoples of Australia and Tierra del Fuego. They observed that the skin—when accustomed to exposure—provides efficient protection for body organs. When covered, however, it loses this ability. In other words, the unintended consequence of wearing clothes is dependence on them; once worn, clothing becomes a necessity. The origin of clothing, the researchers concluded, could not lie in the need to protect the body because the wearing of clothing decreased the body's ability to protect itself.[11]

These scientists also described the elaborate mechanism through which the body attempts to keep the brain, heart, lungs, and abdominal cavity at a constant temperature (37°C, or 98°F) despite fluctuations in the surrounding environment. This mechanism calls for the production of heat by the body at the same rate that it is being lost. Such a balance can be achieved by consuming enough food and engaging in sufficient physical activity to produce the required amount of heat. Another means of preventing heat loss is to use clothing as a barrier.[12] Their discussion concludes with the suggestion that a study of clothing developed by various societies to protect the body against severe climatic conditions may be informative with regard to the impact of clothing on survival.

Although individuals in small groups can survive in a harsh environment, effective clothing makes social life possible and enhances the comfort and quality of life. The Athabascan Indians who live in the frigid Arctic environment of Alaska and northern Canada, for example, have neither housing nor weatherproof clothing. They sleep coiled in front of a fire, keeping only half of the body warm. When awake they are restless and in constant motion trying to keep warm. They seem to be irritable and unable to welcome guests. In contrast, the Eskimo who live in the same large region share a culture that better enables them to cope with their treacherous environment. Moreover, they lead an active social life. The clothing of Eskimo throughout the region is tailored in the same style, they travel by dogsled and kayak, and they heat and cook with shallow open lamps of stone or pottery, in which they burn animal fat. The harpoon is the universal weapon. The myths and legends told in snow huts by central Eskimo are also told by the Eskimo of both the Pacific and Atlantic coasts. Their religious practices are similar, and when rites vary they do so only in detail. The Eskimo religion is predominantly made up of a number of taboos, mainly con-

Eskimo building their winter home. (Reprinted by permission of UPI/Bettmann Newsphotos.)

cerning food and clothing supply. In order to have the raw materials necessary for survival, the unseen spirits of the invisible world must be properly appeased.

The Eskimo go almost completely naked inside their heated winter homes. So effective is the insulation of their housing that outside temperatures can drop to as low as 80° below zero, while inside their homes their bodies exist at a comfortable 80–90°F. Inside the domed snow house in winter and inside tents made of skins during the summer, the Eskimo sit half naked, wearing only knee breeches that extend from the waist to the knees.[13]

Outdoor clothing for men and women consists of two layers of caribou furs. The fur closest to the body is worn facing the skin, trapping beneath it a layer of air and body heat. The outdoor attire encases the body but allows freedom of movement. The looseness of the cut enables the Eskimo, when standing still in the extreme cold, to pull their arms from their sleeves and place them close to the body. When they become warm from working, or when the outside temperature rises, the belt can be loosened, mittens taken off, hood thrown back, and top shirt removed.[14]

Similarly, for people who live in areas with frequent extreme temperature changes—for example, where days are hot and nights are cold—appropriate clothing makes it possible to engage in commercial enterprise. The Rewala Bedouins, cattle-breeding nomadic people who live in the Syrian and Arabian deserts, have to deal with 50° temperature changes between day and night as well as the exigencies of a nomadic and warlike existence. The attire they have adopted is composed of long, loose-fitting layers that can be added or subtracted as the need arises: to combat a sandstorm or a dramatic temperature change, to allow freedom of movement to climb onto a camel or to jump up quickly to defend themselves.[15]

In ancient civilizations such as Egypt and India, and in many parts of the world today, physical labor was and is performed by individuals who are almost naked. Minimal covering allows heat to evaporate more quickly, making work less taxing and physically more tolerable. It also gives the body access to cool breezes when they arise. The white or light-colored clothing typical of countries close to the Equator reflects the rays of the sun, providing protection against solar radiation.[16]

Wandering about almost naked, wearing only a brief layer of leaves or bark, the inhabitants of the rain forests of Africa have survived in a hot and humid climate. Because their body covering is minimal and does not retain water, it does not become cumbersome or inhibit movement. It enables evaporation, the chief means of protecting against overheating, and it is, of course, easily replaced.[17]

Thus, whereas clothing may not always be essential for physical survival, appropriate dress does enhance the sharing of ideas and the development of group life. In this sense clothing may improve the chances of survival.

The Adornment Theory

In the introduction to *Sartor Resartus* ([1838] 1967), Thomas Carlyle complained that "considering our present advanced state of culture and how the Torch of Science has now been brandished about, with more or less effect for five-thousand years and upwards ... it might strike the reflective mind with some surprise that hitherto little or nothing of a fundamental character ... has been written on the subject of clothes."[18] Carlyle proposed that the origin of clothing lies in an adornment hypothesis that derives from the evolutionary theory of change, which was prevalent in the nineteenth century. Scientists asserted that there were fixed stages of development through which all societies must pass. Each stage was preceded by one that was simpler. The theory suggested that since Western society in the nineteenth century represented the highest stage yet in the evolutionary sequence, nonliterate societies were "lawless" ones in which individuals were free to act as they wished. (Research in the twentieth century has, of course, found this theory wanting.)

"Among wild people we find tattooing and painting even prior to clothes" and the purpose of clothing "was not warmth or decency but ornament," Carlyle proclaimed. In such societies, a person's appearance was determined by individual, idiosyncratic behavior based on whim. Among the "barbarians," Carlyle explained, once the pangs of hunger were satisfied, the next need was for ornament. The desire for adornment emanated from "a man's spiritual realm."[19]

Ethnographic reports, however, have revealed that, for the most part, people in nonliterate societies even today modify and ornament their bodies for two major purposes. The first is to make it easier to organize and maintain group life, and the second is to help them cope with a sinister supernatural world.[20]

The appearance of this Indian, a chief from Brazil's Xingu National Park, indicates group membership and social responsibility. (Reprinted by permission of Reuters/Bettmann.)

Members of nonliterate societies find the practice of modifying the body in characteristic patterns necessary for creating their distinct social entity. To separate group members from nonmembers, the Batonga in Africa scar their bodies, the Ibo scar their faces and cut traditional geometric patterns in their hair, and the Mentawei Islanders in Sumatra file their teeth. For the same purpose the Tchikirin Indians of South America pierce the earlobes of boys and girls and insert cigar-shaped plugs of reddened wood into the holes. The plugs are replaced from time to time with larger ones until the holes in the lobes become very large. To place a boy into his gender category, they insert a string of beads into his lower lip at birth.[21]

Among the Nuba, a people who live in southern Sudan, the distinction between the sexes is emphasized as a child approaches puberty. Body adornment focuses on the different responsibilities that adult men and women have.[22] As soon as a girl's breasts begin to develop, the first of a series of scarifications takes place. At this stage cuts are made at each side of the abdomen; they join at the navel and continue to a point between the breasts. Further incisions are made at the onset of menstruation. Nuba men, in contrast, turn their bodies into a canvas. The young man and the artist who will execute the painting decide together on the individual design that will most complement the wearer. Only those with firm, youthful bodies will present themselves in this way. Men of any age who are sick, injured, or incapacitated cover their bodies with clothing.[23]

The Suya, a Ge-speaking people who live in South America, use lip and ear ornaments to emphasize that hearing and speaking are sex-specific. At the first sign of sexual activity the ears of the adolescents of both sexes are pierced. The ear disks are white, a color the group associates with passivity and coolness. In their late teens, when young men begin to be considered as adults, the lower lip is also pierced. The lip disk is red, a color associated with belligerence and masculine self-assertion. Women wear an ear disk but not a lip disk. They are expected to be the audience and supply the food during ceremonies when the men are busy singing. Thus, among some people, adornment places the individual in a gender category.[24]

Adornment also supports desired role behavior. The Kayapo insist that at puberty young men wear a penis sheath to encourage sexual restraint.[25] A vulva closed with scar tissue is considered beautiful among many groups from southern India to northern Africa. To be so ornamented, the women undergo a clitoridectomy, a surgical procedure in which part of the labia majora, the labia minora, and the clitoris are excised and the vulva is completely closed except for a small orifice kept open by a match or a reed tube.[26]

Among many groups in Africa, Melanesia, and Indonesia, new erogenous zones are created to make women more desirous of sex. After menstruation begins, or when plans for marriage have been confirmed, a young woman's abdomen may be scarified or tattooed. The Tiv in Africa, for example, incise a shape called "catfish" on a woman's belly. In the language of the Tiv, this word is similar to the expression used to describe lust. The Tiv report that the scars remain ten-

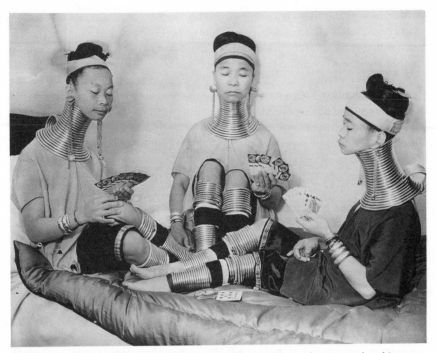

The chokers worn by the Chin women of Burma consist of rings of rattan enclosed in beaten brass. The rings are stacked up from early childhood. They are said to signify wealth as well as submission to men. (Reprinted by permission of The Bettmann Archive.)

der for some years, thus heightening sexual arousal. They believe that the scars make the women more desirous of sex and therefore more likely to bear children.[27]

To succeed in an economic exchange the Trobrianders believe one should be attractive to the trading partner. The Trobrianders will not attempt a transaction, Bronislaw Malinowski (1948) reported, until they have perfumed themselves and rubbed their bodies with coconut oil, medicated leaves, and paint. When going to a faraway island, they will not get on the boat without their cosmetic kits. They adorn themselves again before disembarking, for they believe that their use of cosmetics will soften the hearts of their trading partners and lead to a more valuable exchange.[28]

The Hageners, too, share an elaborate network of exchange relationships with neighboring groups to achieve socioeconomic goals. These relationships are marked by ceremonial get-togethers for which the men decorate themselves lavishly with feathers, shells, and animal ornaments.[29]

Some hunting peoples decorate their bodies to resemble the animal they are after. This decoration provides camouflage and thus enables them to be more successful in the hunt. When stalking game the Australian aborigines evade detection by coloring their bodies with red ocher and earth or clay; when stalking kangaroos, they disguise themselves with blue earth. Bushmen in Africa use paint, posture, sound, and movement to aid them when hunting. They paint themselves in red and yellow stripes to look like a zebra, they sway like the animal and at times remain perfectly still, and they imitate the animal's noises.[30]

In times of war, the Hageners use body painting, facial designs, and accessories to transmit the message of fierceness and aggressive power. Their bodies are charcoaled to a deep black hue. Among the ornaments they wear is one shaped like wings of a particular bird whose presence is seen as an evil omen. Gathered together and identically adorned, the Hageners appear as an overwhelming force. Fulani warriors paint themselves in bright, gaudy colors before going to war because they believe such an appearance will intimidate the enemy.[31] Ethnographic reports thus reveal that groups vary greatly in their use of visual adornment as a means for creating a social entity and for performing particular social tasks.

Some objects that we consider adornment today were originally amulets believed to help the wearer master fears and anxieties relating to the supernatural world as well as those relating to the natural world, such as natural disasters, darkness, illness, and death. Observers of nonliterate societies, including Ruth Benedict, Sir James George Frazer, and Bronislaw Malinowski, have noted that items of dress and adornment are often endowed with supernatural qualities and used to avert fear of sterility, hunger, and failure. The supposed supernatural powers of these items were believed to bolster a person's courage and enable him or her to proceed with the task at hand. Since it was felt that no single amulet could imbue the individual with sufficient power and protection from all nefarious forces, it was usually desirable to wear as many as possible.[32]

To increase personal power, individuals and groups wear distinctive objects that they believe contain special strength that can be transferred to the wearer. The sparkle of rock crystal, for example, suggests that a stone possesses energy that can be called on as needed. Claws of birds of prey and other ferocious creatures and horns and tusks of wild animals are thought to have magical attributes that can empower the person who wears them.[33] Eskimo believe an owl claw will help the wearer have strong fists, caribou ears will make the wearer quick of hearing on the hunt, and the skin of a loon carried in a kayak gives it speed.[34]

For protection against evil and malevolent forces, individuals wear around their neck amulets threaded with grass or a thong made from an animal skin. Leaves, seeds, berries, nuts, and roots with an unusual color or shape, and animals and insects, such as the leopard and scarab, believed to be invested with magical powers, are copied and made into protective images. Earrings fashioned from stones in the color of the sea and sky are attached to newborn babies' ears; black soot from the burning of coconut oil at a religious shrine is put on the bottom of the left foot of babies in India. To protect themselves from evil spirits the Eskimo have foxtails and caribou teeth sewn across their backs at shoulder height and carry bone buttons and weasel tails.[35] For the Navajo, blankets pos-

The horseshoe, four-leaf clover, and rabbit's foot are popular good-luck charms worn with the hope that they will assist the wearer in achieving certain goals. Here, Dawn Bunting-Berry holds a horseshoe ornament she was given after a church wedding ceremony, October 2, 1993. (Photo by Jon Rubinstein.)

sess a force beyond that possessed by any single piece of apparel. They are worn for warmth, for aesthetic expression, and most important, for protection from evil.[36]

To affect the outcome of a specific action the desired result has to be communicated to the powers that be. Today, clothing worn during an interaction that resulted in success, like attaining a desired role or winning a game or a contract, is often worn again when a similar outcome is desired. Items of apparel worn in successful interactions for which the outcome could not have been predicted are more likely than other apparel to become a "lucky outfit." Be it a bracelet, a ring, a baseball cap, a sweater, or even a pair of socks, it may constitute "good luck clothing."

As Laver noted, however, it is often difficult to distinguish protection magic from the impulse of vanity. A necklace made from the teeth of tigers or another strong beast is both an amulet and an ornament. In both cases it has "a life-enhancing value."[37] The wearing of amulets, therefore, not only enables a person to contend with an existing reality but also may have an indirect effect on role behavior.

Part Two:
Characteristics of Modern Social Discourse

3

New Institutional Patterns of Discourse

INSTITUTIONAL PATTERNS of discourse are the organized, formally established procedures for pursuing a given objective. Such patterns consist of the usual and expected methods by which people acquire goods and services, engage in commerce and industry, and obtain official appointments. They form the standard against which the conduct of decisionmakers and other individuals is measured. Clothing is an essential part of the entire process.

What a political authority considers good or desirable is a reflection of the ideas and values underlying institutional patterns of discourse. Significantly, the values of a political authority are portrayed in the basic style of *male* dress. (Female style is another matter.) When impatience with established political authority develops to the extent that a new group with different values gains power, the pattern of discourse is altered, as is the basic style of male dress.

The early church fathers established the human body as the principal expressive vehicle for individual and social values.[1] The monarchs of the royal courts, as well as the Protestant reformers, continued this tradition. The aristocracy, for whom wealth was essential and physical labor contemptible, adored pomp and splendor. In contrast, the Puritans and the bourgeoisie found security and comfort in work. They abhorred ostentatious displays of wealth and power and dressed in attire characterized by simplicity, order, and durability.

The Commercial Revolution of the fourteenth century brought new cultural values: individualism and economic success. With these new values came a basic change in the style of male dress. Loose-fitting monochromatic robes that hid the body were replaced by body-hugging, multicolored attire. The subsequent Industrial Revolution of the nineteenth century introduced rationality as the principal value underlying economic discourse. The basic style of male dress changed again; it became somber in color and was tailored essentially to hide the body. In Western society, therefore, changes in the political power structure and in the mode of economic discourse usually go hand in hand with changes in the basic style of male dress.

Spirituality and the Denial of the Body

Until the fourteenth century spirituality was society's core value, and religious piety, humility, and modesty governed most social discourse. Spiritual authorities thought it appropriate to distinguish between themselves and laypersons.

Further distinctions were made within the ranks of the clergy, such as between cardinals and bishops. Thus the church created a hierarchy of social significance emulating that of the military.[2]

Unlike the Romans, who had conceived of the body as a neutral thing placed between nature and society, Christian leaders saw the body as a clearly visible locus of spiritual order, subject to certain limits with regard to religious teachings. In the first century A.D., the Apostle Paul explained that the body is merely an "earthly vessel" to be infused by the Holy Spirit.[3] Early Christian writers insisted that what separates Christians from non-Christians is spirituality. Sexual desire, the consumption of food, and the longing for sensuous garments must be curtailed, not only to maintain personal spirituality, but to protect the Christian community as a whole. In the second century A.D., for example, the church father Tertullian warned: "With their alluring hairstyles and disturbingly unveiled faces," the women of Carthage could breach the defenses of the church and gain an entry into the "somber assemblies of the male saints."[4]

In the fourth century, Ambrose likened the body to a perilous mud slick on which the individual might slip and tumble at any moment. However, the heaving powers of the flesh could be "reformed." The flesh could be made perfect because it had been taken up, in Christ, by God himself. Conversion and baptism were a means of sharing in the tranquillity that flowed from the spotless flesh of Christ. Christian leaders agreed that sexual continence or long periods of abstinence—that is, suppressing bodily needs—made it possible for a Christian to achieve communion with God. The laity and the married priesthood were advised to live with their wives "as if they were not wives," to bear children yet live the rest of their lives denying sexual intercourse. An orientation toward the spiritual was the expected public and private demeanor.[5]

The connection between religious piety and the nonsexual body was encouraged by pilgrimages to the shrines of the martyrs, which contained the *bones* of "men and women on whom the Holy Spirit has come to rest." In the fifth and sixth centuries, and again during the later Middle Ages, these shrines were visited with increasing fervor. They were portrayed as places where new life and healing bubbled up for the faithful from the cold graves of the dead.[6]

Monochromatic, body-concealing attire that denied the very existence of the physical body was worn from the beginning of the Christian Era until the mid-fourteenth century.[7] It consisted of a tunic with a cloak or a robe of varying length. It was essentially the same for men and women. When minor modifications of style did occur, they were visible only in details, such as changes in the manner of fastening the tunic or variations in the length of the robe. The basic loose-fitting style remained unquestioned and unaltered for more than a thousand years.

Nonetheless, the type of cloth and ornament served to differentiate the social classes. Evidence of superior rank was "carried" on the backs of the nobility. Bedecked with all the jewels and gold they could muster, members of the upper classes competed with one another with their sumptuous garments. By law,

Robed attire from the Middle Ages. (Illustration from W. Bruhn and M. Tilke, A Pictorial History of Costume. *Copyright 1955 [New York: Praeger], an imprint of Greenwood Publishing Group, Inc., Westport, Conn. Reprinted with permission.)*

damask, velvet, and satin could be used only by nobles; broadcloth was reserved for burghers; and the poor wore whatever they could come by.[8] Thus, a fabric hierarchy paralleled the social hierachy.

Renaissance Individualism and Economic Success

In the fourteenth century a politically independent, urban, and affluent commercial class rejected much of the medieval ideology of fixed social positions and strict standards for behavior. Its leaders also objected to the church's attempt to curtail commerce by the usury laws, which stood to prevent economic growth, and other means. Rejecting the church's ideal of modesty, the rising commercial classes wore attire that celebrated individual initiative, announced pride in personal economic success, and demonstrated some degree of freedom from sexual constraints.[9]

Beginning most likely in Italy in the middle of the fourteenth century, young men in the towns abandoned the traditional loose-fitting gown in favor of attire that hugged the body and celebrated its physical attributes. A short, fitted jacket, drawstring shirt, and long, tight hose clung to and exposed the forms of the body. The codpiece, a visible penis covering, was padded and protruding, suggesting aggressive virility. The tight hose, in combination with the codpiece, dramatized male genitalia in a manner and to a degree unprecedented.[10] Male clothing became form-fitting, colorful, playful, and personal. Men could adopt any variation in color and ornament they desired.

Body-hugging attire of the Renaissance shown in illustration portraying reception and banquet at the Court of the Duke of Burgundy. (Miniature from the Geschichte des Karl Martell *[History of Charles Martell]. Painted by Loyset Liédet, 1470. Illustration from W. Bruhn and M. Tilke,* A Pictorial History of Costume. *Copyright 1955 [New York, Praeger], an imprint of Greenwood Publishing Group, Inc., Westport, Conn. Reprinted with permission.)*

In a sixteenth-century Renaissance guidebook to manners for aspiring gentlemen, *The Courtier,* Balthasar Castiglione defended young men against "aging reactionaries" who attacked the new style. He argued that it was appropriate for the young "to strut and swagger in bright colors and snug contours. The attire simply reflected their natural energy, beauty and sexual drive."[11] In addition, the new clothing articulated for the first time "the biological distinctions" between the sexes. Whereas the loose-fitting unisex clothing of the medieval period was replaced by short, tight costumes for men, women's dresses now had snug busts, daring décolletages, and long skirts, the latter hampering physical mobility.[12]

The new Renaissance style symbolized a shift from preoccupation with the spiritual to interest in worldly matters, the here and now. Upper-class and middle-class urban dwellers had found a way to display their new power and manifest their pride in the world they were building.

Modern Rationality

The rediscovery of the classics during the Renaissance, the religious skepticism initiated by the Reformation, and the academic rationalism that had advanced into both the Protestant and Catholic traditions provided groundwork for the belief that objective analysis is the most direct and valid approach to understanding the physical and social universe.

Printing facilitated the spread of new ideas. The Reformation is typically portrayed as a movement that replaced a priestly religion with a *religion of the book.* In a sense, Protestantism was created by people reading and raising questions about religious beliefs and practices. Printing facilitated the dissemination of information and made it possible to evaluate and compare texts. Further, people could respond to written texts with further observations and analyses.[13] Since authors, unlike speakers, could not see their public to gauge their response, they were forced to make more elaborate and extensive arguments so that a more complete idea would be available. Moreover, texts were arranged in chapters and paragraphs and were indexed by page. As Chandra Mukerji (1983) argued, this internal orderliness furthered the impression of a text as a complete system.[14]

Increasingly, European academicians perceived nature as a single system of finite materials and forces accessible to human comprehension. By the beginning of the nineteenth century the scientific method—observation, measurement, and comparison of phenomena—had become widely accepted and rationality had become essential to the study of social and physical phenomena. From this worldview emerged a style of dress and adornment that favored self-restraint.

Until the French Revolution, the image of the proper appearance for a gentleman emanated from France. The attire was elaborate: a waistcoat of rich velvet, damask, or satin embroidered with petit point and emblazoned with gold, silver, or enameled buttons; a shirt with a frilled ruffle; close-fitting breeches buttoned just below the knee, where they met silk stockings; and a coat that fitted the body down to the waist and then flared away in soft folds. Vented in the back and elaborately braided, the coat was always left unbuttoned so the ornate waistcoat could be seen. Gold and silver buckles were worn on belts, garters, and shoes; a heavy gold and silver chain hung from the neck and from waistcoat pockets. The tricorne, or three-cornered hat, weighed down with braid and other ornaments completed the sumptuous outfit.[15]

However, as members of the business and professional classes acquired economic and political power in the late eighteenth century, they rejected the rich color, gay ornament, and embroidered frills of the aristocracy. They discarded the pomp and expense of the traditional style in favor of clothes that proclaimed a more *rational* use of resources. The new style was based on the attire chosen by professional men in England in the second half of the seventeenth century, after the Puritan Revolution. The attire was somber, austere, and nondis-

Costumes Parisiens.

"A Stroll," 1815. The tall hat and long pants indicate the application of the norm of self-restraint and the male as the person of authority. (M. Braun-Ronsdorf [1964] Mirror of Fashion: A History of European Costume 1789–1929. *[New York: McGraw-Hill].)*

"Gentleman's Wear," 1882. By the end of the nineteenth century, color, ornament, and body-revealing styles were rejected. The newly established style was the prototype of the contemporary business suit, signifying rationality and self-restraint. (M. Braun-Ronsdorf [1964] Mirror of Fashion: A History of European Costume 1789–1929. *[New York: McGraw-Hill].)*

tracting—so that people could better focus on the task at hand. The clothing was designed to represent mastery over one's feelings and to demonstrate rationality, the state of making decisions on the basis of calculation, organization, abstract rules, and procedures.

Described by Flugel as "the great masculine renunciation," this change in the basic style of male dress was profound, essentially involving a rejection of sensuality and individuality. Breeches, the style of pants favored by the aristocracy because they revealed the shape of the leg, were rejected in favor of long trousers such as those worn by sailors and farmers. The long pants provided a measure of protection and symbolized activity and utility. Instead of the customary form-fitting style that displayed each individual's physical attributes, a form-following style that hid nearly all personal features, desirable and undesirable alike, was now preferred.[16]

This change in attire involved all social classes, from the king and members of parliament to the fruit and vegetable vendors in the marketplace. Only the quality of fabric and fit differentiated the social classes. Men were now concerned with being dressed in "correct" and useful attire.[17] Renouncing color, ornament, frills, embroidery, velvet, and rich colors in favor of plain dark suits composed of a jacket, vest, and trousers, men left the brighter, more elaborate, and varied forms of ornamentation entirely to women.

Fashion historian René König (1973) described the change in this manner: The 1789 revolution in France set the stage for the Puritans to "steer the course of new developments," and their values came to characterize modern dress. König asserted that "the man's suit of today is fundamentally a direct descendant of the puritan dress, a political demonstration against the ostentation of the courts."[18] Male attire became desexualized and austere. There was another factor that helped establish this style, however: the fact that following the Revolution the nobility in France hid behind long trousers, ragged or dirty clothes, beards, and a generally seedy look to avoid losing their lives.[19]

German sociologist Norbert Elias described the change in attire in a similar manner: "In the industrializing countries the ideals, hopes and long-term goals of the rising industrial classes gradually gained advantage over those seeking to preserve the existing social order in the interests of the established courtly dynastic, aristocratic or patrician power elites."[20] Education and talent largely overshadowed birthright as the important conditions for employment. Hence, the style of dress that proclaimed the aristocracy's values was no longer viable. By the mid-nineteenth century, rationality had displaced feudal loyalty as the principal basis for social discourse and institutional arrangements.

Dressing the Public Self

Clothing discourse in contemporary American society has its roots in the political and economic changes that took place in the nineteenth century. With industrialization and centralization of production the workplace moved out of the home to specialized places. Two distinct realms of interaction emerged, the public and the private.[1] *Goal-directed* behavior and *self-restraint* became the preferred modes of deportment in the public place. A form-following three-piece suit of somber color, a white shirt, and a tie—familiar and often required attire in the United States today—conveyed in a visual form the newly desired modes of conduct.

The Demise of Male Fashion

After the French Revolution, scions of aristocratic families in France and England were ridiculed for constructing highly elaborate sartorial expressions.[2] Literary, academic, and social critics denigrated their attempts. In France they were called the *incroyables et le merveilleuses* (the incredibles and the marvelous ones). In England, Carlyle labeled them dandies, "social parasites who glorified themselves, not God."[3] He called the young men who followed Count D'Orsay (b. 1801), a good-looking man who rejected the somber colors and the form-following suit, "dandiacals—clothes loving men who do not work." Count D'Orsay selected instead shimmering pastels, soft velvet and silks, perfumes and jewels, worn in a form-fitting style. He sought to create an artistic expression that enhanced his physical presence.[4] In the 1880s Oscar Wilde and Max Beerbohm also attempted to challenge the negative image associated with men attractively attired in exquisitely tailored costumes. They claimed that beauty and art were an essential dimension of a well-lived life. The reaction was strong. Men who looked beautiful continued to be denigrated as not being men.[5]

In France, where men were expected to be involved in commerce, business, and the professions, Napoléon III decreed that the only attire appropriate for men were the military uniform, the riding habit, and the English gentlemen's business suit. The task of expressing French taste and the opulent spirit of the period fell on women and was carried out through female dress and a feminine fashion ideal. The French fashion industry continues to receive government support, and it remains the world's most important laboratory for style and fashion.[6]

Thomas Carlyle. In Sartor Resartus *(1838), he observed: "Clothes gave us individuality, distinctions, social polity; Clothes have made Men of us; they are threatening to make clothes-screens of us." (Reprinted by permission of The Bettmann Archive.)*

Goal-Directed Behavior

In the United States, at least since the turn of the twentieth century, goal-directed behavior has been the standard in industrial production. The goal of scientific management studies has been to eliminate wasteful motions. The worker is to perform his or her tasks exactly as described by managers who, through engineers' time and motion studies, possess knowledge of the fastest way to perform them. The studies conducted by Fredric Taylor (1911) were designed to create humans who performed with machinelike precision and speed. Comedians from Charles Chaplin to Lucille Ball have, of course, ridiculed this behavior by dramatizing its inhuman quality.[7]

Goal-directed behavior has also come to characterize business relations. In a recent report on the problems Americans face in conducting business in Eastern Europe, business consultant Fred Martin observed that directness—clearly stated goals—hampered the ability of his client, an American businessman, to secure his goal. The client sought to rent space for a copy shop in Hungary after its move to a market economy. As Martin explained, Hungarians observe formalities, are careful to preserve the dignity of the situation, and are thus circumspect. The American businessman tried to convince the officials that they would benefit by granting him the appropriate space. He kept repeating that this was a mutual partnership, and he told them of the large sums of money he was prepared to invest. The Hungarians, however, viewed his direct approach as an attempt to hide the real purpose of his request and considered him a con man. His lack of proper attire further provoked their suspicion. They believed that any legitimate businessman would wear a suit and a tie. (In general, informal attire is

Time came to be perceived differently in the nineteenth century. Precision timing characterized the reality of urbanization and industrialization. The importance of punctuality is conveyed by the figure of the White Rabbit in Alice in Wonderland. *(Illustration by Sir John Tenniel, 1896.)*

associated with self-expression and personal goals rather than with a more enduring, formalized economic transaction.)[8] In this situation, goal-directed behavior was not accompanied by the restrained business attire of the public place.

The Norm of Self-Restraint

The norm of self-restraint, reinforced by dress, makes possible the achievement of goal-directed behavior. Attire that denies the body leads to self-restraint. The idea is basic to Christian beliefs, including the injunction to modesty, codes of dress devised for priests, and monastic orders requiring that the body be covered from head to toe. Not until the Renaissance, when the notion of individual self-expression assumed importance, were parts of the body exposed. An essential element of male dress that is symbolic of holding in one's feelings is the neckcloth or tie. Historically, some starched the neckpiece to preserve the proper folds. Others, Europeans and Americans, favored wearing two cravats at the same time—a white one wrapped twice around the neck and a black silk one tied over it. A stiff collar and cuffs also became important accessories.[9]

In the United States, it was not until the growth of bureaucracies in the 1940s that the tie emerged as required attire for "white-collar" workers. A *New York Times* Op-Ed article entitled "A Diploma, a Tie, and a Lie," by a graduate student in journalism, described the personal impact of wearing a tie. The author, Greg Spring, complained that when he wore a tie to job interviews he said things that did not reflect his individual concerns and interests. His responses at the interviews were "tailored" to meet the social expectations that he get a job regardless of where it was and what he was expected to do. The attire prevented him from stating his personal preferences. It structured his responses.[10]

Responding to the story, a working journalist, Scott R. Schmedel, affirmed the observation that a jacket, shirt, and tie represent a public self that has incorporated the societal expectation of self-restraint. He wrote that although he does not allow himself the time to put on a tie, he nevertheless mistrusts the "spongy opinions of people committed to jeans, people who let it all hang out—hair, shirttail, shoe laces, moral superiority." To strangers, the manner in which the individual is attired, the author suggested, seems to reflect the hidden self. "When I do put on my pressed suit, instead of my baggy blazer, and my polished shoes and I carefully knot a four-in-hand or a half Windsor, I find I stand a little taller. I am reminded of my professional commitment, my responsibility to society—to be upstanding, perceptive, accurate." The suit, polished shoes, and tie deny personal preferences and feelings; they emphasize the social role. Schmedel continued, "When you feel you are losing your grip the act of tying a necktie may pull everything together."[11] The tie performs the task of integrating the public self.

Conversely, the act of removing one's shirt is associated with the expression of angry personal feelings. Examining the roots of the verbal expression "Keep Your Shirt On," lexicographer William Safire explained the phrase as giving someone an "unshirted hell,"—that is, expressing strong displeasure. The picture that comes to mind when hearing the term is that of a person tearing his shirt off to castigate another. "The unshirted one is angry and ready to give hell to the clothed recipient." In keeping calm, you keep your shirt on.[12] (The origins of the phrase are attributed to nineteenth-century England in Hotten's 1859 slang dictionary.)

The institution of a dress code for taxi drivers confirms the idea that wearing a proper shirt is generally recognized as encouraging self-restraint. In a news story entitled "A Dress Code for Cabbies: No T-Shirts," Richard Levin reported that New York cabbies are prohibited from wearing T-shirts, tank tops, tube tops, and body shirts. They must wear shirts with a collar and sleeves. The purpose of the code, according to the authorities, is "to professionalize the drivers."[13]

Sociocultural Background

The centralization of production in the nineteenth century took place in the cities, and they became magnets for people from rural areas searching for work opportunities and upward mobility. Their new social environment became a place where they could construct new identities. Life in the city necessarily involved meeting a plurality of people and mingling with strangers; it was perceived as full of complexities.[14]

Expressions that were personal and unique were expected to be relegated to the private realm, not made in the workplace. Men had to become actors. Just as in the theater, where actors touch people's feelings without revealing their own offstage character, in the public sphere people concealed private imagery and individual feelings. The desire to suppress and shield the personal self led to common codes of belief, the terms of which were familiar to others. In this public sphere men had to be sociable on impersonal grounds. Their attire acquired new formality. It was contrived with regard to the requirements of a social situation, to the specific status held, and to the officially specified goals of the organization.

In the United States the gradual shift from manufacturing to a service economy further encouraged self-restraint. More individuals became involved in commercial, professional, and technical relationships, as C. Wright Mills observed. The division of labor in modern American society involved a "hitherto unknown specialization of skill: the ability to deal with paper, money and symbols." The new class were "masters at handling people in 'a transient and impersonal manner,'" as Mills pointed out. He called this new occupational category white-collar workers because they wore to work attire generally suitable for street wear—a white shirt, gray wool pants, and a jacket.[15]

The distinction between clothing worn in the industrial production sector and that worn in the service sector was confirmed in a 1955 study of occupational clothing by W. H. Form and G. P. Stone.[16] They found that overalls, aprons, or other protective devices identified manual workers, whereas suits and sports clothes identified service workers.

Presentation of the Public Self

Encouraging the trust of people one does not know is difficult in a world full of strangers and in work relationships. However, the clothing one wears may demonstrate awareness of the expected behavior associated with the particular status one holds.[17] Individuals take great pains to have others consider them rational, noted Erving Goffman. To be accepted, they strive to control the nonverbal aspects of their behavior. They attempt to project a desired image, knowing that people read significance into such cues as manner of dress, body position, gestures, and facial expressions. They may make use of "props," elements not necessary to the performance of a task, such as a beard, a pipe, or an expensive attaché case. The clothing and props reflect the behavior qualities expected in the modern workplace: efficiency and reliability. The meaning and importance of appearance in the public place, however, depend on its relevance to social rewards. Goffman identified three interactional spaces: *front stage, backstage,* and *outside region.* In identifying these three regions of interaction, Goffman inadvertently explained the diversity of appearance on city streets, where the public is left with the impression that "anything goes."[18]

Front Stage

Drawing a parallel between performing in the theater and appearing in public, Goffman divided everyday situations into his three categories of significance. A park setting may be a front-stage situation for members of a sports team who are required to wear appropriate attire to play. Yet a man relaxing in the park may loosen his tie and take off his jacket. He is free to engage in such behavior since he is unfettered by interactional constraints, and his chances of receiving social criticism or rewards for this behavior are minimal.

By wearing the appropriate attire and demeanor, teachers in the classroom, physicians in the office or operating room, and guests at a dinner party promise the audience that they will perform their roles in the socially expected manner. Personal feelings will be withheld and the norms of politeness and decorum will prevail. Before entering the space where front-stage performance is to take place, Goffman pointed out, men usually make sure that they are clean-shaven and neatly dressed, with hair in place and face and hands immaculate. They check their appearance to ascertain, for example, that their trouser zipper is closed. Women are expected to exercise "limb discipline." They take great care that their undergarments and upper thighs are concealed when they walk and sit.[19]

According to Goffman, the dropping of one's "personal front" (a standard regularly employed by the individual, such as gender identity), or the failure to present oneself in a "situational harness" is likely to be taken as a sign of disregard for the other participants and as an act of distancing oneself from the social world of those present on the front stage. People who are unkempt in formal situations, women who wear dresses or skirts but sit with legs wide apart, and men who expose their private parts in public (flashers), all exhibit deviant behavior, though to very different degrees, that disrupts the flow of orderly communication and interaction. The most obvious means by which individuals show their acceptance of a social role and their awareness of the demands of the social situation is through their appearance.

Backstage

Backstage, according to Goffman, is the interactional space in which individuals prepare their personal front for front-stage performance. It is the place where a person can assume that no member of the "audience" will intrude. A beauty parlor, a dressing room, and a locker room are all front-stage areas for the beautician, the salesperson, the coach. However, for users of such services they are backstage areas. Here, an individual is free to dress informally, behave emotionally, and, even when in poor taste, manipulate his or her appearance to create a desired identity. The attire worn may represent the person's feelings, attitude, or mood. In American society, a bathroom is normally a backstage. People expect to clean and clothe themselves in private. Observing someone prepare for a front-stage performance may take away from the desired effect. A young man is

President Clinton dressed for front-stage performance. The president is shown walking to the East Room of the White House, November 10, 1993, for a news conference. (Reprinted by permission of AP Photo/Greg Gibson.)

usually shielded from seeing his date in hair rollers and cold cream, just as the groom often does not see his bride before the ceremony.

In certain settings a backstage can be turned into a front stage. A gym was once a place where people went to keep their bodies in shape for their performance in front-stage situations. How they looked was of little concern. Today's "singles," however, use gyms and health clubs as meeting places. They carefully plan their work-out and warm-up outfits to appear attractive to the opposite sex.

Outside Region

Whereas the front stage is a place where performances take place and the backstage is a place where people prepare for front-stage performances, the outside region is the place where appearance is least socially significant. Attire may be incomplete, Goffman suggested, because the situation is not formally connected to a role performance, and one's appearance is left to the immediate circumstances and the individual's momentary needs. Here, the individual is "outside" prescribed role relationships. There are no social expectations, and he or she need not demonstrate any particular expertise. Models hurrying to their assignments carry the clothing and accessories needed to complete their appearance for the shoot. Individuals often do not bother to dress well to run a neigh-

President Clinton dressed for the outside region, 1993. (Reprinted by permission of AFP Photo/Robert Giroux.)

borhood errand. In cities, women commonly rush to work wearing sneakers with their business suits, their work shoes tucked away in their briefcases.

In an article entitled "Notes on Fashion," Michael Gross complained that jogging suits, sneakers, and T-shirts were worn by audience members at the premiere of *Pygmalion*. He noted that Broadway openings once epitomized cosmopolitan glamour.[20] But things have changed. The well-dressed are a distinct minority. Attending the theater used to be a front-stage performance; hence, the formal attire. The theater has since become an outside region. Many of those who attend do so without concern for possible negative sanctions.

Stability of Appearance

Nursery school teachers, judges, ushers, health care personnel, ward attendants, supervisors, and maître d's, among others, act as gatekeepers, in Goffman's view. They help to create stability of appearance.[21] These guardians of tradition formally or informally identify the boundaries of acceptable appearance. Those inappropriately dressed are threatened with banishment. The media often consider such cases news, making knowledge of them public, as seen in the following examples. The *New York Times* related that the school board in Pharr, Texas, refused to waive the dress code for a four year-old boy whose parents maintained that they had promised God they would not cut his shoulder-length hair until they were certain that he was free from cancer. Under the board's ruling the boy was barred from classes.[22] One of the most publicized examples of trying to maintain stability in appearance involved Don Mattingly, first baseman for the Yankees. In addition to its being a news story and appearing on the sports pages, excerpts of the story were used in the "Quotations of the Day" section of the *New York Times*. The baseball team's manager was quoted as saying: "If someone from management says you need a haircut, then you get a haircut." Mattingly's response was: "Maybe I don't belong in the organization anymore." His response reveals his awareness that standards of appearance affect employment. However, the *New York Times* reported that by the next day Mattingly had gotten his hair cut.[23]

A business suit devoid of ornament has been adjudged by the courts as the proper attire for lawyers appearing in front of them.[24] On March 19, 1980, a New York appeals court ruled that priests who are lawyers may not wear clerical attire to court. In June 1992 a judge in Washington, D.C., banned an African-American lawyer from wearing an ethnic ornament, a piece of Kente cloth, around his neck and over his suit. A suit is also the required attire for lawyers in public employment. On May 2, 1991, a headline on the editorial page of the *New York Times* announced, "Legal Code: Goodbye Jeans." The editorial relayed that a memo had been sent to the 143 assistant prosecutors at the United States District Courthouse in Brooklyn informing them that during business hours they were to wear "dress appropriate for a law office." Coming to work at the office (when not scheduled to appear in court) in jeans and open-collar polo shirts was described as "a little too laid back" and nonprofessional.[25]

Clothing Signs in the Public Place

Established by those in authority, clothing signs are required attire that have only one meaning and indicate expected behavior. A study conducted at the University of Nevada over a four-year period found that the more clearly an attire was associated with a status, the greater the sharing of meaning. Pictures of a nun, policeman, bride, and rodeo rider were easily recognized by the subjects of the study. However, they could not place the picture of a woman wearing stretch pants and a ruffled blouse in an occupational category. Clothing signs imbue strangers with known characteristics, making them less threatening.[26]

Because clothing signs identify expected role behavior, their significance is not limited to the specific situational context. The attributes of a clothing sign are relevant and carry weight beyond the boundaries of front-stage performance. They also enable individuals to *fabricate* an identity. By wearing the appropriate attire a person can convince others that he or she has the special qual-

Fabricating an identity: A quack surgeon in fashionable clothes, ca. 1696. Here the costume and full wig of a physician cover up for an absence of medical qualifications. (P. Cunnington, C. Lucas, and A. Mansfield [1967] Occupational Costume in England from the Eleventh Century to 1914 *[London: Charles & Adam Black]. Reprinted by permission of John Johnson [Author's Agent] Ltd.)*

ities and skills the clothing signifies. To impersonate a physician, a police officer, a priest, or a person of another gender is not difficult, but it is usually illegal.[27]

In an article concerning burglars, Susan Black pointed out that good burglars affect an appearance that will get them into the buildings they are interested in robbing. On countless occasions, clerks in the best hotels have allowed access to thieves dressed in well-fitting, high-quality suits because they did not look the part of a thief.[28]

Believability concerning a particular identity depends on coherence between the impression one gives (a conscious effort to communicate a certain image) and the information one "gives off" (the not-so-conscious nuances that may cut away at the desired impression). Goffman cited examples from verbal discourse as sources of discrepancy, but the manner in which one is dressed may also discredit a claim to a social identity. To protect themselves from being duped, people usually look for corroborative evidence. An authentic cowboy, unlike a dude, wears his pants long to protect himself from the brush. He has no time for well-polished boots, and his Stetson will have accumulated fingerprints, for it is used as a water bucket, waved in the air to steer cattle, and tipped to keep off bugs and supply shade. The extent to which a performer is capable of imitating a real appearance and demeanor determines his or her credibility and successful fabrication of an identity.[29]

To summarize, as contractual relations became central to interaction in the economic and political spheres in the nineteenth century, the structure of daily life changed. A person's social realm became differentiated into the public self and the private self. The role of informal social control mechanisms, such as community and home, diminished, and the public realm consisted of two spaces, formal and informal. Two types of rhetoric came to characterize the public self: one *contractual and formal,* the other *noncontractual and informal.* A dress code governs dress in the formal realm, where clear lines are drawn between acceptable and unacceptable attire. Gatekeepers and other social control mechanisms offer feedback and are ready to apply negative and positive sanctions. Social roles, power, authority, gender, and seductiveness are governed by this rhetoric. In the informal realm, rewards and punishments are less exact and less certain.

Part Three:
Clothing Signs and Social Imperatives

The Image
of Power

$\mathbf{P}$OWER, observed German sociologist Max Weber, is the ability to realize one's own will even against the resistance of others.[1] The image of power stems from the desire for obedience and personal loyalty. The ability to reward and the ability to impose the threat of physical harm are the animating forces behind the image of power. The details of the image are dependent on the source of its legitimacy and the right to exercise physical force.

Power relations are asymmetrical: the power holder exercises greater control than the power subject over the subject's behavior. Legitimacy, however, must be demonstrated for one to achieve and maintain a position of power, according to Weber.[2] The validity of the legitimacy claim may be based on (1) charismatic grounds—resting on the devotion to heroism, exceptional sanctity, or exemplary character of an *individual;* (2) traditional grounds—resting on an established belief in the sanctity of long-held *traditions* and the legitimacy of those exercising authority under them; or (3) rational grounds—resting on a belief in the *enacted rules* and the rights of those elevated to authority by those rules. These three types of authority are pure types, two of which, charismatic authority and traditional authority, are dependent on personal loyalty. In their desire to remain unchallenged, dictators and monarchs dominate the image of power. In their appearance, they make their ability to reward or inflict harm obvious to increase the probability that their commands will be obeyed. Their dress contains elements that extend the body's reach; and when they appear in public they (and their appearance) are supported by attendants.

In a democracy, obedience is owed to the established rules. The exercise of power is impersonal; the ability to inflict harm is displayed only by those charged with that responsibility, usually the military and the police. A plurality of power centers exists, each strong enough to compete with the others but not strong enough to undermine the entire political system. The responsibility of wearing or carrying elements that extend the body's reach and increase one's physical ability to control the environment is confined to attendants.

Charismatic Dictatorship

A dictatorship may have its roots in charismatic leadership. A charismatic leader, with the intent of transforming society, preaches, creates, or demands new obligations to which the populace must accede. Members of his party or group who are familiar with his ideas consider obedience to them and to him their duty. Those who do not recognize or who reject the leader's superior or extraordinary qualities are forced into submission. The threat of physical force or death encourages such obedience.

The dictator usually adopts a military uniform, the elements of which reflect his ideology. The choice of a uniform is designed to impress both his followers and his antagonists. To his followers the uniform represents the "cause." It signifies single-mindedness, discipline, and self-restraint. To his detractors the uniform is intended to denote a superior commitment to the collectivity, to the society.

Twentieth-century dictators such as Joseph Stalin, Adolf Hitler, Benito Mussolini, Mao Tse-tung, and Fidel Castro began their careers as charismatic leaders. Their followers considered them to have exceptional powers and extraordinary qualities. Each claimed legitimacy and was acclaimed in turn by a community of "believers." Others, however, had to be "convinced" to comply. The uniforms with their implements capable of inflicting physical harm encouraged pride among supporters and fear among dissenters.

Monarchy

Traditionally, the royal court was the residence of quasi-divine monarchs at the center of political and administrative power, national and international in range. No group was more acutely aware of the way in which images had to be deployed and manipulated for political effect than these ruling aristocracies.[3] Artistic spectacle, the dress and ornament of the monarchs, performed at least three major tasks: It protected and sustained the sacred character of kingship; it served to demonstrate political and administrative power; and it constituted an exemplary appearance for foreigners and nationals alike.[4]

The sacred character of kingship and its legitimacy were signified by a crown, a scepter, and a chain worn around the neck. These emblems served to display and justify the exercise of power. Both in formal ceremonies and in the organization of the household, the monarch was presented as God's representative on earth, the center of a universe carefully designed to duplicate the harmonious ordering of the heavens.[5]

The relationship between the monarch and his subjects was characterized by the threat of force, according to French historian Michel Foucault. The sword in royal regalia was designed to encourage voluntary obedience. It exhibited the right of seizure—of a person's belongings, body, time, and ultimately life.[6] In Western society, however, from the fourth century A.D., when Roman Emperor Constantine crowned himself as the first Christian ruler of Europe, the crown rather than the sword signified royalty. Whenever a pope or an emperor awarded a kingship, the appointment was accompanied by the gift of a crown. The crown established the king as the legitimate ruler and upheld his claim to reward as well as to punish. The details of crowns differed from one kingship to another,

Wearing uniforms with military and fascist insignia: dictators Benito Mussolini of Italy and Adolf Hitler of Germany in 1936. (Reprinted by permission from The Granger Collection, New York.)

but the elements from which they were constructed and their basic structure remained the same. Made of gold, the radiance of which is associated with the heavens, and encrusted with jewels, which were thought to contain the creative powers of the universe, the crown indicated access to both divine powers and superhuman force.[7] The crown invested the monarch with authority to grant individuals and groups the right to engage in commercial or industrial enterprise, and economic exchange occurred mainly between persons so designated. The monarch thus had the power to enrich and give life, as well as to destroy it.[8]

The scepter, another integral part of royal regalia, was a staff, or batonlike implement, that signified the king's right to exercise authority. It was used to delegate permission. When a king invested an organization, such as the British Parliament, with royal approval, he often accompanied this announcement by the award of a scepter.[9]

Court etiquette, with its fine hierarchical gradations and its exact delimitation of functions, proved—whether in London, Paris, or Madrid—to be an important device for inculcating social discipline. It provided education in politeness, taste, and service. Court behavior thus became an example for others to follow. Supported by monarchical power, the court played a vital role in the "civilizing process," as Norbert Elias pointed out.[10]

Power in the American Presidency

By contrast, visual images of power are deliberately limited or absent in the context of the office of president of the United States. Whereas monarchs had personal ability to punish those who violated the law or threatened the integrity of the state, presidents are limited in their ability to exercise physical force to secure a course of action. Regardless of whether a monarch acquired the crown through inheritance or conquest, his power was unrivaled. The will of the people was subject to his desire or whim. Equating monarchy with tyranny and subjugation, the Founding Fathers insisted that rationality and democracy were necessary to ensure liberty. The signers of the Declaration of Independence rejected the notion of a divine right to rule. The U.S. Constitution and the Bill of Rights specify protection for individuals and minorities. Under the Judiciary Act of 1789, the first Congress emphasized the rule of law. It created the federal court system, the Supreme Court, with a chief justice and five associates, and the office of attorney general. The chief justice, John Jay, adopted the black robe and cap as the appropriate judiciary attire.

The framers of the Constitution rejected the traditional nature of the monarchy and thus, too, the attire of power.[11] They insisted that power be shared in an effort to guard against its concentration in the hands of one man. Policy, they decided, should be the sum of the visible and formal decisions of the three branches of government: the executive, the legislative, and the judicial. The Constitutional Convention of 1787 created a government of limited and separate

Codex Manesse, *illuminated between 1298 and 1304, Heidelberg Library. King Wenzel II sits on the throne, dominating the picture due to his size and ample clothing. Like the Egyptian pharaoh, he wears a crown and carries a mace.*

powers, thus limiting the president's power to command. Influence, rather than coercion, and leadership through persuasion and bargaining became the principal means to power for the president.[12]

In organizing the proceedings of the Constitutional Convention, however, the delegates employed some elements connected with monarchical power. They placed sentries—armed guards—at the State House doors so that only official delegates would be allowed in, the proceedings would be kept secret, and "some headway could be achieved." But to encourage the free exchange of ideas, the sign of royal authority, the mace, was removed from its place in front of the speaker.[13]

On ceremonial occasions, the president's three leadership roles are each signified to some degree in images: As commander in chief of the army and navy of the United States, the leader of the forces of peace and war, for example, the president is attended by uniformed members of the armed forces. As chief of state, the symbol of the sovereignty, continuity, and grandeur of the American people, he is accompanied by an honor guard holding swords. As chief executive, the leader of the executive branch, who shapes policy, takes care of the government's administrative tasks, and signs legislation into law, he wields a special pen that is often sought as a symbol of presidential favor and power.

People in power exercise it by virtue of the offices they hold; their commands are exercised only within the *legal* scope of those positions.[14] Accordingly, the attire of modern power holders, the somber suit, has its roots in the values that

President John F. Kennedy signing the Test Ban Treaty, which limited the testing of nuclear weapons, July 1963. (Reprinted by permission of UPI/Bettmann.)

underlie the institutional context and guide organizational behavior. It denotes holding back personal feelings, or self-restraint, and focusing energy on achieving organizational goals, or goal-directed behavior.

Looking the part is important, as was suggested by a Defense Department publication, *The Armed Forces Officer 1965*, which was distributed to all branches of the military. It advised that as far as being a leader is concerned, "It is good ... to look the part, not only because of the effect on others, but because from out of the effort made to look it, one may in time come to be it."[15]

Origins of the Image of Power

The word "origins" means both beginnings and causes, and there is frequent cross-contamination of the two meanings. With regard to the origins of the image of power, historical evidence suggests that both meanings apply. Perhaps the first instance of an image of power is seen in the *Palette of Narmer*, a pictorial record commemorating the consolidation of Egypt under the rule of a pharaoh in B.C. 3300–3100. On one side of the palette, Narmer wears a tall double crown, the conical white crown of upper Egypt and the superimposed red one of lower Egypt. Together they signify that the nation has been unified under his rule. At

Palette of Narmer, *ca. 3000 B.C., Egyptian Museum, Cairo. Wearing the tall crown, the king dominates the palette. He holds a mace aloft with his right hand, about to smite a captive held in his left. At the back of his kilt, he wears a bull's tail, a symbol of power and strength. Holding the king's sandals is his attendant. He is diminutive in size and wears little clothing. The captives at the bottom of the palette are nearly naked. (Reprinted by permission of Giraudon/Art Resource.)*

Codex Manesse, *illuminated between 1298 and 1304, Heidelberg Library. The image of power applies to the classroom. Magister Henricus (the teacher), holding a birch branch in his left hand, lectures from a high chair. The birch is an emblem of Gramatica, one of the Seven Liberal Arts. Some students wear ragged clothes and appear to have suffered under his hand.*

the center of the palette, occupying his own distinct space, the pharaoh is bigger and taller than all the other figures. His raised arm wields a club and he threatens a captive. His posture signifies his ability to inflict harm. At a distance stands an aid, smaller and with his body turned toward the pharaoh, as if ready to serve him. The vanquished warriors, naked and small, have been hurled to the bottom of the palette. The pharaoh and the men he defeated provide the interrelated images of power and victimhood.[16]

According to Henri Frankfort, the crown has its origins in the semi-sacred occupation of the boatmen on the Nile. This river and its canals were the sole roads in ancient Egypt. When people died, their bodies, accompanied by statues of the gods, were carried to the place of interment by boat in religious processions. To prevent the strong north wind from blowing hair in their eyes, the boatmen plucked weeds from the river's edge and wove them into circlets, which they tied over their brows with a bow in back, the ends dangling. Lotus flowers, tucked into the headband, were often used as amulets to provide protection. This headdress was transformed into a crown by the pharaoh, who sought to demonstrate that power is sacred in origin. Access to nonhuman powers was demonstrated in the royal headdress. Seeming to rear itself up on his brow, a jeweled image of a brightly colored poisonous snake often adorned the pharaoh's headdress as a warning to potential enemies. The pharaoh's wife wore a crown in which the vulture, a sacred bird that shielded the pharaoh in battle, appeared to spread its wings over her head, suggesting that she too was similarly protected.[17]

Outside the palace the pharaoh was carried on a gilded chair held aloft by eight pole-bearers. Wearing his golden skirt, a sword, a crown, and a gold ring, he shone like the sun. Because gold embodies all the fire and glory of the sun, the attire indicated access to superhuman powers and signified his divinity and sovereignty. Like the sun, the pharaoh had power over life and death. Worn by the pharaohs for two thousand years, the short, royal skirt, called Shend'ot (Shenti), was made of gold cloth and decorated with gold embroidery. This type of garment predates the development of agricultural communities and the pharaohs' rise to power; it is based on a skirt worn by chieftains that consisted of two pieces of matting that hung from a string around the waist. The chieftains' skirt had a lion's tail on the back panel signifying a strong and successful hunter.

When appearing in public the pharaoh induced in those around him a sense of their own insignificance. His crown, his body raised high on a throne, and his demand that people kneel before him made him appear bigger, extending his space and his reach. The other royal insignia—a scepter, a crook and a flail—symbolized his loyalty to his subjects and his intent to defend and protect them as a shepherd protects his flock.

The personal nature of royal administration was seen in the pharaoh's granting of the right to wear elements of royal attire. When individuals outside the royal family were given the task of administering the land, the pharaoh bestowed upon them the right to wear a skirt in the style of the Shend'ot or to wear his signet ring, which indicated that the individual's decision-making powers had been expanded.[18] The warrior's sword, which made possible the centralization of power, and the other signs and symbols of royalty were based on existing notions of sacredness and emanated from the wishes of the monarch to indicate a monopoly of force. In the ancient civilizations those at the top of the social hierarchy were the first to adopt clothing signs, initially used only for ritual and ceremony.[19]

Images of Power in Christian Art

The sword, crown, and scepter, signs of royal power and authority, were popularized through Christian art.[20] They were used to portray the attributes of saints and martyrs and to indicate the role they played in church history as well as for eternity. A jeweled crown, or a diadem, denoted divine powers and spiritual force. When the Madonna is evoked as Queen of Heaven, she is portrayed wearing a crown. When the heavenly messenger Saint Michael is depicted as the defender of the church against Satan, he is shown wearing a crown and dressed in the clothing of a warrior or a knight.[21]

Prior to the Renaissance, paintings of the Annunciation nearly always showed Gabriel, the chief messenger of God, richly robed, wearing a crown and carrying a scepter. His majestic appearance is intended to signify that he had been invested with divine and royal authority.[22] Other depictions of the archangels also demonstrate this point. When the archangel Raphael is portrayed as the protec-

Painting of Saint Michael, with a sword, armor, and scales, by Domenico Ghirlandaio, 1490. (Portland Art Museum, Gift of Samuel H. Kress. Reprinted by permission.)

tor of the young, innocent, pilgrims, and wayfarers, ready to come to their aid, he is dressed in the attire of a pilgrim or traveler and wears sandals. His hair, however, is bound with a diadem. He carries a staff, indicating formal authority, and there is a gourd of water or a wallet slung on his belt, indicating access to a necessary scarce resource. When Raphael is portrayed as a guardian spirit he is often shown richly dressed with a sword in one hand and the other raised in a warning gesture, as if he is saying, "Take heed." The sword is interpreted as an instrument appropriate to a knight or warrior, defender of the forces of light against the forces of darkness.[23]

Power and Victimhood

There are two basic images of Christ: the victorious Christ and the suffering Christ. The image that prevailed during the first thousand years A.D. and celebrated in Coptic and Byzantine churches is that of the victorious Christ. He is depicted sitting or standing, tall, often splendidly dressed, holding a cross. Prior to the eleventh century, even when nailed to the cross, he is portrayed alive and upright. His eyes are open, his arms straight. A halo encircles his head like a crown, and sometimes it seems as if it emanates from within him. His image is that of a triumphant sovereign.[24]

When shown in the second image, that of a victim, Christ is portrayed as dead on the cross with his head slumped on his right shoulder, his eyes closed, and his face twisted. Often he wears a crown, but this one is of thorns. Tears and blood are often visible. Except for a loose-fitting loincloth that looks like it can be easily unraveled, he is naked. He is the object of attention in these paintings, and the demeanor of all those who are gathered around him is one of sorrow.[25]

In Western secular art, too, the image of power has been supported by its counterpart, victimhood. Rape is often used to convey violence. Paintings of rape by Rubens, Poussin, and David, for example, portray male warriors on horseback wearing military helmets and shields, swinging swords and spears, while unarmed women on foot gesture distress. Their clothes are torn and their breasts are often revealed. Similarly, Madonna's 1989 video *Like a Prayer* (Sire Records) depicts rape and contrasts modern images of power and victimhood. Policemen with guns, clubs, whistles, and screeching police cars are juxtaposed with images of people with clothing torn off their shoulders, Christ-like stigmata, and tears of blood. In both realms, religious and secular, in the past and today, the image of power is more commanding and its impact stronger when accompanied by the image of the victim. When the image of power is divorced from that of victimhood, brutality and violence are less discernible. The threat of harm that underlies all explicit images of force becomes less overtly fearful, less likely to be a source of terror.

The "suffering Christ" and the "victorious Christ." Details from The Crucifiction and Last Judgement *by Jan van Eyck, ca. 1420–1425. (The Metropolitan Museum of Art, Fletcher Fund, 1933. All rights reserved, The Metropolitan Museum of Art. Reprinted by permission.)*

Nicolas Poussin's Rape of the Sabine Women, *1636–1637. (The Metropolitan Museum of Art, Harris Brisbane Dick Fund, 1946. All rights reserved, The Metropolitan Museum of Art. Reprinted by permission.)*

The Image of Authority

THE TERM "AUTHORITY" has three distinct root meanings, as sociologist Richard Sennett observed.[1] In one sense, the word is related to the Latin word *auctor,* which means to begin, to create, to author something; in this sense the word implies productivity. Another set of meanings derives from the Latin *auctoritas* (the actual source of the English word), which means coming from an author. Here, an authority has legal powers and is in a position to grant permission; that is, an "authority gives guarantees to others." In this sense, the term connotes something permanent, stable, solid, and, hence, of lasting value. Finally, the term is used to describe a person who has power over other people. In this situation, the individuals on the two sides are perceived as unequal. All three meanings are encapsulated in the role behavior expected of those holding positions of authority. Authority holders represent a social entity: They are required to be concerned with production—the achievement of an organization's goals— and as members of a hierarchy they are expected to relate differently to those below and those above.

In Western society, as Flugel observed, the image of authority is characterized by form-following rather than form-fitting attire. The image consists of vertical continuity of fabric, a generalized unity from head to toe. The style increases the size and volume of the person, effecting a commanding presence and making it easier for the office holder to perform his or her expected task.[2]

The image of authority has two distinct manifestations in attire. One is the uniform. Each person's attire is identical in style and detail, and expectations for role performance are explicit—for example, the clothing worn by police officers. The attire indicates the person's right to represent a group. With the second manifestation, the "nonuniform uniform," dress and behavior are less specified, but in style and sentiment the image demands respect, as in a businessman with a three-piece suit.[3]

Uniforms

This category of clothing encompasses required attire. Formal, negative sanctions follow acts of omission or commission, that is, not wearing an element of the attire, adding to the specified dress, or modifying it in any shape or form. Emblems, implements, and other visual elements identify the extent, sphere,

*Representation of Adam and Cain in the at-
tire of workers of the land, ca. 1330. Adam,
the father, is more completely covered. Over a
tunic, stirrup, and hose he is wearing a
sheepskin cloak, which offers protection
while the side vents enable him to move
freely. He is thus portrayed in the image of
authority. Cain wears only a tunic hitched up
by a belt. (P. Cunnington, C. Lucas, and A.
Mansfield [1967]* Occupational Costume in
England from the Eleventh Century to 1914
*[London: Charles & Adam Black]. Reprinted
by permission of John Johnson [Author's
Agent] Ltd.)*

and boundaries of social control. The extent of deference accorded to the status holder may thus vary.[4]

The attire required of workers by sanitation departments, hospitals, airlines, hotels, and restaurants, for example, identifies *the right to enforce policy.* Company badges, logos, and special insignia on ties, blazers, and coveralls mark those with such privilege. Uniforms can also identify *the right to interfere with an ongoing action.* Here, the uniform includes implements such as batons, whistles, timers, whips, or axes. These instruments enable orchestra conductors, umpires and referees, equestrians, and firefighters to perform their roles. Similarly, the display of keys in areas where admission is legally limited—in mental hospitals, prisons, and stockrooms, for example—proclaims *the right to control access.*

*St. Patrick's Day Parade marshals wear attire
showing the right to enforce policy, 1993 (*New York
Times, *March 18, 1993; reprinted by permission of
Fred R. Conrad/NYT Pictures.)*

The right to exercise force is demonstrated by uniforms that include coercive instruments, tools capable of inflicting harm. Armed guards, police, and uniformed military personnel support the operations of justice, peace, and public order.

The Social Meaning of Uniforms

In his study of uniforms Nathan Joseph (1986) pointed out that uniforms are a device used by organizations to distinguish members from nonmembers and inform the actor and the audience of what behavior to expect.[5] A uniform exerts a degree of control over those who must carry out the organization's tasks, encouraging members to express the ideas and interests of the group rather than their own and thus enhancing the group's ability to perform its tasks.

The conferring of a uniform or the salient parts of it, such as a police officer's shield or a nurse's cap or pin, signifies that legal rights have been transferred from the institution to the individual who represents it. The attire authorizes individuals to act on the organization's behalf. Because they represent the organization, those in uniform are not permitted to wear buttons and other insignia that announce a political or other loyalty.

When an organization authorizes an individual to wear its uniform, it certifies that the person has acquired relevant values and skills and that the group will assume responsibility for the person's conduct. In turn, by wearing a uniform a person outwardly displays acceptance of and allegiance to the organization's goals. The individual signals his or her intention to abide by and adhere to standardized expectations for role behavior and to be guided by the group's ideas, beliefs, and values. Suppressing personal choice of dress, the organization binds the individual to his or her peers, underscores common membership, and encourages a sense of loyalty among members and faithfulness to the same rules. The uniform serves to integrate wearers into a cohesive unit that will act to ensure that organizational goals are attained. The withdrawal of the right to represent the group is accompanied by a ritual that involves removing parts of the uniform. Police officers lose the authority to arrest when they are asked to turn in their guns and shields.

To summarize, a uniform designates membership in a group and is a certificate of legitimacy. It shows that the individual has mastered certain essential skills and values. By wearing a uniform an individual displays adherence to group norms and standards. The uniform embodies the attributes of the group and affects the wearer's behavior. Through the uniform, the individual signifies that all other allegiances will be suppressed.[6]

Displaying Rank and Power

In work that involves emergency conditions and in situations that require quick response, such as military and police work, fire and marine services, the display of rank is necessary and made clearly visible. Through insignia, the line of command in the heat of "battle" is always in evidence, ensuring that there will be un-critical obedience.[7]

Where uniforms are required, only those with the highest rank can avoid wearing the attire. Julius Roth, in his study of a tuberculosis hospital, discovered that physicians were the least likely of all individuals to put on the protective gown and mask required by hospital rules because not wearing the attire indicated their freedom from gatekeepers and other social control mechanisms. In their behavior they laid a claim to their true status, power—the right to exercise force. Similarly, the New York City police commissioner and other security chiefs appear in public in white-collar attire, that is, civilian clothes.[8]

Nonuniform Uniforms in the Corporate World

The image of authority, because it denies the personal, was chosen as the preferred mode of dress by the business class of nineteenth-century England. The men's suit in its form-following style denied the body; in its somber color it repudiated public expression of feelings. It indicated that, so attired, the individual would suppress personal desires and sentiments and conduct himself or herself in the expected "professional" manner. A somber-colored suit with all elements coordinated to create a unified whole emerged as *respectable* attire in the white-collar workplace.[9]

In pairing men with types of neckties, fashion reporter Ruth La Ferla identified four general categories of tie wearers: the collegian, the corporate worker, the cosmopolite, and the iconoclast. The collegian's tie is diagonally striped ribbed silk (rep) or embroidered with shields or heraldic insignia (club ties). It communicates that the student wearing it is ready to meet the scrutiny of a vigilant parent or headmaster. Invariably the tie is worn with a neat, button-down collar, and the wearers often prefer ties in school colors. Brooks Brothers and other college stores carry such ties. The corporate worker's tie suggests "power, authority and unflappable decorum." Its message is conveyed by a suitably weighty pattern on a background of blue or claret-colored silk. The cosmopolite, more dashing than the corporate worker, wears solid-color satins or crisp knit ties. The rich luster of the fabric betrays a love of finery, La Ferla observed. Finally, the convention-flouting iconoclast prizes wit and inventiveness above stiff propriety. He uses the tie to set the tone for the rest of his ensemble.[10]

Although personal preference can determine the color and pattern of the tie one will wear, as well as the style of shirt, collar, and cuffs, one's occupational group seems to have a major impact on these choices. A 1989 study of American male attitudes, purchasing patterns, and behavior patterns with respect to ties, commissioned by the Tie Rack, found that American men believe that the type of tie a man wears often reveals his occupation and title. The more elevated he is, the more likely he is to wear an expensive tie.[11] The study found that civil servants, on the average, spent no more than $13.00 on a tie, whereas chief executive officers (CEOs) spent $31.00. Conservative colors, such as blue, were associated with investment bankers (53 percent), lawyers (59 percent), and corporate executives (62 percent), whereas the study participants believed that advertising executives were almost as likely to wear red ties as blue ties. The participants believed accountants and advertising executives, of all the occupational groups, were most likely to prefer bow ties.

American men also felt that different occupational groups typically wear particular styles of ties, with the civil servant maintaining the most downscale, unimaginative profile. Over 90 percent thought that his tie would be a standard type, and just about half (49 percent) indicated that it would be made of polyester. Only 10 percent felt that a civil servant would wear a silk tie. By contrast, CEOs were thought most likely to wear silk (71 percent). Blue was the most dominant color selected for them (71 percent).

In his well-attended seminars and workshops, John Molloy (1978), the author of *Dress for Success*, has insisted that his research shows that the appropriate mode of dress for those who wish to command respect continues to be the somber business suit. The attire conveys authority because in the public mind it is associated with knowledge.[12] Banker J. P. Morgan insisted that his employees dress in a solid patterned, dark, three-piece suit because it conveys stability and reliability. Lawyers, conversely, have adopted a pin-striped pattern, perhaps a symbolic reference to "straight as an arrow," or honest. Those working in the entertainment and cosmetics industries often choose a more stylish appearance— body-hugging attire with a more visible fabric motif or texture.

The general assumption is that, as in the theater, many roles cannot be believably performed without the aid of a costume. It enhances credible performance. Similarly, the quality of fabric and fit makes rank visible in the corporate hierarchy.

Members of the corporate world generally recognize that the better the quality of cloth and the better the tailoring skills, the more likely the attire is to cover body imperfections, a paunch, or sagging muscles. Usually it is the older, more established executive who recognizes the need to conceal the ravages of time; moreover, he usually has the resources to purchase the more costly attire. Whereas most junior executives buy their clothes ready-made, their immediate superiors often have theirs made by custom tailors. The superiors' superiors may secure theirs from even more exclusive tailors who provide even better quality and fit. Through their more imposing appearance, the higher level executives limit the threat of competition from the younger, more energetic men.

The Executive Role

"An orderly and handsome" appearance seems to have been imperative for men in authority before and after the American Revolution, as historian Alice Morse Earle observed.[13] With new wealth from bountiful crops and growing industry, these men replaced the durable leather doublets and breeches with suits of plush velvet and silk damask, their brocade coats trimmed in lace and embroidery. Governor John Winthrop (1588–1649), a leading Puritan, had several dozen scarlet coats sent from England. In the colonial towns of the North, shops offered imported fabrics, a rich assortment of ornaments, and the latest fashions. In the South, planters had to wait for their crops to be sold before they could have the means to buy luxury clothing from London merchants. Because of this time lag, their clothing was more often sumptuous than fashionable.[14]

In sharp contrast to the plain attire of persons lacking an official position or wealth, the attire of the signers of the Declaration of Independence "showed no Republican simplicity," observed Earle. John Hancock's attire was of the richest material available and striking colors. The scarlet velvet suit he wore when he was declared governor (October 26, 1780) was designed to "make an impression, and yet not to appear over-carefully dressed."[15]

The importance attributed to "executive" attire may be appreciated from the following story: On the eve of the Revolutionary War, George Washington wrote a letter to his nephew (George Steptoe Washington) in which he told him that to be considered for a leadership position he must abstain from pursuing the latest fashion. His choice of dress must conform to the prevailing fashion to "stand well in the eyes of other peoples" and to "impress the simpler of their own folk"; he must be aware that distinct situations require different attire.

> A conformity to the prevailing fashion in a certain degree is necessary—but it does not follow from thence that a man should always get a new coat, or other clothes, upon every trifling change in the mode, when perhaps, he has two or three very good ones by him.—A person who is anxious to be a leader of the fashion, or one of the first to follow it, will certainly appear, in the eyes of judicious men, to have nothing better than a frequent change in dress to recommend him to notice.—I would always wish you to appear sufficiently decent to entitle you to admission into any company where you may be:—but I cannot too strongly enjoin it upon you—and your own knowledge must convince you of the truth of it—that you should be as little expensive in this respect as you properly can;—you should always keep some clothes to wear to Church, or on particular occasions, which should not be worn everyday.[16]

Knowingly or unknowingly George Bush took heed. In a report on the then-president's style of dress, Ruth La Ferla observed that when William Thourlby, a New York image consultant and a former actor, said that George Bush had "taken an adjustment," he was not talking tailors' talk. He was using a fancy thespian term for slipping into character—one that aptly described the president's shift of gears sartorially to match each occasion. He wore a hard hat when touring a Kentucky steel plant, a ten-gallon hat in Texas, a lab coat when warranted, and he changed into camouflage when going hunting. Moreover, he followed a deliberate sartorial strategy during his campaign. Mr. Bush wore a nondescript tan jacket, button-down collars, and bright-red regimental ties. His style said, "We are second in command," Thourlby explained. After the election, the public saw a one-hundred-day metamorphosis from a modestly outfitted Everyman to an icon of power in pinstripes, straight collars, and subtle ties. His switch to blue was significant. It ascribed to the president a stronger look, Thourlby suggested.[17]

Origins of the Image of Authority

In artwork from ancient Mesopotamia and Imperial Rome, those with social responsibilities that entailed a public role are presented in erect postures and in torso-concealing attire. In reliefs, monuments, statues, and commemorative plaques of the Sumerian and Assyrian civilizations, the military uniforms and the battle formation of warriors convey an image of solidity. In identical-looking garments—tunic-gowns to the midcalf and nail-studded leather stoles—the warriors are shown marching in columns; moreover, the king's voluminous presence appears in sharp contrast to the scantily dressed captives.[18]

In the *Stele of Hammurabi*, ca. 1792–1750 B.C., Hammurabi, the ruler, is shown representing his people before an enthroned sun god as he receives the code of laws. He stands erect. His attire is long, form-following, and body-concealing. The priests and rulers of Mesopotamia (the land between the Euphrates and Tigris Rivers) saw themselves as leaders by virtue of greater knowledge. Their authority came out of their ability to provide for the economic and spiritual needs of the population and their desire to protect the people from natural disasters.

As a result of swollen rivers and mud brought down from the mountains, crops were often threatened in Mesopotamia.[19] The desire of the priests and rulers to overcome the precariousness of the physical environment is mirrored in the strong, emphatic images they created in sacred and secular realms. The most dramatic example is the raised temple known as the ziggurat. Built on stepped levels, as if to unite the world below and heavens above, the ziggurat resembled the solid structure of a mountain, as Joseph Campbell suggested.[20]

In the Roman Republic and during the early empire, the toga was a sign of citizenship. It consisted of a large piece of off-white cloth worn over a tunic. It enveloped both shoulders, wrapping the left hand against the chest. Only the right hand was left free. All male citizens were required to wear the toga for public ceremony. It was the "standard uniform of all classes from a senator to the lowest plebeian." A man banished from Rome would first be stripped of his toga.[21]

Togas distinguished Roman citizens from the many visitors and the barbarian slaves that thronged Rome. To receive respect, Roman men had to present a dignified appearance, and wearing a toga helped. The toga limited the number of tasks a citizen could perform. Also, because the toga was held together only by draping, movement and gesture had to be refined and poise maintained, lest the dress come apart. The toga style of dress could be adopted only because Roman citizens did not have to engage in physical labor; they could leave that to slaves.[22]

The Christian sects that hid in the catacombs in Rome took on the humble tunics of the servant class. These "servants of the Lord" replaced the toga with a symbol of asceticism. The early Christians also adopted a rectangular pallium

Stele of Hammurabi, *ca. 1780 B.C., Louvre, Paris. The earliest written body of laws is engraved on a diorite slab. At the top is an engraving of Hammurabi standing in front of the sun god, Shamash, who is seated on a mountain. The god's hand holds a staff and is outstretched toward Hammurabi.*

wrap, rejecting the Romans' new emphasis on status symbols, such as blond wigs, makeup, jewels, and silk. They also rejected Persian regalia, barbarian wool cloaks, and the bright plaids and trousers that were worn during this period.[23]

During the first centuries of the Christian Era, Roman costume in the countries conquered by the empire as well as in Rome was of two types: long for the wealthy and cultivated classes, short for workers and soldiers. By the sixth century, liturgical costume consisted of several layers of garments worn one on top of the other, concealing all personal characteristics. The style, embroidery, and other details of these garments signified *the right to represent the church.*

Throughout time, authority has been carried by the garment: More complete covering and uniformity conveys more authority. The individual must measure up to the garment, or rather must *appear* to become the garment. If it is worn constantly, clothing of authority will ultimately be dehumanizing, subsuming the person it contains.

Sociocultural Background of Uniforms

In the early twentieth century, members of the medical profession wore white uniforms to promote the image of a scientific approach to illness and of themselves as professionals whose ministrations in hospitals would result in healing.[24] Similarly, as social life began to acquire a new complexity after A.D. 1050 and pilgrim traffic, industry, agriculture, and trade began to encourage the development of distinct occupational groups, each group sought to make its authority visible.[25] Uniforms emerged as a means of centralizing authority, identifying hierarchy, and claiming expertise over a specific body of knowledge. The belief prevalent at the time, that God's universe is orderly and each person has a place within it, made possible the institution of a mode of dress that categorized people by occupation and rank.[26]

The Spiritual Realm: Monastic and Priestly Attire

Within the spiritual realm, between 1000 and 1350 B.C. two basic uniforms were confirmed—monastic attire and priestly dress. They represented the two different paths to religious training and life in the church.

From reading the Gospels, the founders of monasteries concluded that a life that was contemplative in nature and lived alone in austere and ascetic fashion was the only true path to God, who alone can fill "inner emptiness." Monks acquired their religious education individually, under the guidance of a spiritual father and through reading the Bible within the liturgical framework of monastic life. Within the monastery walls they copied manuscripts and set up libraries, keeping alive an intellectual tradition.[27]

Later clerics acquired their education in theological schools near the cathedrals in cities. Already versed in the liberal arts, they were prepared for an active life in the secular world. The Christian bishops decided the clerics should make visible the ideas and power of the church to enlighten the population and increase its involvement with religion.[28]

In the medieval period, almost as soon as children were weaned, they were regarded as small adults. They were dressed in adult styles, and as they got older they mingled, competed, worked, and learned expected adult behavior in interaction with adults. Through close supervision of the offspring's attire the family guided a child's orientation to adult roles. One of the earliest examples of the use of dress to encourage a very young child to assume clerical vocation can be found in the memoirs of Abbot Guibert of Nogent. Written in 1115, when he was in his forties (b. 1066?), the memoirs tell of Guibert's childhood experience. His mother's difficulty in giving birth led his father to pledge the unborn child to the service of God. Before Guibert was a year old his father died, and thus the pledge could not be revoked. When he was a young child, his mother dressed him in rich clerical garb to promote the kind of self-control he would need as a priest— his anticipated adult role. So attired, the boy remained on the sidelines, but he watched the other children in their "games and merrymaking." Talking to God through his memoirs, he wrote, "O God, Thou knowest what warnings, what prayers she daily poured into my ears not to listen to corrupting words from anybody. She taught me how and for what I ought to pray to Thee."[29]

Monastic Attire   Monastic life required detachment from the world. It demanded vows of poverty, chastity, and obedience and a life of prayer rather than the act of prayer. The principles of monastic attire were set down during the rule of Saint Benedict (A.D. 480–543) and were followed by all the orders created in the eleventh and twelfth centuries. Monks were to be clothed in long, loose-fitting, wide-sleeved habits made of plain wool. The habits were to be simply belted with leather or with a knotted rope. The cut of the monks' hair, the shape of their hoods, and the color and weave of their habits distinguished the various orders. Saint Benedict believed that the vice of private ownership would be avoided if the abbot supplied all necessary clothing: two cowls, two tunics, stockings, shoes, and a belt. When monks received new clothes they had to return the old ones to the clothes room for donation to the poor. Saint Benedict was concerned about the image monks presented to the outside world; he did not want them to be considered negligent in their appearance. Monks traveling abroad or receiving important visitors to the monastery were allotted better quality clothing, but it had to be returned after use.[30]

Three of the major monastic orders had female counterparts, and the nuns wore plain, inexpensive dress that enveloped the body from head to toe. In the case of Benedictine and Cluniac nuns, it consisted of a white undertunic, a black gown, and a black veil with a white wimple (headcloth) that covered the head completely except for the face. Cistercians dressed entirely in white and were called the "white ladies."[31]

Franciscan monk's habit. The clothing reflects the monks' vows of poverty, chastity, and obedience.

Priestly Attire   In addition to negating sexuality, as monastic attire did, the clothing of the priesthood emphasized the *act* of prayer and connectedness to spiritual and supernatural powers in the liturgy. Hierarchy and access to wealth were also visible.

Ecclesiastical authorities viewed Roman attire as dignified and carrying the image of authority, which was in contrast to that of the invading barbarians, who wore pants. They adopted the Roman style and created the priestly uniform. In A.D. 573 the Council of Braga ordered that the cassock, an ankle-length, long-sleeved tunic, be worn underneath liturgical vestments. By A.D. 600 the ecclesiastical authorities had designated the chasuble the garment required for cele-

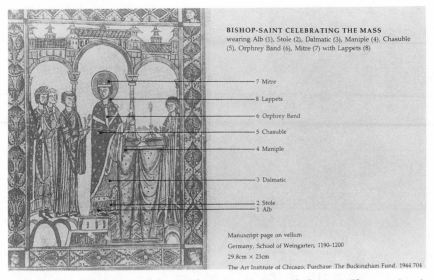

BISHOP-SAINT CELEBRATING THE MASS
wearing Alb (1), Stole (2), Dalmatic (3), Maniple (4), Chasuble
(5), Orphrey Band (6), Mitre (7) with Lappets (8)

7 Mitre

8 Lappets

6 Orphrey Band

5 Chasuble

4 Maniple

3 Dalmatic

2 Stole
1 Alb

Manuscript page on vellum
Germany, School of Weingarten; 1190–1200
29.8cm × 23cm
The Art Institute of Chicago; Purchase: The Buckingham Fund. 1944.704

Priestly attire. Bishop-Saint celebrating the mass, 1190–1200. (C. C. Mayer-Thurman [1975] Raiment for the Lord's Service: A Thousand Years of Western Vestments *[Chicago: The Art Institute of Chicago].)*

brating mass. From the Latin word *casula,* meaning "little house," the chasuble projected a sense of solidity. It was worn over the cassock, which was lined in fur to suit the colder climates of northern Europe. The surplice and the alb, overtunics with wider sleeves, white and ornamented, were also worn over the bulky cassock though under the chasuble. The amice and the dalmatic, too, added to the size and volume of the priestly appearance.[32]

Emulating military hierarchy, the church mandated that those at the top, such as the pope, for whom the white cassock is still reserved, and cardinals and bishops, should dress differently from those farther down the ecclesiastical order. With the strengthening of church authority in the late Middle Ages, the color and the sumptuousness of the clothing began to be used to create distinctions between occasions and ranks. Silk, elaborately embroidered with threads of gold, was reserved for the most solemn affairs. All colors were worn by everyone who said mass, but when clerics were in "regular dress," white was reserved for the cassock of the supreme pontiff. Cardinals wore scarlet, bishops purple, and abbots green.[33]

Pope Leo IX (1048–1054) introduced the miter, a tall gilded hat, as part of the distinctive liturgical dress of bishops. In 1049 he placed a miter on the head of the archbishop of Treves, saying: "We adorn your head with a Roman Miter which you and your successors will always use in the ecclesiastical office after the Roman manner in order to remind you that you are a disciple of the Roman See."[34] The cope, the most opulent outer garment, together with the miter, pectoral cross, pastoral staff, and jeweled rings bishops wear on gloved fingers are all indicators of rank and bear witness to the bishops' spiritual marriage with the church. As vestments have gradually become more elaborate and costly, they have acquired more mystical associations and sacred connotations.[35]

For many years, during mass, priests presented their backs to the congregation. Consequently the backs of their vestments were elaborately embroidered with Christian images. In 1963, when the church moved toward more direct communication, the priests were expected to face the congregation. Since then the front and back of their vestments have been decorated more or less the same, and the vestments have been less richly ornamented.

Ecclesiastical attire increased the body's dimensions and thus its visual significance. It also served to distinguish laity from the clergy, creating a clear line of demarcation between the secular and the sacred and between personal attire and attire that represents the group. By identifying the particular rank of each member of the priestly hierarchy, it specified degrees of authority, which, in turn, identified the extent of deference due an individual wearing some type of priestly attire. The specialized dress for priests of different ranks thus came to control their interaction with one another and with the public.

The symbolic significance of priestly attire can be gathered from the following historical evidence: In the past, when a priest was punished, he was required to remove his garb so he could be whipped without demeaning the office or damaging the vestments. When an individual wore the priestly garb, he ceased to be seen, or to function, as an individual. Instead he became the embodiment of the church, speaking for it and *vested* with its power.

The Economic Realm and Guild Attire

The term "guild" is usually taken to mean an organization of those engaged in a particular craft. In the Middle Ages there were many guilds, among them those of carpenters, weavers, shoemakers, goldsmiths, and ironmongers.[36]

The guild had two principal aims, both of which were reflected in the members' attire. First, the guild acted to maintain its economic position in society by regulating who could produce a specific object and how it would be produced. Second, it tried to preserve equality among the masters of the craft. Each guild developed an insignia or a dress that identified the product and the task and allowed for little distinction in rank. This uniform was worn to guild meetings, which were held outside the workplace. For example, the shoemakers guild, organized in 1272, had the motto "Leather and Skill." Its insignia was a golden chevron and three goats' heads. It was different from the insignia of the cobblers, whose task it was to repair shoes rather than make them.[37] So important was the guild's uniform that "to be clothed" meant that one had attained membership in the guild. As a social observer in 1347 remarked, a uniform was a means of "cherishing the unity and good love among guild members and the common profit of the mastery craft or group of craftsmen."[38]

Because of the advantages that guild membership conferred, the right to wear the uniform was restricted. Although some women developed the skills necessary to excel at a craft, men disregarded their proficiency and discouraged their admission to the guilds. The few women who did belong were not allowed to wear the group's attire because it would have given them a valued social identity.[39] For the most part, women's economic activity was expected to take place in the home. The word "spinster" indicates that spinning was the habitual means of support for many unmarried women.[40] But such women could not use their skills for entrepreneurial enterprise. A statute of the Siena guild of wool merchants that covered the period from 1297 to 1309 read: "No one subject to the guild of wool merchants can or should lend any money to a spinster (woman who spins), nor pay for any wool or carded wool until she has done the work. Whoever violates this rule must pay 5 soldi in deniers to the Guild."[41]

The decline of the guild system led to the demise of guild uniforms. Guilds began to diminish in importance in the sixteenth century when widening horizons and increasing trade led to a demand for new products. The manufacture of these products often necessitated importing expensive raw materials, which entailed increased costs that the guilds could not bear. Guild members became employees of merchant entrepreneurs—men with capital who could carry the costs of the productive process and wait for the return on their investments. The ultimate dissolution of the guilds, however, did not occur until long after the triumph of industrialism.

The Governmental Realm: Judicial and Military Attire

In the early Middle Ages law was the province of the kings' courts, clerics, and wise old men. Justice was administered by feudal lords, noblemen, and others enjoying the kings' confidence. As cities, states, and nations developed, the information necessary for the performance of judicial, military, and police tasks became specialized, requiring special learning. Specialized clothing naturally followed.

Judicial Attire   By the twelfth century, law became a matter to be treated with scientific accuracy, and justice was administered by judges trained in the law and legal thinking. From the twelfth century on, judges were juristic professionals who were expected to know by heart all the pertinent laws. As the number of years of required study and the number of doctors of law increased, the jurists demanded to be called lords, rather than doctors or masters, although that title was usually reserved for noblemen and prelates. The attire they adopted was like that of the nobility they succeeded. It resembled court dress.[42]

In all the countries of Western Europe, a new status was created—professional judges. They replaced the feudal lords as administrators of justice. During the fourteenth and fifteenth centuries, judges were understood to be the legal representatives of the monarch. Elements of dress were part of the drama used to show transfer of the monarch's power to the judge. By wearing robes of the royal ermine, judges showed that they had the right to decide the fate of many. The

*Britain's chief legal officer, Lord Mackay, shown in April
1989. Wigs and robes are mandatory dress in all British
courts above the lowest level. (Reprinted by permission of
AP/Wide World Photos.)*

king continued to be present vicariously in the law courts, through a state portrait, coat of arms, or the color of judicial robes. Moreover, when judicial decrees
were promulgated, armed guards stood by ready to enforce the court's decision.[43]

For the most part, sovereigns clothed their judges. By the sixteenth century judicial robes in England were no longer bound to the fashion popular among the
nobility. The robes assumed the general shape they possess today, with the color,
shoulder piece, hood, and wigs marking levels of authority. In England, scarlet
silk was and still is reserved for those of the highest judicial rank.[44]

After the French Revolution, with the rejection of the aristocracy in France,
traditional judicial attire was abolished. It was later reconstituted, in altered
form, because government leaders considered it vital to preserve the dignity of

the law. The black robe that judges now wore was free from the implications of court dress and military uniform, yet it conveyed solemnity.[45]

In the New World, the colonies of the South continued the pomp and ceremony established in the English court. Scarlet robes identified judges; lawyers who argued cases wore black.[46] In Massachusetts, where the monarchy was rejected as a source of law, traditional judicial attire shared the same fate. Since the Bible was regarded as the appropriate source of law, the clergy assumed judicial positions. Judges appeared in public wearing black robes, which had earlier identified the clergy of the Church of England. In 1789, John Jay, the first chief justice of the United States, instituted the black academic gown as the appropriate judicial attire in the new nation. The voluminous black robe hides the physical characteristics of the body, denies the personal being, and offers the image of solidity.[47]

Military Attire Military service grew out of loyalty to the feudal lords. As knights became involved in the Crusades, they were also considered soldiers of the church. After the Crusades knights were replaced by retainers, who fought as soldiers when needed. Their attire proclaimed their relationship to a particular lord because they wore his colors or his coat of arms. In fifteenth-century England many lords had private armies to protect their economic and political interests, and the retainers wore distinctive uniforms. In 1458 the earl of Warwick insisted that his six hundred retainers wear red jackets with an embroidered badge; the marquess of Winchester had his gentlemen and yeomen wear uniforms of "Reading Tawny"; and the earl of Oxford had his entourage wear embroidered suits with the image of a blue boar on the left shoulder and chains of gold around the neck.[48]

Henry VII of England clothed his retinue in white satin. When he visited the French king, the uniforms of the kings and their armies were so lavish that historians called the meeting "the field of the cloth of gold."[49] As the power of monarchs increased, so did the splendor of their armies' uniforms. By the end of the fifteenth century, the king of England and the king of France each had developed a standing army with uniforms so dazzling that the uniforms themselves were expected to intimidate the enemy. Military uniforms were patterned after the sumptuous attire of the aristocracy with arms added.[50]

English and French soldiers on the American continent wore the colorful, fashionable attire prevalent in their countries at the time, as Alice Morse Earle observed. The first inkling the English had that their army uniforms were not conducive to winning a war came during the American War of Independence. Redcoats became easy targets for the nonuniformed, volunteer American soldiers.[51]

The extension of royal power to the seas and the founding of the Royal Navy led to the adoption of seamen's informal garb as the new naval uniform. The officers, as holders of a higher rank, demanded a distinct appearance; they were dissatisfied with the "Quaker plainness" of the blue uniforms assigned to them.

Justice Byron White, June 24, 1993. John Jay, the first chief justice of the United States, designated a simple black gown as appropriate judicial attire. (Reprinted by permission of Jose Lopez/NYT Pictures.)

Occupational attire acquired new precision and importance in the nineteenth century, as seen in the shift from the watchman's uniform to that of the policeman. (P. Cunnington, C. Lucas, and A. Mansfield [1967] Occupational Costume in England from the Eleventh Century to 1914 [London: Charles & Adam Black]. Reprinted by permission of John Johnson [Author's Agent] Ltd.)

In 1775, they petitioned for gold epaulets, which to this day characterize naval officers' attire both in Europe and the United States.[52]

In response to the rise in crime in England in the early part of the nineteenth century, a formalized police force was developed in 1840. A special uniform was designed that was intended to provide an image of discipline and strength: a dark suit with a tall hat, special insignia, a club, and a whistle. The police officer replaced the earlier informal status of watchman or parish constable, who made nightly rounds wearing a simple cloak and carrying a rattle. Through the organization of the new police force and the use of uniforms, the government extended its power.[53]

7

Gender Images

CENTRAL TO A DISCUSSION of the relationship between clothing and gender is the understanding that sexual characteristics at birth are the basis for the "script" identifying social expectations for sex-appropriate behavior.[1] Recent research has shown that very early in life, before children are aware of sexual differences, they are alerted to differences in dress, and that as early as two years of age they classify people according to gender.[2] Gender scripts help to create two social categories, the members of which deal with their bodies differently, as Goffman observed. Men are socialized to use their bodies in a straightforward manner; they learn to manipulate, grasp, and hold. Women learn to convey the feeling that their bodies are delicate and precious; they are supposed to caress objects and people.[3]

Psychologist J. C. Flugel suggested that the basis for sex-specific attire is sexual *interdependence*. He noted that visual distinction between the sexes has been seen throughout history and in most places and in most parts of the world. Everyone assumes that people wear sex-specific attire because doing so follows "the natural order of things." Sex-specific attire was, and is, intended to alert an approaching individual about *suitability for sexual intercourse*. Even articles of clothing associated with a specific sex have the power to arouse passion in members of the other sex. The tie, jacket, trousers, and shoes of the male, for example, and the high heels, garter, and girdle associated with the female have been found to elicit sexual responses. Hence, the purpose of sex-specific attire is to spur interaction between the sexes. Survival of the species depends on such a distinction.[4]

British costume historian James Laver suggested that sex-specific attire identifies the social spheres in which men and women function. The "hierarchy principle" underlies male dress: Men wear class-conscious attire that reflects their standing in the wider social sphere. Female attire is governed by the "seductive principle": It is designed to make women attractive to men and hence less significant.[5] The meaning of appearance, thus, is closely tied to gender expectations for behavior.

Socialization to Gender

Clothing is used to create a gender distinction, as noted by Gregory P. Stone. He observed that dressing a newborn in blue begins a sequence of interaction that is different from the one experienced by a baby dressed in pink. The infant's appearance in clothing of a sex-specific color sets up expectations about how the child should act, think, and feel. Among other things, it is anticipated that a baby dressed in blue will be handsome, strong, and agile, whereas the pink-clad infant will be beautiful, sweet, and graceful. The color acts as a cue or stimulus that influences how people behave toward the child and how that child is expected to conduct himself or herself. It is the response of others to gender-specific attire that encourages gender-appropriate behavior, Stone concluded.[6]

Norms governing gender-appropriate attire are so powerful, Stone pointed out, that male participants in a study he conducted were able to recall the revulsion they experienced when as children their mothers dressed them in "fussy" attire. They wanted to be clothed in what they had learned was "manly" attire. Sex-specific attire, Stone maintained, enhances the internalization of expectations for gender-specific behavior. Through subtle rewards and punishments, such as those given through tone of voice, parents encourage or discourage specific behavior, which leads to the development of a gender identity.[7]

Gender-Specific Toys

In early childhood the clothing worn in play and the toys children play with may be important means of encouraging gender orientation. Girls are more likely than boys to play dress-up. Many also have fun creating ensembles for their dolls, coordinating the color and style of the doll clothes. Playing with Barbie, an extremely popular doll (more than 600 million Barbies have been sold worldwide since 1959), encourages awareness of textiles and fabrics. Barbie has kept up with the times and has been portrayed as an astronaut, a business executive, and a pilot, among other things. Her wardrobe, in appropriate colors and fabrics, covers everything from space travel to summit meetings. Playing with Barbie, however, requires staying close to home, limiting the opportunity to explore the outside world.[8] Moreover, since Barbie's body was designed principally to look good in clothes, she is tall and the dimensions of her body, 36-18-33, are unrealistic. She embodies a standard that is almost impossible to achieve, and thus she encourages a sense of inadequacy.[9]

The physical characteristics of the toy figures that boys carry around are often menacing. Batman, Superman, G. I. Joe, the Masters of the Universe, and the recent Killer Tomatoes are characters of power and action.[10] Boys' toys are thus characterized by activity and toughness, even those played with indoors, like Nintendo. Functionality and goal-directed appearance inform boys' orientation to clothing.

Children's Picture Books

Children's storybooks also offer two distinct orientations to appearance. *Confluence* characterizes the portrayal of men, and *contrast* typifies that of women. In these books, the father is portrayed wearing form-following, body-concealing attire coordinated to create a unified whole. Dressed in a housedress or a skirt and blouse in contrasting colors, the mother is often depicted wearing an apron. Visually, these outfits cut the body in half, dwarfing the person and intimating a

In children's books aprons often identify housewives, whereas self-restraint characterizes the appearance of the male figure. (Illustration by T. Hutchings in Chippy Goes to the Dentist, 1985. *Reprinted by permission of Joshua Morris Publishing, Inc.)*

figure of less significance. The apron, moreover, has always been associated with physical labor, which is considered less important than "head work." It identifies people in service occupations who lack authority.[11] From aprons to business suits, gender-specific attire varies along with the dimension of authority. Even when animals are used in place of humans, their identity is made visible through gender-stereotypical attire.

As they get older, children increasingly associate dress with stereotypical behavior patterns.[12] They feel that "feminine" means a docile demeanor and that negative sanctions follow women who behave in gender-inappropriate ways. When young girls, ages seven through thirteen, were asked to select one of four clothing styles for a girl who is "bossy"—bossy being a characteristic expected of a male—77 percent chose one of the two most extreme styles: jeans and a T-shirt (the most androgynous outfit) and a frilly dress (the most feminine). From the girls' comments, it became clear to the investigator that they viewed only two kinds of "scripts" leading to bossiness: a prissy, spoiled girl who is likely to wear frilly dresses, and a tough person, tomboy, or bully who is not afraid to get on the ground and get dirty. The respondents viewed "bossiness" as an attempt to exercise control, a negative female attribute.[13]

The findings of this study bring to mind the fact that "tomboy" was coined in sixteenth-century England. It was used to describe a bold and immodest girl, one who violated society's expectation for meek behavior. That the phenomenon was recognized and given a name suggests that there were many young women at the time who engaged in such behavior. The word was coined during the reign of Elizabeth I, who inherited the throne and successfully ruled for over fifty years. When badgered by parliament to marry in order to assure succession, she publicly prayed to God "to continue me still in this mind to live out of the state of marriage."[14]

Religious Injunctions

The church fathers have always insisted upon a visual distinction between the sexes and have submitted guidelines to the church for sex-appropriate appearance and behavior. Three beliefs have underlain their use of dress to establish gender distinction: that real differences exist between the sexes; that the male is the more superior being; and that women's social participation should be limited to reproduction. Saint Paul, for example, criticized the practice current during the first century of men and women wearing each other's clothing. He claimed that this habit violated the order of nature because each sex has its own place in the universe. He implored men and women to dress in a manner that demonstrated the superiority of men. Men, he said, must keep their heads uncovered when praying, whereas women must cover their heads as a sign of subservience to men:

> Any man who prays or prophesies with his head covered dishonors his head, but any woman who prays or prophesies with her head unveiled dishonors her head—it is the same as if her head were shaven. For if a woman will not veil herself, then she should cut off her hair: but if it is disgraceful for a woman to be shorn or shaven, let her wear a veil. For a man ought not cover his head, forasmuch as he is the image and glory of God; but woman is the glory of man. For man was not made from woman, but woman from man. Neither was man created for woman, but woman for man.[15]

Later he said:

> As in all the churches of the saints, the women should keep silence in the churches. For they are not permitted to speak, but should be subordinate, even as the law says.
> If there is anything they desire to know, let them ask their husbands at home. For it is shameful for a woman to speak in church.[16]

And in Paul's Epistle to Timothy, he explicitly demanded women's submissiveness:

> Let a woman learn in silence with all submissiveness. I permit no woman to teach or to have authority over men; she is to keep silent. For Adam was formed first, then Eve; and Adam was not deceived, but the woman was deceived and became the

Bess Truman, Eleanor Roosevelt, and Edith Wilson, all in hats (1954). (Reprinted by permission of UPI/Bettmann; photo by Jack Larz.)

transgressor. Yet woman will be saved through bearing children, if she continues in faith and love and holiness, with modesty.[17]

Clement of Alexandria, a church father of the first century A.D., declared that beards were the badge of masculinity and that it was sacrilegious to trifle with them because they were a symbol of man's stronger nature. He claimed that "by God's decree hairiness is one of man's conspicuous qualities. ... Whatever smoothness or softness there was in him God took from him when he fashioned the delicate Eve from his side ... his characteristic is action; hers, passivity."[18]

The Seven Deadly Sins were a set of guidelines for appropriate appearance and behavior. The sin of pride advocated humility and modesty in dress for both men and women. The prohibition against sloth, another of the deadly sins, supported the idea that males should play an active role in social life and was designed to encourage males to take part in the socioeconomic process.[19] Medieval literature depicted idleness, or sloth, as the "feet of the devil that halt man in his tracks" and declared that it demonstrated a lack of feeling for the world, the people in it, and oneself.[20] Church authorities in medieval times interpreted Saint Paul's dictum, "He who shall not work will not eat," as a universal injunction against the withdrawal from society. Monks were enjoined to remain in touch with secular matters in order to gain better control over "satanic forces."[21]

*In preparation for her role as a wife, Lady Diana Spencer had to acquire hats, visually af-firming the traditional wife's role. (*New York Times, *June 5, 1981; reprinted by permission of UPI/Bettmann; photo by R. Letkey.)*

Thomas Aquinas preached that work was essential for the survival of the individual and the community. Protestantism subsequently viewed labor as glorifying God and proclaimed it the moral duty of every man. Resistance to one's calling was considered blasphemy.[22] *Rational piety* and *worldly engagement,* the expectations for male behavior, were supported by attire that conveyed obedience to the injunction to modesty and self-effacement.

Morality Tales

Prior to the sixteenth century (before the Protestant Reformation and printing), when most of the world's population was illiterate, paintings of religious themes warned men and women against the pursuit of sexual and other personal interests. One popular account portrayed in paintings was the story of Salome, which alerts men to female trickery and seduction and informs women of their power and their ability to get things they want despite disapproval and objection. For example, in the *Altarpiece of St. John the Baptist and St. John the Evangelist, 1479* by Hans Memling, King Herod and the soldiers are depicted in the attire of power. Salome is demure and tentative in manner, with eyes cast down, as she stands with a platter to accept the head of John the Baptist.[23]

The cautionary tale of Saint Ursula directs young women to obey their fathers. The Saint Ursula Shrine, now in the Memlingmuseum in Bruges, Belgium, is a glittering miniature house of the late Gothic period (before 1489). The shrine consists of small-scale sculpture and paintings that depict how Ursula went to Rome with ten thousand virgins to appeal to the pope to override her father's decision that she marry. Pope Cyriac is shown blessing Ursula, who is kneeling before him dressed in feminine attire and submissive in posture. He is giving her the Sacrament and bidding her to return home and obey her father's wishes. She complies, but on the way home the travelers are attacked by the Huns and Ursula is killed by an arrow. By disobeying her father she opened herself and her followers to misfortune.[24]

Chivalry and Courtly Love

Between the tenth and fifteenth centuries, in the feudal courts of medieval Europe, gender expectations gradually changed. Female submission, male modesty, and self-effacement evolved into a new form: chivalry. Members of the nobility who acquired the title of knight acquired a new set of expectations for gender-appropriate behavior and appearance. These warriors on horseback viewed women as an inspiration to heroism. The code of chivalry, their rules of conduct, included a pledge to *protect* women.[25] The initial phase of training entailed service in the house of the lord, where the aspiring young knight acquired more polished manners and an appreciation of the important part women played in his culture.

A different kind of relationship between the genders is seen in the courtly love ideal, which existed alongside chivalry. It consisted of the idea that love between a man and a woman is of supreme value to life on earth and that love uplifts and ennobles the lover. The courtly love ideal led to the elevation of women as objects of devotion. Today, the customary signs of deference toward women— holding the door for a woman, lighting her cigarette, and so on, are reflections of the code of chivalry and courtly love. Etiquette books continue to espouse these practices but in a somewhat diminished form.

To be a knight was a male privilege that had to be individually earned and personally given. Horsemanship and swordsmanship were part of the training. From early childhood on, male members of the nobility jousted, wrestled, and exercised to develop coordination and strength. Medieval jousts and tournaments pitted one man against another. Combative games were played during solemn occasions and social events, such as coronations and royal marriages, and physical prowess became a virtue. In his erect posture, with armor, shield, and sword, the knight conveyed an image of invulnerability.

In contrast, beauty was the desired characteristic for women. A woman was beautiful if she was small, well-rounded, slender, and graceful, "with a small willowy waist."[26] Delicacy and refinement were the desired qualities of female attire in the feudal courts. Long hair was often braided with ribbons or enclosed in long tubes of silk or leather. Women adorned themselves with splendid necklaces. Dresses were made of wool, linen, and sometimes leather and were completed with embroidery, precious jewels, and fur.[27] The floor-length jumperlike garment was the style of the time. It had a long, fitted bodice, low neckline, and very deep armholes. It was figure revealing.[28] The generous open expanses around the neck suggested vulnerability.

Thus, highly contrasting images of masculinity and femininity emerged from the feudal courts. Desired appearance and behavior for each gender diverged radically.

Masculine Physical Ideal

The erect posture, agility, and strength of the nobility became an ideal for the mercantile middle class during the Renaissance. Pope Pius II (1458–1464) recommended that schools adopt games and exercises to develop "the general carriage" of children. They should be trained to hold their heads upright and to look straight ahead, unafraid. Whether walking, standing, or sitting, children should bear themselves with dignity.[29]

Male members of the royal courts exercised and played sports. The kings of England saw tennis as essential for developing agility, speed, and the kind of strategic thinking they believed would help them run the country. Henry VIII even had thin-soled shoes designed for himself to help improve his chances of winning.[30]

In the United States the masculine ideal emanates from two sources. One is the need for simple physical strength. Among those making their way to the West, a strong physique symbolized the victory of man over nature.[31] The election of President Andrew Jackson (1829–1837) represented the ascendancy of the brawny man, whose rough-and-tumble image diverged dramatically from the refined sensibility of the European aristocracy. Later, an interest in muscle power was brought to the country by new immigrants from Germany and Ireland, who competed physically among themselves or against others. Youths seeking to distance themselves from an older immigrant generation they considered sedentary seized the opportunity to engage in sports. They believed that to be successful in life they needed to develop a physically strong body.

The second source for the masculine ideal is the desire for agility and strength. A German professor at Harvard University, Charles Follen, a German immigrant, introduced his students to fitness. He met with them twice a week, on his own time, to do gymnastics. A formal physical education program was instituted in 1861. All students were required to appear at the newly constructed gym for half an hour four times a week. Erect posture, agility, physical strength, and competition were in this way incorporated into Ivy League education.

In the 1870s athletic clubs and baseball leagues were established in many American cities. In the 1880s football gained importance at American colleges, and working out with weights became a key part of programs at Young Men's Christian Associations (YMCAs). Famous weight lifter Eugene Sandow popularized bodybuilding among men. Those who relentlessly pursued muscle power and achieved their goal were admired for their "iron will."[32]

Finally, connected with the masculine physical ideal in American society is a moral strand. Current actors like Clint Eastwood, Charles Bronson, Sylvester Stallone, and Arnold Schwarzenegger continue the medieval knightly tradition of righting wrongs. They often portray the idea that the male role entails competition and physical strength in the service of some higher ideal.

Female Images

The belief on the part of church fathers that men were unable to control sexual passion underlays their demand that women cover their bodies. The specific evil evoked by lust was its mastery over the whole man. Saint Augustine wrote:

> This lust assumes power not only over the whole body and not only from the outside, but also internally; it disturbs the whole man, when the mental emotion combines and mingles with the physical craving resulting in pleasure surpassing all physical delights. So intense is the pleasure that when it reaches its climax there is an almost total extinction of mental alertness: the intellectual sentries, as it were, are overwhelmed.[33]

Christian thinkers argued that a man's affections should be expressed in the love of God. Shame was expected to accompany even the lawful practice of procre-

ation. To help men remain pure and reach spirituality, women's attire had to obscure the body and be drab and colorless.

Although new opportunities were opened for the male in the medieval period,
roles available to women seem to have decreased.[34] Rules for female deportment during this period held that women's "eyes must be cast down, they must
not glance left or right, ... they must neither look at nor address a man, and must
not swing their arms when walking, or cross their legs when sitting, their hands
must be hidden in their cloaks." These expectations for female deportment in effect limited women's involvement with society, according to M. von Boehn.[35]

The rules for female deportment were reinforced in religious art, especially art
depicting the Holy Family and Nativity scenes. In the Book of Hours, an illuminated prayer book that first appeared in the second half of the thirteenth century, women are shown in domestic settings, praying and reading the Scriptures,
or working in the fields. The message conveyed is that women are pure, pious,
and submissive. Often women are pictured holding babies. Spirituality, motherhood, and submission to those in higher authority were the characteristics of the
ideal woman.[36]

The church's definition of modest attire that hides the female body was integrated into secular life. Even today, it continues to guide female role behavior.[37]

The Secular Sphere

Female labor was essential in medieval times. In most social classes, men were
dependent on their wives for doing household chores. Tasks assigned to wives
varied from manor to manor, from region to region, and from countryside to
city. Within a manor women always had control over the production of dairy,
poultry, and vegetables. In the cities they were involved in the home brewing of
beer and the making of cloth.[38] Wives were dependent on a husband's protection and support. Men monopolized the more lucrative and rewarding trades
and professions, leaving unattached women economically vulnerable. According to French historian Philip Aries, they were also physically vulnerable. Impoverished and with no family protection they were subject to rape. The community
saw itself as a vast gathering of householders; living within a family context was
the ideal. Departure from this ideal was unacceptable. For an unmarried woman
living alone, a house of prostitution became a "safe harbor."[39]

Clothing regulations recognized that to attract a husband women had to wear
more frivolous attire than at other times. Women in the courting stage were allowed to make use of color and ornament different from what a wife could use. A
woman remained under the jurisdiction of her father and was entitled to wear
the attire of his rank until she married. Once married she was under the control
and protection of her husband and wore the clothing of *his* rank.[40]

Although women could not be party to a business contract, buy or sell land, or
control significant amounts of money, they sometimes could do so through an
inherited position. In the "Wife of Bath," Chaucer (1342–1400) wrote about a
widow, a merchant's wife, who took part in the pilgrimage to Canterbury. She
carried on her husband's business after his death, "making cloth that bettered of

Ypres and of Ghent." In company she loved to chat and laugh. She was skilled in love, having had five husbands, and knew how to take care of "love's mischances." Chaucer described her attire in this manner: Her kerchiefs were finely woven, her hose of the finest scarlet red, and her shoes soft and new. He concluded that her attire testified to her income. Yet she contrasted herself to those who decided to live in virginity, "as clean in body as in soul, and never mate. I'll make no boast about my own estate."[41] The Wife of Bath clearly viewed the body as a source of sensual pleasure. This pleasure carried over to her joy of dressing and clothing herself in a manner that would attract male interest. Her resources, of course, made that possible.

The Procreative Role

Throughout time women have been expected to marry and assume their biological role of procreation. In Indian art from prehistoric times, an emphasis on the hips, breasts, and belly alluded to women's biological ability to bear and nurture children. In the late Middle Ages, when plagues decimated the European population and an iconography of death was a popular subject in art, the prevailing style of dress focused on women's abdomens, simulating a "pregnant look." Breasts as "containers of nurturing" were a subject frequently portrayed in art. It was as if to remind women that bearing and nurturing children was their unique privilege and responsibility.[42] After World War II, in the late 1940s and through the 1950s, fashion styles again alluded to pregnancy. Yves Saint Laurent's 1953 "Trapeze line" consisted of clothes that emphasized wide hips and called attention to the abdomen, glamorizing maternity and womanhood. The breasts assumed new importance. It was during this period that the large bosoms of Marilyn Monroe and Jayne Mansfield were celebrated.[43] The exhortation by those in authority in the workplace that women return to the traditional female role, leaving the jobs to men, and the fact that men were back from the war resulted in the so-called baby boom (1946–1960).

The Wife's Role

With the advent of commerce and the growth of monarchies, it was no longer sufficient for a man to dress himself in attire that supported his claim for rank. To demonstrate his power and wealth a husband had to dress his wife and other members of the household well. The family members' appearance signified the consciousness of a "we." Their lavish attire was similar in style, texture, and color. To create dynasties, monarchs established the right to rule through birthright. The royal wife wore sumptuous garments and dazzling jewelry, supporting the king's claim to the monarchy and helping to create an image of stability, power, and wealth.[44]

The Female Authority Role

In the sixteenth century three women ascended the throne: Isabella of Aragon/Castile, Catherine de Médicis in France, and Elizabeth I in England. They wore female attire—dresses, in a style that extended the body but de-emphasized the

Jan Arnolfini and His Wife *by Jan van Eyck, 1435, London, National Gallery. It was fashionable to stress the woman's abdomen in art during this period.*

*The "Trapeze line" by Yves Saint Laurent, 1953 (*Jardin des Modes). *The focus is again on the abdomen.*

maternal and nurturing role. A high-necked masculine bodice flattened the chest and its V-shaped padded front resembled the armor of noblemen. The bodice extended over a voluminous skirt and was supported by a farthingale, a structure of stiff hoops. Like the high neck and skirt, puffed sleeves served to draw attention away from the body, thus forcing distance and creating a sense of amplification. The many gemstones the women wore provided the brilliance characteristic of male monarchs. Unlike male monarchs, they carried no arms, but they were surrounded by attendants who did.[45]

Women of the nobility in other European courts also dressed within this new paradigm. The image they adopted was that of confluence: the breasts flattened, the waistline repudiated, their dress form-following, coming straight down and just touching the floor. A stiff white ruff effectively denied access to the expression of feelings.

Similarly, in the 1970s, women in managerial positions observed that a key to being considered professional was dressing in a manner that minimized the maternal, nurturing, and sexual dimensions of their appearance. A form-following jacket over a blouse concealed the contours of the female body and, like a shield,

Actress Jayne Mansfield (1932–1967), whose large breasts were celebrated by the media. (Reprinted by permission of The Bettmann Archive.)

The 1959 Barbie doll displayed the traditional emphasis on female breasts. (Barbie® doll photo used with permission of Mattel, Inc.)

Queen Elizabeth I *by Cornelius Ketel, n.d., Pinacoteca, Siena. The queen's breasts are deemphasized by the dress, but her ability to extend her reach is emphasized by both the dress and the attendants seen in the background. (Reprinted by permission of Alinari/Art Resource, New York.)*

*Women who hold authority positions in contemporary society are expected, like men, to project self-restraint. In her chambers at Federal Court in Washington, D.C., Judge Ruth Bader Ginzburg wears a form-following jacket that hides the waistline and obscures the breasts. (*New York Times, *June 27, 1993; reprinted by permission of Paul Hosefros/NYT Pictures.)*

created distance. They felt that this distance strengthened their ability to give orders and the probability that they would be carried out.[46]

Adopting Male Roles

Rejection of the traditional female role has usually been accompanied by a change in dress. For example, prior to the Renaissance the church allowed women who renounced their sexuality and publicly announced their virginity to wear male attire and to preach. The Acts of the Apostles, a text thought to have been written about A.D. 160, tells the story of Thecla, a beautiful young woman engaged to be married. One day, by chance, she heard Paul preach chastity. Enthralled, she rejected her suitor. When an attempt to burn Thecla at the stake failed, she appealed to Paul and was accepted as his student. After she completed her training, she went out to teach dressed in male attire.[47]

Historian Marina Warner observed that there is ample evidence to suggest that many women who escaped arranged marriages cropped their hair in male fashion, donned male attire, and arrived at monastery gates disguised as men. Often their identity as women was not discovered until their death. Margaret of Antioch, bearing the name Brother Pelagius, lived quietly as a monk until she was accused by a young woman of fathering her child. Margaret suffered the accusation in silence and was condemned to solitary confinement for the rest of her life. With death at hand, she wrote a letter revealing her innocence. She was then recognized as a woman and honored as a saint for her suffering.[48]

The most celebrated example of a woman who rejected female passivity is Joan of Arc. After proclaiming her virginity, and thus her right to wear male attire, she donned a knight's armor and led men into battle on a white horse. Because a woman bearing arms was not acceptable in the church's view, she was accused of immodesty. Refusing to the end to change into women's clothes, Joan was burned at the stake.[49] It was not until World War I that women could formally wear military attire.[50]

Decline of Passivity

At the beginning of the twentieth century, the expanding economy and increasing military needs in the United States encouraged women to move out of the home and into factories, offices, schools, hospitals, and shops. The Gibson girl attire signified the change. It consisted of a shirtwaist blouse and a tailored skirt. It was a practical style preferred by working women and women serious about sports. Artist Charles Dana Gibson popularized the style by portraying beautiful young women so dressed. Feminists at the time saw the Gibson girl as the prototype of the new woman—"braver, stronger, more beautiful, and more skillful and able and free, more human in all ways" than the traditional woman.[51] According to the November 1911 issue of *The American Businesswoman* there were five million self-supporting women in the United States employed in 295 occupations. Mass manufacture made shirtwaist blouses available for as little as $1.50 and suits for $10.00.

The movement of middle-class women into the full-time labor force has been increasing throughout the twentieth century. The 1970s women's movement and the civil rights acts made it possible for today's women to wear police and other uniforms that say that they have right to exercise force. The capacity of women to think rationally and make effective decisions was also recognized. The Puritan rejection of waste and its emphasis on individual determination, together with higher education, legitimated the movement of women into positions of authority. Arguing that national security was undermined by putting sex ahead of talent, the U.S. Senate voted on July 31, 1991, to remove the ban on women as combat pilots.[52] Nearly five hundred years had passed since Joan of Arc was burned at the stake for donning a knight's armor and leading men into battle.

Demise of Subservience and the Active Ideal

Women had been required to cover their heads in public as a sign of submission and obedience to men since early Christian times. In the United States, hats, which some women had interpreted as symbols of middle-class respectability, were repudiated in the 1950s.[53] As the wife of President John F. Kennedy, Jacqueline Kennedy did popularize the pillbox hat, which sat on her well-groomed hair like a crown. But by the end of the 1960s, no hat was in sight. (Journalists may describe the distinction as Jackie Kennedy versus Jackie Onassis.) By the late 1960s women also rejected other upper-class refinements, such as the attire consisting of a basic black dress, white gloves, and strand of cultured pearls. That attire was generally replaced with pants suits and slacks.

In 1982 actress Jane Fonda brought out her first aerobics videotape, helping to bring exercise to a whole new segment of the population, those who never venture out to an exercise class. Youthfulness and health were emphasized by women's magazines and the cosmetics industry, which encouraged more women to join exercise classes. The popularity of working out resulted in what reporters call "the fitness craze."[54]

Actress Jane Fonda in aerobics garb, December 15, 1983. (Reprinted by permission of The Bettmann Archive; photo by Susan Ragan.)

As aerobics and working out became popular, the dancer's black leotard and tights and the sweat suit were gradually replaced. In fabrics that stretch and styles that are comfortable, the unisex capri-length "wrestler" unitard is now worn over a cropped top. The unitard and similar two-piece sets are skintight. They hug the body and allow no place for bulges to hide. In addition to allowing for a greater range of motion, the attire encourages restraint in the consumption of food. The newest exercise attire, a thong-style brief or leotard with high-cut legs, permits a critical view of upper thigh muscles. This attire makes long, well-toned legs, a current fitness ideal, highly visible.

🐦   🐦   🐦

Throughout the many centuries, the Church's injunction to sex-specific attire has remained essentially unchanged. Like church fathers decreed long ago, the body continues to function as a blackboard upon which values and expectations for behavior are signified. Within the secular realm, styles of dress have at times differed from church prescription, dependent upon expectations for participation in the public sphere. As the male role became autonomous from that of the female, men's style of dress became visually independent from that of women. Images of masculinity and femininity evolved to support the expectation that men and women would function in separate spheres. Visual interdependence existed in the monarchic courts, where men were dependent on women to support their claim to the right to rule. Female attire developed around the same principles of power and authority as did male attire.

Economic and political conditions in the United States in the twentieth century gradually made it possible for women to reject visual signs of submission. Further, public education made it possible for American women to reject relegation to the domestic sphere. Women are now more than ever able to dress in attire that allows them greater ability to participate openly in decision-making roles.

The women's movement for the past two decades has sought to modify the powerful influence of traditional male role models such as kings, warriors, and lovers, whose response to women has been that of tyrants, killers, and seducers. The movement has sought to legitimate feelings of tenderness and care, which had usually been stifled in the contemporary male gender role. And today, a new direction in male dress—a masculine translation of female style—is appearing.

In 1991 Italian and American designers seemed to respond to women's complaints and to their own experience. They addressed the man who is unashamed to acknowledge his vulnerability, as well as his virility, and to make light of gender distinctions. In a news story on male style, Ruth La Ferla reported that designers showed men's clothes in shapes and colors borrowed from a woman's wardrobe. Krizia embellished sweaters with nosegays, and Versace showed shirts, shawls, and vests in kaleidoscopic hues "as resplendent as a rajah's." Giorgio Armani altered the mood of the business suit by adding a shirt in a bright woodsman plaid. Keith Varty and Alan Cleaver of Byblos (a design company based in Italy) paired blazers with tapered ski pants. Similarly, Krizia, Ferre, Gucci, and others showed loosened jackets and track pants.[55]

American designers Donna Karan, Calvin Klein, and Michael Kors have moved in another direction. They are attempting to introduce sexiness and flexibility into male dress. Donna Karan pants for men have no creases, eliminating the rigidity and stiffness of the image of authority. Klein is also introducing an extra measure of softness in men's wear. Michael Kors's collection includes separate pieces that can be combined as suits. "As in his women's wear collection, stretch fabric will play a part as will sexiness," reported Woody Hochswender. He quoted Kors as saying, "There is nothing wrong with dressing with a provocative edge," and, "Men want the same comfort level as women." According to Kors, the lycra and stretch fabrics used in women's fashions can give men a new level of comfort. At the same time, these fabrics provide a tighter fit, exposing shape and allowing pride in the physical male body.[56]

Although the norm of gender-distinct attire continues, the injunction to modesty is being rejected. Expectations for women to renounce their intellectual capacities and for men to repudiate humane, emotional dimensions are slowly diminishing. More important, perhaps, the 1992 U.S. presidential election and the appointments made by then president-elect Bill Clinton suggest that the talents and strengths of both genders will be more equally respected in the future.

Seductive Images

FOR MOST PEOPLE, defining seductive attire appears to be extremely easy: Clothing that arouses sexual desire is, of course, seductive.[1] However, people from different countries or different time periods may disagree about which styles of clothing are truly seductive. Each culture develops its own definitions of attire that provokes sexual interest; those who wear such attire within that cultural milieu will be seen as inviting onlookers to engage them sexually. Alluding to the body beneath it, seductive clothing is part of sexual foreplay.

Seductive images are different from pornographic ones. Seductive images are designed to elicit interest in further communication and interaction, are "homemade," and can even be found in family gatherings and ordinary snapshots. Pornographic images, in contrast, address an already positioned audience interested in sexual acts. They are commodities constructed by professionals within distinct social and economic circumstances and are designed to furnish sexual pleasure.[2]

Feminist scholarship suggests that in Western society the role of seductive tempter has been assigned almost exclusively to women.[3] This designation stems from the early church theologians who placed Eve in this category. She not only succumbed to temptation and disobeyed God, but, even worse, she tempted Adam to do the same.

Although Adam and Eve were themselves condemned for disobeying God, it was through their sexual union that their Original Sin was transmitted to all humankind.[4] From this Augustinian perspective, every sexual act could be viewed as a repetition of Original Sin. Because every human being must, of necessity, be conceived by such an act, we are all born in sin and subject to death. The resulting hostility to sex has become, in turn, justification for disdain of the body and antipathy to pleasure of any kind.

With knowledge of pagan sexual practices and biblical prohibitions, church fathers sought to prevent women from serving as a source of carnal temptation. They designated as seductive the use of color that inflamed lust, certain ornaments, and styles of dress that exposed the body or emphasized its curves. Women were not to wear such attire.[5] The basic and most important category of seductive attire consisted of *alluring images designated by the church*. These images are discussed in the next section of this chapter. The church fathers' claim that style of dress had the capacity to equip the wearer to think, feel, or act differently than otherwise is basic to the conception of alluring images.

The prohibition against color, ornament, and style placed women in a difficult position. Because they were dependent on men both socially and economically, they had to attract male attention. To attract the attention of a male, a woman needed to stand out. Over the centuries, Western European women developed modes of attire that remained within the bounds of modesty yet simultaneously enhanced their physical appeal. Such styles sometimes become popular and then disappear, only to be rediscovered later. These styles belong to a second category, *alluring images developed by women.* They are discussed further in a later section of this chapter.

In contemporary America deviant sexual preferences of some men have been legitimated by mainstream culture; they have become part of the vocabulary of seductive images. They form a third category, *alluring images initiated by men.* This category, too, will be discussed in detail later in this chapter. All three categories of images have become part of public memory and provide sources for today's designers.

Alluring Images Designated by the Church

Between A.D. 100 and 500, the church fathers defined the fundamental characteristics of seductive attire as ornamentation, varied colors of clothing, and styles of dress that exposed body parts. Clement of Alexandria (ca. A.D. 150–220) argued that to prevent male transgression, women should cover their bodies from head to toe. However, "their dresses should not be overly soft and clinging and should be hemmed below the ankles rather than above the knees. ... For that style of dress is grave, and protects her from being gazed at." "And," he added, "she will not fall who puts before her eyes modesty and her shawl; nor will she invite another to fall into sin by uncovering her face."[6]

Clement required that women wear veils but forbade them to circumvent the purpose by wearing purple ones because colors attract attention and "inflame lusts." As Enoch, another of the church fathers, argued, "If God wanted dresses made of purple and scarlet wool, he would have created purple and scarlet sheep." In a diatribe against jewelry, Clement complained that certain ornaments used by women served as symbols of adultery. In a similar vein, Tertullian attributed to Enoch the observation that women learned about cosmetics from the fallen angels.[7]

The objection to ornament and the injunction against adornment were clearly expressed by Cyprian in his work, *The Clothing of a Virgin:*

> Let your countenance remain in you incorrupt, your neck unadorned ... let not rings be made in your ears, nor precious chains of bracelets and necklaces encircle your arms or your neck; let your feet be free from golden bands, your hair stained from no dye, your eyes worthy of beholding God.[8]

Similarly, in the first *Epistle to Timothy,* women are advised to "adorn themselves modestly and sensibly in seemly apparel not with braided hair or gold or pearls or costly attire but with good deeds, as befits women who profess religion."[9]

The church's desire to dampen women's sexual allure by requiring that they keep their heads and bodies covered has had several unintended consequences. First, the woman's body has become like a chalkboard upon which she can write or erase sexual intentions. For example, after World War I, women wearing high heels and tight-fitting dresses with low necklines or sideslits that allowed some of the bosom or thigh to be discerned, as well as women letting their hair down when it was normally held up, were interpreted as announcing sexual desire.

The second obvious consequence is that because body parts that have been covered can be uncovered, all parts of the female body have been sexualized. A hemline shortened to expose the ankle or the removal of a glove to allow a glimpse of hand and wrist can arouse sexual interest. Likewise, a person who is partially clad usually provokes sexual interest. (In contrast, costume historian Lawrence Langner [1959] found that in cultures whose members do not usually wear clothing, it is the covered or clothed body that arouses sexual desire.) Thus, the church's insistence on covering the body had the paradoxical result of providing women with a means of contravening its original intention.[10]

A third consequence is that proscribed attire became the category of dress identified as likely to arouse sexual desire; it was cataloged, recognized, and used deliberately for that purpose. This logical consequence was not necessarily unforeseen, since those who chose to wear such clothing provided a warning as well as an invitation: People knew which women to shun, and men knew which women to avoid or to seek out after dark. A law in England from 1352, for example, acknowledged that prostitutes needed special clothing to elicit sexual response. It stated: "No known whore should wear thenceforth, any hood except red or striped of divers colors, nor furs, but garments reversed or turned the wrong side outward upon pain to forfeit the same."[11] The regulation thus recognized that both color and a style signify seductive intent.

In the nineteenth century, prostitutes' attire demonstrated the same characteristics as were stated in the 1352 law. It was made of cheap, flashy material (brightly colored and, as it were, turned wrong side out to suggest its closeness to the body) and "nothing besides in the way of undergarments. Bonnetless, without shawls, they presented themselves 'in their figure' to male passersby."[12] All of the early church fathers, of course, would have recognized from only their lack of head covering that such women represented the temptation of the Devil.

Alluring Images Developed by Women

The medieval whore in her gaudy headdress and the unbonneted nineteenth-century prostitute readily attracted male attention: Each stood out in stark contrast to the norm. But attracting the attention of a desired male was also a goal of ordinary, "modest" women who sought access to wealth, power, and prestige. In a crowd of women covered from head to toe in dark-colored clothing, how was one to stand out? A woman's appearance had to be interesting and had to differentiate her from the others, and yet it had to avoid evoking disapproval or censure. To achieve this goal, her clothing had to remain within some definition of "respectable."

The women best known for achieving this goal were those who were "certified seductive"—the royal courtesans. They were women who sought to attract the attention and interest of a monarch and succeeded. Their success in attracting a king and gaining legal recognition of their status legitimized their clothing style; consequently, they became what is today called trendsetters. Other women sought to copy their style. The courtesans were responsible for initiating and popularizing three distinct tactics (images) that were then adopted by more modest women: adapting elements of male dress, creating an image of harmony, and creating a glamorous look. These tactics, rediscovered in the twentieth century, continue to influence contemporary styles.

Adapting Elements of Male Dress

This tactic first appeared during a period of social and political change. The fourteenth century was a time of increasing prosperity in Europe. With the growth of commercial centers, such as Venice, Genoa, Barcelona, and Marseilles, and with the establishment of the great northern ports of Bruges and Antwerp, the feudal system began to disappear. Royal and princely courts were created in which political power was increasingly centralized. These courts were supported by a prosperous mercantile class and an ambitious bourgeoisie.

With the resulting growth in the number of powerful and wealthy families, members of the nobility felt it necessary to distinguish themselves from the rich merchants. Distinctions in clothing provided a readily available means by which the court nobility could assert its higher social rank, and copying the court styles became the means by which the rich bourgeoisie, in turn, could identify itself with the nobility and its privileges.[13] Almost inevitably, the clothing worn by these groups displayed their wealth and power. As the new look of luxury in courtly attire spread across Europe, it became known as the International Gothic Style. For men, the wearing of jewelry embellished by precious gems, such as diamonds and pearls, became a mark of status.

In paintings from the fifteenth, sixteenth, and seventeenth centuries, women are sometimes depicted wearing elements of male dress. The credit for making such daring behavior acceptable usually goes to the first official courtesan in the French Court, Agnes Sorel (ca. 1444). To set herself apart, she borrowed diamonds from the men in her family and had them mounted into a feminine-style necklace. By wearing the unexpected (diamonds had hitherto been worn exclusively by the male members of the royal family), she succeeded in catching the eye of the French king, Charles VII. As M. Baerwald and T. Mahoney (1960) noted, *the charm of the unexpected* is at work when women adopt elements of male dress.[14]

Because Sorel succeeded in becoming the king's mistress, she quickly became a fashion leader. Other women copied her appearance. She popularized the high-domed forehead, a hairstyle that required that the forehead be immacu-

Virgin and Child, *Jean Fouquet ca. 1480, Antwerp Museum of Fine Art. Agnes Sorel, the first officially recognized courtesan of Charles VII of France, is thought to be the model for the painting.*

lately plucked. It is the style she is wearing in the painting *Virgin and Child* by French painter Jean Fouquet (ca. 1480). In this painting she was elevated by the painter to the highest status available to a woman—placed "on a pedestal" as the Virgin Mary. Although the dress she wears in the painting is simple, its curved seams outline her figure smoothly, and one of her breasts is exposed. Round and seemingly full of milk, it is directed toward the baby on her lap. As befits the Queen of Heaven, a crown studded with gems and pearls sits firmly on her head.[15]

Gloves, hats, and hoods were the other elements of male dress that women adopted in this period. In a painting called *Hunting with Falcons at the Court of Philip the Good* (ca. 1442), all the guests are dressed in white as part of the theme of the festivities. The focal point in the painting is Duke Philip the Good, who is lounging elegantly against a banquet table in the center of a magnificent ensemble of courtiers. In different parts of the painting are clusters of guests, all in elegant costumes that seem more appropriate for display than hunting. In one cluster, among a group of couples participating in a stately dance, is a woman wearing scarlet gloves. Traditionally only cardinals wore scarlet gloves.[16] But by the fifteenth century so many women had adopted this element of male dress that the cardinals refused to wear theirs. Despite their protest, the pope ordered them to continue wearing scarlet gloves.[17] Masculine headdress, specifically the bourrelet (a round, padded roll placed over the hair), is worn by a few of the women in the painting, and women wearing this style of headdress appear quite frequently in other northern European paintings as well. Hoods worn by men were also adopted by women of the nobility.[18] The trousseau of Agnes of Cleve included several hoods, at least two of which had bourrelets attached.[19]

In a chronicle describing the customs and habits of the people of Venice, Cesare Vecellio reported that by 1590 the prostitutes had adopted elements of male dress as part of their seductive attire. Made of silk or other cloth, depending on the prostitutes' social class, their "vests were padded and fringed in the style of young men, particularly Frenchmen." Next to their bodies they wore a man's shirt "more or less delicate according to what they can spend." Instead of wearing a skirt, many wore men's breeches, which made them instantly recognizable.[20]

In a double portrait of the Flemish painter Peter Paul Rubens and his wife Isabella Brandt (1610), Isabella is wearing a man's hat. It rests precariously on one side of her head over a traditional female bonnet. It seems that by the seventeenth century women of the bourgeoisie had also discovered the charm of wearing elements of male dress.

The practice does not appear to figure into the art and fashion of the eighteenth or nineteenth century. But at the beginning of the twentieth century Gabrielle Chanel discovered its allure. Attending the races at Deauville one chilly day, so the story goes, she was cold. She borrowed a polo player's sweater, belted it, and pushed the sleeves up. Chanel was so entranced with the image that she soon produced similar sweaters for other women, and they sold immediately.[21]

Hunting with Falcons at the Court of Philip the Good *(also known as* The Marriage of Philip the Good to Isabella of Portugal*), French School, 1430, Versailles Museum. (Reprinted by permission of Giraudon/Art Resource.)*

Marlene Dietrich in 1933 adapting male attire to the female body. (Reprinted by permission of Culver Pictures, Inc.)

At the races she could be seen wearing a shetland sweater and pearls while other women wore silk and lace. Other elements of male dress that she introduced into female fashion were the leather belt, sailor pants, and the twin set, a combination of matching cardigan and pullover worn together. Chanel was also one of the first women to cut her hair short.

Elements of male dress worn by women call attention to the wearer because they are unexpected; since they are utterly contrary to the norm, they are "so absolutely daring." The novelty is disarming and sexually alluring. So found actress Marlene Dietrich, when in 1933 she made international headlines when she appeared offscreen in mannish attire. Warned by the Paris chief of police that she would be asked to leave town if she continued to wear pants, she changed into a skirt, but she still wore a man's hat, collar, and tie. The tight-fitting jacket that she had worn came from a boy's clothing store. It emphasized her female curves.[22] Perhaps male clothes make "femaleness" all the more obvious.

The oversized male shirt, or pajama top, the fedora hat, baseball and sailor's caps, the tie (worn loosely), and the male-style leather jacket were adopted by

Designers Joan & David adapt male attire to the female body. (Wom-en's Wear Daily, August 23, 1993; photo by George Chinsee; reprinted by permission of Fairchild Syndication.)

women in the 1970s. Giorgio Armani's use of haberdashery fabrics and Ralph Lauren's form-fitting tuxedo suit are 1980s examples. Designers had thus come to realize the seductive charm of the unexpected engendered by women who wear elements of male dress.

Creating an Image of Harmony

Creating an image of harmony was a tactic adopted by one of the best-known French courtesans, Jeanne-Antoinette Poisson, known as Madame de Pompadour.[23] Two ideas seemed to animate her style. The first was that "the sensual and lighthearted" are "delightful"; the second was that "the elements of appearance should be fused to create a whole greater than the sum of its parts." These two principles were embodied in the clothing she wore when she set out to establish herself as Louis XV's mistress. The story goes that the king, long estranged from his Polish wife, Marie Leczinska, and brooding over the death of his most recent mistress, was restless and devoted much of his time to hunting in the Forest of Senart. Jeanne-Antoinette Poisson would follow the hunt in a brightly colored carriage. One day she would dress in light blue and ride in a rose-colored carriage; the next, she would wear a rose-colored dress and the carriage would be light blue. She followed a similar procedure in Paris, where she would arrive at the theater in full view of the king. She succeeded in catching his eye; then, under the cover of festivities and masked balls celebrating the marriage of the dauphin, she lured him to her bed. Shortly thereafter she was publicly acknowledged, and in 1745 the king awarded her the title Marquise de Pompadour. For nearly twenty years, until her death in 1764, she was considered de facto Queen of France.[24]

In her time many court observers paid tribute to Madame de Pompadour's extraordinary beauty; however, despite their praise, her facial characteristics, as depicted in portraits and sculpture, were less than beautiful, scholars have insisted. They noted that the accuracy of the depiction is not in question. A number of artists (including Nattier, Boucher, Van Loo, Cochin, Droiuais, Lemoyne, and Pigalle) portrayed her at different times. Each depicted her with the same facial characteristics—a round face with even features and a dazzling complexion, eyes not very large but most "brilliant, witty and sparkling."[25]

Reports by court observers have suggested that it was her style of dress that attracted the king's attention and led, in turn, to the many tributes to her beauty. Following her belief, which was in keeping with the time, that the elements of appearance should be fused to create a whole greater than the sum of its parts and that the individual should be in harmony with nature, she chose fabrics of pale and delicate shades that complemented her dazzling pink and white complexion and her sparkling eyes. To provide a sense of playfulness, she wore her richly decorated, low-cut gowns adorned with many ribbons, flowers, ruffles, and lacy flounces. This profusion of exquisite tiny details, like those in the world of nature, was arranged to convey the impression of a unified whole. People who knew her almost never mentioned her beauty without also mentioning the "consumate elegance with which she dressed."[26] Although the *robe à la française* (a dress of tight-fitting bodice, a low square décollete, and a ladder of bows down the front), which Madame de Pompadour adopted, had already come into fashion, her preference for it had an impact on other women. Throughout Europe, for the remainder of the eighteenth century, women's fashions were inspired by her clothing.

The desire for harmony in attire grew out of the rise of new ideas and disturbing questions about freedom, responsibility, and ethics in eighteenth-century

Mme. de Pompadour *by François Boucher, n.d., Louvre, Paris. The color, material, and trimmings of the decorations on Madame de Pompadour's head and around her neck correspond to those of the dress, leading to unity and harmony. (Reprinted by permission of Giraudon/Art Resource.)*

France and England. Enlightenment thinkers argued that the development of science obviated the need for supernatural guidance. Instead, humans were urged to rely on the power of reason. These thinkers pointed out that the study of nature, unaided by divine guidance, had revealed it to be both knowable and regular—and hence predictable. For many of them, the study of nature through the use of reason and logic replaced the study of the mysteries of God.[27] In keeping with this change, writers began to emphasize that individuals were in and of themselves increasingly capable of good and that when they at last reached harmony with nature, they would be judged perfect. This desire for harmony also reflected a desire for political and social accord, the roots of which lay in classical Athens. When Athens was established as a democracy in the fifth century B.C., its citizens sought to limit dissonance among families and groups. Balance and order were viewed as essential for social life. In response to the value placed on harmony, artists of classical Greece strove to represent strength balanced with grace and gentleness in their statues of the gods. Symmetry and just proportions (in which the parts are subordinate to the whole) became the classical period's criteria of beauty.[28]

Eighteenth-century philosophers who valued the harmony and regularity that they believed existed in nature readily adopted the classical Greek principles of beauty. In 1756 Edmund Burke suggested that beauty comprises a "smoothness" such that parts melt into one another.[29] The definition of beauty by J. Barry in 1784, cited in the *Oxford English Dictionary,* similarly focuses on the unity that emerges when variety exists. The result, in art, is resolution—a static, balanced artifact.

In the 1960s, with the "youth revolution" and the call for an "authentic self," women outside fashion centers were encouraged to reject fashion as "conspicuous consumption."[30] Women in small towns and suburban communities were listening to Suzanne Caygill, who toured the country lecturing on natural color harmonies. The principle underlying her talks was the Enlightenment idea that harmony with nature is basic to happiness. She lectured that the most effective way for a person to be in harmony with the environment is for him or her to dress and live in the appropriate color and style. In the natural world, she noted, the palette of each season consists of harmonious colors. Each individual's skin and eye coloring, hair, body contours, and personality can be complemented by a palette existing in nature. The effect engenders in both wearer and onlooker a feeling of being at peace—with oneself and with nature. Wearing these colors conveys a sense of unity and harmony.[31] Caygill evolved and eventually codified for the public the principles that Madame de Pompadour had utilized so successfully. In *Color Me Beautiful,* Carol Jackson popularized Caygill's ideas about color and personal appearance.[32]

Creating a Glamorous Look

A third tactic developed by women to make themselves stand out in the eyes of men can best be described as the creation of a "glamorous look." Glamour is particularly difficult to define. *Webster's* describes it as "mysteriously exciting and often illusory attractiveness that stirs the imagination and appeals to a taste for the unconventional, the unexpected, the colorful or the exotic." The term may also connote personal charm and poise, and may imply unusual physical and sexual attributes.[33]

The nineteenth century witnessed a turning away from the profusion and richness of the Pompadour style. Decent, modest women were expected to wear structured dresses in dark, somber colors. Such colors and styles were in harmony with society's conception of the proper place and role for women. Women's styles in this period were not expected to create the impression of an individual as a harmonious whole. Rather, style served to express conformity with society's expectations for women. The dark-colored, enveloping garb appealed to middle-class women because it was practical, useful, and economical. During long, cold winters in small, drafty, sometimes smoky houses, the warmth of the relatively coarse, heavy fabric in such garments was useful. Equally important, most of the fabric was produced locally, as was the clothing itself, and production of the preferred dark-colored cloth did not require the use of costly dyes or dyeing processes. Hence, the garments were practical, useful, and inexpensive.[34]

Wearing such garments, however, forced women to confront once again the problem of how to stand out among a group of women wearing the same "practical" clothing. To make matters worse, their voluminous, heavy-looking dresses, broad-brimmed bonnets, and enveloping capes in dark and gloomy colors stood in stark contrast to the white, light yellow, light green, and orange satins worn by the courtesans. The courtesans set out to look sensual. They decorated their clothing with dainty bows, ribbons, and frills. Trimmed with lace, their dresses emphasized their bosoms. Frivolity and lightheartedness characterized their appearance. Their attire glistened; it was soft and encouraged touch.[35]

The courtesan was less than a mistress and more than a prostitute. As J. Richardson reported, "She is less than a mistress because she sells her love for material benefits; she is more than a prostitute because she chooses her lovers. The courtesan is a woman whose profession is love, and whose clients may be more or less distinguished."[36] Often the women who became courtesans sought to escape the traditional constraints of poverty and marriage. Born between 1814 and 1830, they grew up in a time of economic and political change. The monarchy had fallen; the old aristocracy was discredited; and Napoléon's meteoric rise and fall served as a warning to any who might attempt to reach the heights of the pre-1789 nobility. Instead, industrialization, trade, and the burgeoning cities were the new sources of opportunity and wealth.[37]

The courtesans sexualized sensuality. They reddened their cheeks and nails to stimulate passion and widened the pupils of their eyes with atropine, simulating sexual excitement. They were reputed to have raised interaction with men in general, and sexual intercourse in particular, to an art.[38] They acquired the reputation that they were beautiful, talented, imaginative, and fun to be with. They were identified as "*les grandes horizontales.*" Aided by being glamorized in the

Marguerite Bellanger (1840–1886), mistress of Na-
poléon III, was known for her playful use of dai-
sies. She wore them in the form of pins and hats. A
sense of enchantment is conveyed by the shimmer-
ing satin, light colors, and playful delicacy of her
dresses. (Reprinted by permission of The Hulton
Deutsch Collection.)

poetry, literature, and visual arts of the period, they became members of the
fashionable set. They were international in origin, and they each had their own
distinct features and style. They were described as *"grandes coquettes"*; they
were flirty, gay, witty, and entertaining. As Richardson described:

> All of Paris turned out to see the glorious sight of the courtesans in their handsome
> carriages and impeccable horses. Excluded from formal ceremonies by those who set
> the standards for respectability, this was most evident when they were not allowed to
> enter the grandstand at the Longchamps races. They had to park their carriages on
> the other side of the track. To offset this humiliation, the courtesans saw to it that
> their return from races would be like a triumphant procession. Reclining languidly
> against the plump cushions of their satin upholstered carriages, attended by
> footmen in elaborate and colorful uniforms and powdered wigs, they competed and
> often outshone the more respected wife. They drove from Longchamps to the Place
> de la Concorde, to the Bois de Boulogne and back again until nightfall imparting ra-
> diance as they and their carriages reflected the last rays of the sun.

Esteem accorded to a man from other men often depended on how well he had
provided for his courtesan. For her services she would often receive financial support

in the form of a well-appointed home, liveried servants, art objects, magnificent clothes and jewels.[39]

To some women the courtesan's ability to attract a man, receive his gifts of support, and maintain his interest became proof of the desirability of the courtesan style. Many women, among them members of the court, tried to adopt a glamorous look.

In the United States, the radiance of satin, the zest of champagne, costly furs, and wealthy admirers characterized the image of chorus girls and movie stars.[40] The media conveyed the message that any woman with beauty and talent could dance or sing her way to the top. They encouraged the notion that the United States was indeed a land of opportunity. Newspapers presented movie stars and chorus girls as modern Cinderellas, and the clerks and secretaries who swelled the ranks of women workers from 1900 to 1920 read with envy about their exciting lives, freedom, romance, and adventure.[41] Female movie stars were presented as radiant and larger than life, and movies were capable of transporting viewers across all barriers of time, space, and class. Evoking the magic world of fantasy, the luminous quality of the stars' images modified the drab confinement of everyday life.[42]

Women regarded movie stars as experts on appearance. Everything Gloria Swanson did was news. She became the epitome of elegance and feminine enchantment. When she bobbed her hair in the early 1920s, millions of women rushed to have their hair cut. Until then, throughout the centuries, women had kept their hair long and their heads covered. Short hair had been considered an affront, a violation of the norm of modesty. Suddenly it was seen as romantic, chic, and classy. The lacy, black negligee worn by Mae West in *Night After Night* (1932) was celebrated and copied by many women.

Two distinct seductive images were made popular by the show-business industry: that delineated as sexy by the church and that appraised glamorous by the media. The former consisted of sequins, color, plunging necklines, and dresses draped to swathe the body snugly. The latter was constructed with much less emphasis on female attributes; it merely alluded to the body underneath. Satin and makeup conveyed radiance and sensuality.

Alluring Images Initiated by Men: The Vulnerable Look

In the 1800s and 1900s sexual liaisons between older males and young females were satirized and usually discouraged. The term "dirty old man" reflects such sentiments. In a February 6, 1799, advertisement in *Diario de Madrid* for the *Caprichos,* a set of satirical prints by Francisco Goya, many of which mock older men who attempt to seduce young women, Goya described his art as deriding "vice and error." Goya was a keen observer of society and confronted directly the

Mae West in a glamorous and revealing negligee, 1932. (Still from the movie Night After Night.*)*

darkest and most basic human impulses, according to art historian Reva Wolf, who in 1991 curated an exhibit of Goya prints at Boston College.[43]

In the art and literature of the 1950s, however, a liaison between the older, sophisticated male and the young teenager was legitimized. The status of the young teenager as seducer was first seen in ballet, which had acquired a new importance in the post–World War II period. Designer Clair McCardle offered the "ballerina" look for everyday attire, making it popular. The style emphasized long limbs, flat-chestedness, ballet slippers, and hair swept back to reveal a long, delicate neck.[44]

Embodying the essence of youthful innocence and the vulnerability of a new bloom, Audrey Hepburn, a former ballet student, was chosen by the writer Colette in 1951 to play the character of Gigi in the play by the same name on Broadway. *Gigi* is the story of an older, sophisticated male captivated by the innocent, childlike charm of a teenager. At the heart of all twelve romantic comedies in which Audrey Hepburn later starred is the same fantasy: a coy and playful relationship between a young teenager and a mature, sophisticated male. Her attire in each of the movies denied the attributes that traditionally anchor a woman in society: her breasts and hips.[45] In the film *Funny Face*, for example, Hepburn is wearing a ballerina-style tunic, black turtleneck, and tights. Whether running with balloons in the rain, looking pensive in a railroad station, or floating down the steps in the Paris Opera, Audrey Hepburn gave to the films an aura of "enchanting innocence," as noted by reviewers. She was described as waif-like—an image supported by her long arms, neck, and legs. Her popularity and success surprised her. She repeatedly insisted: "I have no illusions about my looks" and described herself as a "skinny broad." To her amazement she was chosen to represent a new seductive ideal. The *vulnerable look* was one that inspired the older adult male to view a woman as a child and perhaps as "Daddy's little girl," an immature being in need of care and instruction.

Cultural fascination with adolescent sexuality is reflected in the success of *Lolita*, a 1954 novel by Vladimir Nabokov that was initially banned, and in the "baby-doll" fashion that was popular by the mid-1960s.[46] The baby-doll style featured little girls' attire. It consisted of a very short skirt, high waistline, puffed sleeves, jumper or apron effects, lots of lace and ruffles, and sometimes even bloomers. Legs were clad in lacy, pale stockings and feet in Mary Jane shoes. Geoffery Beene, Chester Weinberger, and Bill Blass designed attire in the baby-doll look. The clothing was accessorized by elaborate makeup providing a doe-eyed look, and by spiky eyelashes; the latter were sometimes painted on in a doll-like fashion. Cheeks were rosy and lips pale frosted, and hair was worn in ringlets around the face.[47]

Without really knowing it, high school and college women offered a different version of the vulnerable look. Rebelling against fashion magazines because of their emphasis on gender differences, they rummaged in thrift stores and family closets for oversized men's shirts, sweaters, and coats. Their image was seductive for two reasons. First, it was familiar yet unfamiliar, because we are used to see-

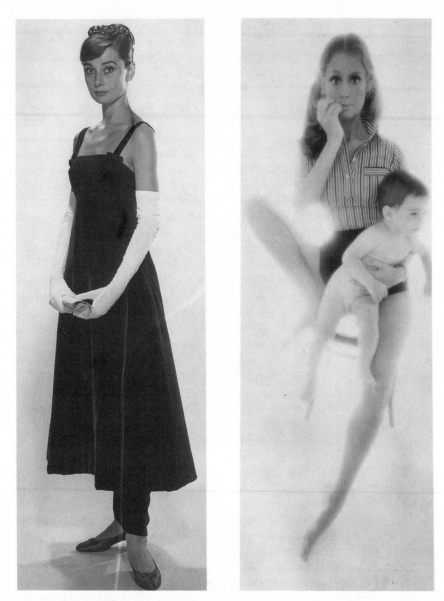

Audrey Hepburn (left) shown personifying the vulnerable image. Ballerina slippers with droopy leggings nullify the elegance of the dress, an "A"-line designed by Givenchy. The delicate long neck and bare shoulders suggest access to youthful delicacy, hence vulnerability. (Reprinted by permission of UPI/Bettmann.) Lauren Hutton (right) portraying the "babysitter" image in Esquire, December 1968. *(Photo by Carl Fischer; reprinted by permission of Ken & Carl Fischer Photography.)*

ing women in women's clothing and men in men's clothing. Second, the teenager's body inside unstructured, oversized shirts, coats, or jackets seemed small and vulnerable, waifish. The softness of the look made her seem to be wearing her father's or big brother's hand-me-downs. She appeared lost and in need of male protection; some men would want to hold and comfort her.

Several cultural forces offered legitimacy to this image of vulnerability, giving it a place in the gallery of seductive images. Chosen by a panel of "analysts and sociologists" consulted by *Esquire*, it was included in the December 1968 issue of the magazine. The headline read: "Season's Greetings! 4 naughty dreams to last you till March." Lauren Hutton, a model and actress, used makeup and costume to represent four different seductive images, including the "baby-sitter." The teenager is portrayed in short shorts, bare feet, and an innocent-looking blouse partially unbuttoned. She is sitting at the edge of a kitchen stool holding a naked baby on her precariously stretched leg. Large parts of her body are exposed, and she looks directly at the viewer, unaware of danger. Since at least the eighteenth century a woman's extended pale leg, exposed to the thigh, and an undone bodice have alluded to sexual availability.[48]

To summarize, the art and literature of the 1950s initiated a cultural dialogue that rejected old definitions and sexualized the "childlike" look. Adopted by teenagers, the vulnerable look represents the incorporation of a deviant male desire into the realm of public fantasy. This amalgam helped to widen the boundaries of the acceptable.

Further Implications

Seductive images designated or initiated by men differ from those developed by women, and they seem to have different effects on the the male-female interaction. Alluring images that emanate from men call attention to the body and define the male-female relationship more fully in terms of sex. Nourished by the view that sexuality is a biological drive pressing for release, or orgasm, the focus of the interaction is sexual satisfaction. Fulfillment entails mastery over the other, or the use of women as sexual objects.

Male-initiated seductive images can be seen as transporting men from "triumph to trauma." The male, in comparison to the female, enters a male-female interaction from a position of greater access to wealth, prestige, and power—or triumph. Reaffirming such superiority, sexual intercourse may likely preclude female sensuality, warmth, and caring. Interaction with an "object" is likely to result in paultry long-term rewards. The rejection of an opportunity to take advantage of the nourishing qualities of women limits the experience, ultimately leaving men with a sense of unfullfilment and insufficient mastery over the situation. Such feelings may do violence to the male's sense of personhood, hence a "trauma."

Alluring images that women develop, in contrast, employ attire that encourages sensual pleasure. They can be described as enabling a woman to shift her lot from "trauma to triumph." The trauma stems from the recognition that she is shut out of significant social realms such as wealth and power. The clothing that women adopt allude to play and encourage eroticism, fun, and gentler sex. The courtesan's interactions with the king or other suiters enabled her to overcome her sense of humiliation over the condition of her birth. These women were given the opportunity to influence policy, to develop their talents and abilities, and to achieve economic independence. Their relationships with men made it possible for some of them to resolve the initial trauma and secure personal triumph.

Part Four:
Clothing Symbols and Cultural Values

ANNO ·ÆTATIS ·   · SVÆ · XLIX ·

Wealth and Beauty

CLOTHING SYMBOLS reflect cultural values that one has achieved, and their use is largely a matter of personal choice. Unlike clothing signs, the use of which is governed by norms specifying what people ought or ought not wear, no rules govern the wearing of clothing symbols in contemporary society. In small tribal societies ritual and ceremony reaffirm meaning; the visual representation of a value through appearance tends to be constant. In societies with limited ritual and ceremony, and where change is constant, as in the United States, the meaning of cultural representations of values, as through clothing symbols, is likely to vary; it is specific to the individual, the group, and the period.

Dressing in the attire of a class higher than one's own has been recognized as wearing a clothing symbol. According to Erving Goffman, "Symbols play a role that is less clearly controlled by authority." Rather than having a direct impact on behavior, "class symbols ... serve to influence ... in a desired direction." The wearing of clothing symbols, according to Goffman, evokes *feelings* rather than behavior.[1] Thorstein Veblen also suggested that the impact of symbols lies in the feelings they arouse rather than in behavior elicited. In *The Theory of the Leisure Class* ([1899] 1953) he argued: "In order to gain and hold the esteem of men it is not sufficient merely to possess wealth or power. The wealth or power must be put into evidence for esteem is awarded only on evidence."[2] The wearing of attire that suggests the achievement of cultural values, what a society considers good and desirable, leads to a positive social evaluation and response. Because physical labor was defined unworthy by the "warrior class," the wearing of attire that signifies *leisure* demonstrates worthiness. In Veblen's words, "No apparel can be considered worthy or even decent if it shows the effect of manual labor."[3]

Veblen used the term "status symbol" to designate elements and styles of dress that reflect the achievement of cultural values. To identify the meaning of a symbol one must consider a person's primary group; its resources, information, and experience; and the political, economic, and cultural forces of the period. The social situation in which the symbol is worn must also be taken into account. A particular visual construct may, however, reflect more than one cultural value and thus have more than one meaning. In contemporary society, for example, the wearing of "Michael Jordan" or "Bo Jackson" sneakers may reflect racial pride; a desired alliance with a sport, a person, or male success; a desire to feel "with it"; or simply access to wealth. The wearing of Porsche sun goggles, similarly, may suggest a desired association with male success or the lifestyle that ownership of the car suggests, or it may reflect an association with sports

cars in general. The wearing of a "Chris Evert" $1,000.00 diamond tennis brace-
let, marketed for women, may simply reflect that one is in love.

In addition, a different type of evidence is typically required of each social
class to convey the same message. To demonstrate the realization of economic
success, for example, a member of the Du Pont family and the owner of a small
hardware store would be required to present different "proofs." A Du Pont would
likely wear understated attire, whereas a hardware store owner may wear heavy
makeup and jewelry.[4] The purpose of wearing a clothing symbol may be personal, but its larger meaning and significance depend on its connotation with
respect to an audience.

Values are central and distinguishing characteristics of a culture. In the form
of ideas and images, they represent societal goals and encourage individuals to
act on their behalf. From early childhood on, children are exposed to these ideals and are consciously and unconsciously encouraged to pursue them. Continuity in value orientation enables a society to re-create itself.[5]

As new "aristocracies"—religious, political, or economic—acquired power in
Western society, they gave voice to their own values and goals. For example, the
accumulation of wealth and the desirability of beauty, along with coordinated,
understated attire, emerged in the Middle Ages; hierarchy and leisure, that is,
freedom from physical labor, arose in the monarchical courts; artful display and
fashion developed in the newly prosperous commercial centers; beauty as the
perfection of the physical form, as well as youthfulness and health, emerged
with the rise of the middle class and modernity.[6] Each of these elements is a subject of a chapter in Part 4. The cultural values of wealth and beauty are discussed
here.

ક્ર   ક્ર   ક્ર

A central feature of the economic and political life in medieval society, according
to Michael Mann, was that neither economic power nor political power was centralized.[7] In A.D. 1000 European society was characterized by a number of small
interaction networks. The organization forms of the barbarian invaders (Visi-
goths, Vandals, Franks, Celts, and so on) were confined within the local relationships of the village or tribe, with only loose and unstable confederations beyond.
No single group had a monopoly or control over social life.[8] Because no one possessed monopoly powers, almost everyone could have private economic resources hidden from the control of some authority. The lord, vassal, town,
church, and even the peasant village were all power actors with autonomous
spheres and resources to contribute to a delicate balance of power, explained
Mann.[9]

Christianity provided a broad framework for the emergence of cultural values.
The economic development that the church facilitated made it possible to accu-
mulate wealth and the refined symbols of wealth that demonstrate an awareness
of beauty. Three factors contributed to the emergence of market relations, according to Mann. The first was literacy; ecclesiastical Latin was a stable means of

communication beyond face-to-face relations. The second was the church's emphasis on moral conduct: its concern for "just" behavior; its preaching for consideration, decency, and charity toward all Christians. Together with the threat of excommunication, this emphasis on moral conduct facilitated long-distance control and regulation of behavior. The third factor encouraging markets and trade was the existence of a monastic-episcopal economy underpinned by Christian norms.[10]

In its retreat from the Roman world the church had created networks of monastaries; each monastary had its own economy, yet none was fully self-sufficient. Trade developed among monastaries, the estates of bishops, secular estates, and manors. By 1155, individual families, local villages, and manor communities were participating in a wider network of economic interaction that was governed by institutionalized norms concerning property possession, production relations, and market exchange.[11] Towns emerged between 1050 and 1250, as did merchant and artisan institutions. Economic success and awareness of beauty, and in the religious realm spirituality and asceticism, were the first cultural values to which individuals aspired. By making spirituality a goal that one must strive to achieve, the church fathers supported the emergence of achievement as a basic value of Christian culture. Achievement can be understood as a "master value" in the sense that it is important to accomplish one's goals no matter what the particular goals are.[12]

Wealth

Five lines of evidence suggest that the accumulation of personal wealth emerged as a value by the eleventh or twelfth century: (1) the sin of pride, (2) ascetic and heretical movements, (3) legal property rights, (4) luxury dress, (5) the regulation of dress.[13]

The Sin of Pride

The church fathers have always associated luxurious dress with the sin of pride. The increased vigilence against pride in the twelfth century suggests that, indeed, the demonstration of wealth was becoming socially important. One of the earliest Christian thinkers to employ a hierarchy of sins, Evagrius Pontus (died ca. A.D. 400), distinguished between vainglory, which included luxurious dress, and pride, an attitude of arrogance; he listed them, respectively, in sixth and seventh place in the hierarchy of sins. Gregory the Great (590–604) rearranged the order of significance. He combined vainglory with pride and elevated this cardinal sin to first place. He argued that pride, the attitude of arrogance, and luxurious dress were "at the root of all evil."[14]

A twelfth-century theologian, Alanus de Insulis, who wrote extensively on the sin of pride, identified the elements of this most cardinal of sins: a haughty mode of speech; a manner of silence; and the wearing of fashionable dress, ornament, and cosmetic beautification. "An inner demeanor of pride" could be signified by the outer personal demeanor: "looking up to the things of heaven, lifting of eyebrows, turning up of chin and holding arms as stiff as a bow." According to Alanus, the body was "pressed into service on behalf of arrogance."[15] Humility in deportment and modesty in dress signified the absence of the sin of pride. This sin thus came to include wearing elements of dress that enhance self-importance at the expense of religious authority.

Ascetic and Heretical Movements

The years between 1050 and 1200 marked a turning point in the history of religious devotion, as English historian Collin Morris (1972) suggested. The focus turned to the suffering of Christ. The individual strove imaginatively to share in the pain of the Lord.[16] A new pattern of interior piety developed that was characterized by a growing sensitivity, marked by personal love, for the crucified Lord. Regular use of the confessional, the position of homage as a posture for prayer, and the increasing popularity of the "dying Christ" style of crucifix were aspects of this new piety. Devotion was compassionate but directed inward. Instead of depicting a living Christ, victorious over the forces of evil and radiant with vitality, works of art portrayed Christ as dead on the cross. An early surviving example is a wooden crucifix made for Archbishop Gero of Cologne (969–1076). Christ's head is slumped on his right shoulder, his eyes are closed, his face is twisted, and his jaw is hanging open. Morris suggested that this style of crucifix was designed to encourage personal grief and a personal bond to Christ.[17]

The new style of devotion was also a result of the growth of education, trade, and industry, the rise of towns, and the incorporation of new territories, all of which led to social dislocation, tension, and reorganization of group life.[18] Angered by the wealth and the moral laxity of the clergy, heretics rejected the claimed privileges of the official priesthood. In part, heretical movements were an attack upon the abuses by the system. Heresy offered a social protest for the poor, the rich, and the nobles. Merchants joined the protests, angered that they were denied respectability because the church claimed that wealth earned in the marketplace did not assure them a place in heaven. To members of the nobility who envied the property and power acquired by the church, heresy offered a justification for seizing the wealth of the corrupt church for themselves. For many of the laity, moreover, the mystical and emotional rewards of religion were lacking; the church gave them "no opportunity to study the Bible, to hear it read in the vernacular, or to be moved by sermons."[19]

The rise of religious sects, such as the Waldensians and the Albigensians, led to an association of asceticism with spirituality in the popular mind. The Waldensians, or "the poor men of Lyons," emerged around 1170, when a rich merchant from Lyon, Peter Waldo, not only denounced the church, which had been done by many others, but offered a solution to its problems: a life of absolute poverty. He attacked the moral laxity of the clergy and denounced the sacra-

The Gero Crucifix. *ca. A.D. 975–1000, carved from wood, Cologne Cathedral. (Photo courtesy of Bildarchiv Foto Marburg/Art Resource.)*

ments it administered. His preaching attracted followers, and the group was declared heretical by the Lateran Council of 1215. The Church of Rome, however,
never succeeded in suppressing the Waldensian Church. Its theology was later
absorbed and transformed by Protestant reformers.

The Albigensians, like the Waldensians, denied the value of the sacraments
and priesthood of the established church. True Albigensians led a life of rigorous
asceticism. They sought to help the god of light vanquish the evil god of darkness, who had created and ruled the material world. Sexual intercourse was discouraged, even within marriage, because it served only to propagate matter and
thereby extend the dominion of darkness. Considered tainted because animals
reproduce, all animal flesh was also forbidden.

Angered by the luxurious dress, wealth, and moral laxity of the clergy, some
monastic orders also rejected the privileges claimed by the official priesthood. A
leading proponent of "drabness in dress," Bernard of Clairvaux (1090–1153), was
concerned not with people's external actions but with their inner motives.[20] A
member of the Order of Templars, he argued that the proper role of clothing is to
demonstrate obedience to higher authority. To that end, Templars wore only the
clothes their commanders gave them and sought "neither other garments nor
other food." "They cropped their hair close because their Gospels tell them that
it is a shame for a man to tend to his hair. They are never seen combed or rarely
washed, their beards are matted, they reek of dust and bear the stains of heat
and harness," noted Michael and Ariene Batterberry.[21] Saint Bernard criticized
the immodest size of churches, their enormous height and their immoderate
length, their vacant immensity, their paintings, and their sumptuous finish. The
purpose of showing these riches, he argued, was to draw more riches, to gorge
the eyes so as to open the purse strings. He saw monetary profit rather than veneration of what is sacred as the goal of such ornamentation.[22]

In addition, a Cistercian statute denounced the use of silk, gold, silver, stained
glass, sculpture, paintings, and carpets in churches. Similar denunciations were
made by others who argued that these superfluities merely distracted the faithful from their prayers. The basic concern of the ascetics, Umberto Eco (1986)
pointed out, was whether the churches should be decorated sumptuously when
the children of God were living in poverty.[23]

Despite criticism, church authorities were proud of their ownership of scarce
resources. One of the best known church authorities, Suger, the abbot of Saint-
Denis (1133–1144), argued that the House of God should be a repository of all matter that would show our affection "for the church our mother." He proceeded to
identify each of the gemstones and precious metals used in the ornament of
"that wonderful cross of St. Elloy."[24] Since the church's focus in this area was on
accumulation, church treasuries contained functional objects, beautiful objects,
and some that were merely curious. According to Eco, in acquiring objects medieval people found it extremely difficult to distinguish between those of utility or

goodness and those of beauty. They mingled the two because of "a unitary vision of the transcendental aspects of being" and took joy in enumerating these riches. They viewed the act of collecting these objects as a "reflection of, and participation in, the being and the power of God."[25]

Legal Property Rights

Medieval Europeans were primarily concerned with utilizing the land in their own locality. Their agriculture focused on the penetration of nature, on bringing more land into cultivation.[26] They learned to cultivate heavier, wetter soils and harness more effectively the energy of their animals, skills that enabled some lords and peasants to acquire additional property and wealth. They possessed sufficient autonomy and privacy to be able to keep the fruits of their own enterprise. By A.D. 1200 property possessors, lords and wealthy peasants, revived Roman law on private property as a means of regulating their relationship with the state; the law based ownership claim on custom and tradition. The legalization of private ownership suggests that the acquisition of personal wealth was emerging as a desirable social attribute.

Luxury Dress

Until the twelfth century, dress was socially stratified. Cost, custom, and law controlled consumption. The wealthy among the Romans wore their dress ankle length; workers and soldiers wore theirs to the knee. Monks' and peasants' attire was made of a coarse grade of cloth, whereas the attire of the wealthy was made of a finer grade of wool or linen.[27] The luxury of sable, ermine, miniver, and vail was limited by law to the elite in rank and riches. The easy availability of pelts, such as sheepskins, made it possible for the poorer classes to keep warm and at the same time to be recognized and defined as a class.

Social rank determined the quality of cloth one received even as a gift. Charlemagne, for example, chose the highest grade of fabric for himself and to send off as gifts. He gave fabric of a coarser grade to the officers who lived with him at the palace, and he gave an even coarser grade to his servants on feast days, when gifts of cloth were customary.[28]

When the manufacture of cloth was established in Frisia (in the area that is Belgium today) in the tenth century, awareness of social class and differing degrees of access to wealth governed production. Wool was woven into various grades of cloth, enabling the wealthy to acquire a "finer" image.[29] Two levels of clothing consumption affected production: that by the manor and that by the village. Whereas local weavers met the clothing needs of the near-subsistence peasant, the consumption of more expensive attire by the manors encouraged formal production and organized trade.

By the twelfth century, increased exposure to novel artifacts brought in through trade created an interest in luxury dress and ornament. Barbarian chiefs, while maintaining their traditional style of dress—breeches and tunic—had their attire reproduced in fine, luxury-grade silk that came from Byzantine workshops. It was "outstanding for its bright and varied colors."[30] They also ornamented themselves in gold and precious stones acquired at market fairs, where foreign merchants exhibited spices, perfumes, strands of pearls, and fantastic clothes made of powdered ermine, ethereal silks, and the lustrous feathered skins of flayed birds.[31] As Michael and Ariene Batterberry stated in *Fashion: The Mirror of History*, "The rich wore all the jewels, pearl necklaces, and heavy gold bracelets they could lay their hands on."[32]

The Regulation of Dress

Clothing regulations in the Middle Ages either prescribed what one could or should wear or proscribed what one could not wear. They were used by ruling authorities to control competition for scarce resources, to support differences between classes, and to maintain a superior position at the top of the social class hierarchy.[33]

The clothing regulations were based on two ideas: The first was the belief that each person had a predetermined place in God's orderly universe and that each must uphold this order by leading an exemplary life, which involved dressing in rank-appropriate clothing; the second involved mercantilism, the economic ideology of the time. The basic premise of mercantilism was that the world contained only a given amount of wealth and that each nation could enrich itself only at the expense of others. This belief led people to hoard gold and silver rather than spend it on imported cloth, attire, and jewelry. Sumptuous attire, since it was imported from the East, was expensive and required an "excessive" expenditure of bullion.[34]

The emergence of wealth as a cultural value encouraged individuation in two paradoxical ways. Ownership of material objects, on the one hand, invited personal experimentation, comfort, and pleasure. Asceticism, the denial of material objects and normal pleasures of life, on the other hand, emerged as a means of achieving what some felt was a deeper and more significant kind of satisfaction than that derived from consumption. It spoke of a state of spirituality and of a moral good.

Beauty in the Early Middle Ages

Between the fifth and eleventh centuries, church theologians feared that a keen interest in earthly and physical things might endanger the soul. They urged their followers to resist the lure of beauty and to attend to spiritual matters. They associated beauty and art with the pagan cultures of Greece and Rome; replacement of those cultures with Christianity required that pagan ideas and artifacts be obliterated. However, the Synod of 1075 recognized that art offered the illiterate peasant population a legitimate aid to piety. Sculpture, pictures, color, and light were increasingly seen as facilitating religious endeavor, and art began to acquire status. Theologians sought to help by providing a theory that explained the beauty of art, as described in the section that follows.[35]

Saint Thomas Aquinas on Beauty

Saint Thomas Aquinas (1225–1275) taught that beauty and art are within the realm of the transcendental, that the beautiful is "good" because it is capable of affecting the human soul. He claimed that in creating works of beauty the artist is dedicated to the humble service of faith; the artist is an associate of God and is, in fact, continuing his work.[36] When creating an art object, the artist achieves "a mean," controlling the extremes of excess and defect, which is a moral virtue.[37]

"Beauty is the splendour of form shining on the proportioned parts of matter," wrote Saint Thomas. He quoted Saint Augustine as saying that "unity is the form of all beauty. ... If beauty delights the mind, it is because beauty is essentially a certain excellence or perfection in the proportion of things."[38] The mind likes the beautiful because it likes unity, order, and brightness or clarity of color, explained Saint Thomas. Defining the nature of the beautiful, he identified four qualities: (1) excellence in the perfection of proportion; (2) integrity of design, order, and unity of form; (3) brightness, clarity in color; and (4) a degree of splendor, something luminous in itself.

The bearer of beauty, according to Aquinas, is the concrete organism in *all the complexity of its relations.* Deciding that an image is beautiful requires judgment, not intuition, and involves "a dialogue" with the object. Beauty is what pleases when it is seen, "not because it is intuited without effort, but because it is through effort that it is won." He warned that however beautiful a created thing may be, it may appear beautiful to some but not to others "because it is beautiful only under certain aspects which some discover and others do not."[39]

To touch beauty is to ascend to the realm of God. The presence in the organic whole of all its parts is essential to beauty. The human body, for instance, is considered deformed if a limb is missing. Eco supported this contention with his comment, "We call mutilated people ugly, for they lack the required proportion of parts to the whole."[40]

The Acceptance of the Ideal of Beauty

In the thirteenth century, the ideal in art and attire changed from merely showing off one's wealth to creating a harmonious unity. The term "elegance" was incorporated into the French language to describe this ideal, according to Michael and Ariene Batterberry (1977).[41] It referred to gracefully refined and luxurious attire. Such attire can be seen in a medieval miniature of Tristan and Isolde in conversation. Isolde is wearing a crown and a dress of simple line with a high waistline and wide sleeves lined in fur. In the fourteenth century, gowns were less elaborate than before but made of soft golden cloth called *panno d'oro.* With

simple dresses women wore a *demi cient,* a chain with hanging pendants of precious metals that draped loosely on the hips.

The Renaissance inspired further explorations of style by artists. Jewels continued to be used sparingly. The emphasis was on creating a harmonious appearance by the careful use of details. Depictions of dress and ornament considered the interplay of texture, color, and pattern. Sandro Botticelli (1445–1510), a
painter of line and grace in movement, sought a perfect harmony between the
person, costume, and environment. Antonio Pisano, known as Pisanello (1395–
1455), focused on precise contour and balance in his designs for male costumes.
The asymmetrical hosiery-shoes worn by the men were remarkable in their
highly contrasting designs. In the painting *Lady in Green* by Raphael (1483–1520),
a woman's bare white neck and shoulders are framed with a contrasting rich but
dusky dress. In contrasting her dark eyes and her white face, the artist repeats
the theme. Taken together, the image conveys a sense of unity.[42]

The Book of Hours and the
Diffusion of the Beauty Ideal

The Book of Hours encouraged awareness of art and taste within an upper social
class that had spread across large geographical areas. This illustrated prayer
book for the laity first appeared in the second half of the thirteenth century and
was reissued regularly. It enabled individuals to commune with God directly,
without benefit of clergy. It was the most popular book read for nearly 250 years,
and its popularity was due largely to the illustrations. The text was supported by
richly elaborate, brightly colored paintings, which helped to tell a complete
story. The goal was to create a unified visual whole.[43]

In addition to prayers to the Virgin Mary, arranged by the time of day, and
other prayers such as Litany and the Office of the Dead, the Book of Hours included a calendar of the cycle of the seasons to remind the individual of farming
tasks, feasts, and holidays. Commissioned by the nobility, the book also contained stories and paintings commemorating events enjoyed by the patron's
family, such as weddings, births, and travel. The cost of the book was such that
for the first 150 years of its life only the nobility of rank and wealth could afford it.
The inclusion of prayers created especially for the patron and the depiction of
the patron in the paintings suggest that the book was the product of a consulta-
tive effort between consumer and artist.

During the fifteenth century, changes in the method of manuscript production enabled the book to be produced in larger numbers and more locations,
making it possible for those of lesser social rank to also acquire it. Merchants,
shop owners, and lesser rural landowners could now order the prayer book from
French and Flemish centers and request that their own portraits or events that
they wanted to commemorate be added to the book's existing illuminations. Urban dwellers could acquire the book from scribal shops. Produced from stan-

Detail from The Trials of Moses *by Botticelli, n.d., Vatican Museums, Rome. Two young shepherdesses display elegant hairdos that were inspired by the embroidery on their clothing. (Reprinted by permission of Alinari/Art Resource.)*

dard exemplars, their copies were more mundane.[44] The cost, however, made it impossible for an ordinary peasant or urban worker to own a Book of Hours.[45]

Art historian Lawrence R. Poos (1988) pointed out that the Book of Hours was a possession prized for far more than its spiritual function. Its ownership, he suggested, is the earliest example of conspicuous consumption. People carried it around to show off. It became what Veblen called a status symbol. The fact that medieval piety incorporated a substantial emphasis on public display prepared the ground for people to "show off" ownership of the book, Poos pointed out. He observed, "More than one satirical broadside aimed at the social pretensions of the urban middle class singled out the vogue for carrying about richly adorned Books of Hours."[46]

In a 1989 exhibit at the Walters Art Gallery in Baltimore, Maryland, entitled "The Medieval Clothes Horse," the curator called attention to what we call today "nostalgia dressing"—the phenomenon of reaching back and "resurrecting" a fashion popular in an earlier period. The pages of the Books of Hours portrayed customary dress as well as fashionable attire and current trends. They became sources of style and an important example of what Maurice Halbwachs called public memory.

10
Leisure and Political Hierarchy

Leisure

The dress and adornment of the nobility, according to Veblen, exhibited the following characteristics: It was expensive; it was in the latest fashion; and it signified in style and detail that the wearer could not possibly engage in manual labor and was thus a member of the leisure class.[1] He identified the nobility's preference for expensive materials as conspicuous consumption and its pursuit of fashion as wasteful, calling it conspicuous waste; he regarded the impractical style of the nobility's dress as indicative of *conspicuous leisure.*[2]

The origins of the clothing of the leisure class, in Veblen's view, go back to the time when "a warlike habit of life" was considered more worthy than the drudgery and toil involved in working the land. To prove that they had successfully ravaged the enemy, warlords returning from military exploits paraded their newly found treasures. Property ownership became associated with the receipt of honor, and one's social worth depended on the amount of property one owned. As ancient society became differentiated there were those who periodically went on military forays and acquired wealth. There were also those who stayed home, worked hard on the land to eke out a living, and had little property. Those who were free from physical labor and did not have to produce their own food became respected socially. To receive the desired respect, one had to do more than possess wealth and power; they had to be exhibited, because "esteem was accorded only on evidence."[3]

Political Hierarchy

As discussed earlier (Chapter 5), shifts in the fortunes of war weakened the power of the autonomous feudal lords and the knightly class and encouraged the growth of monarchical courts and commercial centers. Beginning in the fourteenth century, a time of increasing prosperity in Europe, royal and princely courts each attempted to concentrate power under the rule of one man. Exaggerated ceremonial etiquette, lavish banquets, and entertainment were used to persuade the court and noble guests of the power of the ruler. Sumptuous courtly processions and extravagance (in dress and other areas) were used to impress the people. In the courts of France, England, and Spain and in the local dukedoms of Italy, cultural ideas, objects, and resources were carefully manipulated to convey the appropriate image. The wealth, physical force, and political and religious authority of the ruler were the intended messages.

Evidence of these spectacles can be found in historical documents and in paintings. At a meeting between Francis I of France and Henry VIII of England in June 1520, the rulers relied on such spectacle to conduct "international affairs." The meeting was called "The Field of the Cloth of Gold"; it lasted for twenty days, during which "the kings visited, dined, jousted, and excelled in theatrical acts of courtesy, and friendship," to quote Phyllis Mack (1987).[4] Henry held court

The Field of the Cloth of Gold, *ca. 1520, anonymous, from the collection of Her Majesty the Queen. Henry VIII and his entourage of five thousand are winding their way to the Castle of Guiness (left), headquarters of the French. On the right stands the temporary "palace" and the wine-spouting fountain of the English. At least 820 tents*

in a palace specially built for the meeting. It was ornamented with statues of men in various attitudes of war; its ceilings were covered with white silk, and its roofs were studded with roses on a ground of gold. A great pillar wreathed in gold and surrounded by four gilt lions supported the whole edifice. Francis rested in a tent "as high as the tallest tower" with thirty-two sides covered in golden cloth that had stripes of blue velvet "powdered" with golden fleurs-de-lis. Nearly four hundred other tents surrounded Francis's, creating an appearance of "an entire town of silver and gold, of silk and velvet, of floating tapestries."[5]

were brought by the English to accommodate the troops. Many of those who came to observe the spectacle, knights and ladies, had to sleep on hay and straw. (Reprinted by permission of Royal Collection Enterprises.)

Francis I, *ca. 1525, attributed to Jean Clouet, Louvre, Paris. The king's attire is made of rich satin and is soft and flowing. The black satin stripes provide contrast and restrain the color, which might otherwise seem too pert. The doublet, an outer garment, has a wide-cut neck so the embroidered shirt can be seen. The sleeves are full but slump off the shoulders, suggesting laxity. The ensemble is sensuous and somewhat seductive. (Reprinted by permission of Alinari/Art Resource.)*

Henry VIII, *1536, by Hans Holbein, Walker Art Gallery, Liverpool. The king's attire is richly embroidered and perforated, allowing the fabric of his shirt to come through which makes the garment look as if it is bejeweled. The chain around his chest, padded doublet, puffed sleeves, and fur coat increase his bearing. The hat continues the details of the garments, emphasizing a unified whole. (Reprinted by permission of Alinari/Art Resource.)*

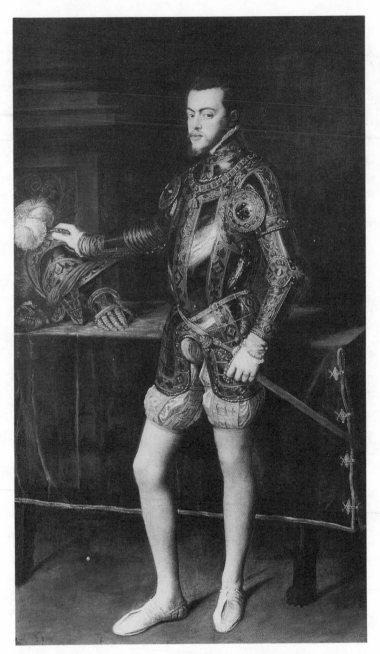

Philip II of Spain, *n.d., by Titian, Prado, Madrid. The king is shown in armor and codpiece. (Reprinted by permission of Lauros-Giraudon/Art Resource.)*

Court Style, Decorum, and Manners

Dress signified the distinctive style of each court in relation to the population and to its governmental functions, as historian J. H. Elliott (1987) pointed out.[6] The French style was that of public kingship. The monarch lived out his life beneath the public gaze, and the nobles were grouped around the highly visible monarch. Hence, all were sensitive to aesthetics. Competition for patronage was part of the lifestyle of those dependent on the monarchy, including courtiers, artists, and those of the nobility who were financially strapped.[7] The Spanish style, in contrast, was that of private kingship. The tenures of Philip III, Philip IV, and Carlos II were characterized by the kings' social distance. Court ceremonies and rituals were used to isolate the sovereign; his company was limited to a few privileged aristocrats. A somber style of dress prevailed in the Spanish court. The attire included a ruff that imprisoned the neck and made both expression and carriage rigid and dramatic. Pleats were heavy; diamonds, rubies, and emeralds were used lavishly; earrings, diadems, and necklaces oppressed the silhouette.[8]

Veblen argued that "in the last analysis the value of manners lies in the fact that they are a voucher of a life of leisure."[9] Knowledge of good form, he claimed, is prima facie evidence that a portion of a person's life was spent in acquiring accomplishments that were of "no lucrative effect." In *The Civilizing Process* (1978), Norbert Elias argued that political rhetoric underlies the expectation for "civility" and "refinement," terms that describe the conduct and attire required of the leisure class. The demeanor expected of the attendants serving those in authority was also expressed in dress.[10]

Within the households of the great barons of feudal Europe, loyalty was the expected conduct, and the most familiar embodiment of this value was the knight. Knighthood was a privilege. It was not automatically bestowed on members of the nobility; it had to be specifically earned and individually given. To be invested, a novice knight had to pledge to be unflinchingly steadfast in his loyalty to his feudal lord and to be ready to fight and lay down his life. A knight had the right to confer the rank on any man he considered worthy, but he also had the responsibility of giving him guidance.[11]

Knighthood and loyalty declined with the decline of the feudal households.[12] In the fourteenth and fifteenth centuries a new aristocracy came into being that had new patterns of association and interaction. Composed of members of the landed nobility, members of the middle class who had acquired wealth, and government officials, this aristocracy came to inhabit a new space, the semiurban courts of princes and kings. A nobleman was no longer the master in his own castle. He now lived at the court, serving the sovereign and waiting on him at the table. At the court he had to behave in exact accordance with his own rank and the rank of those who surrounded him. Unlike free lords and knights who were largely unrestrained in their ability to act, be fair, or feel compassion for the downtrodden, the members of the new aristocracy were dependent servants of the king. They were constrained in their behavior and in their freedom to ex-

Philip II of Spain, *n.d., by Sanches Coello, Prado, Madrid. The king is shown wearing the characteristic black and white "Spanish habit." It consisted of a padded black parabola, a cone-shaped structure, with a white ruff around the neck. It was starched to rigidity, immobilizing its wearer. The somberness and volume of the attire suggest a desire for distance and self-restraint.*

press emotions. Sycophancy, self-restraint, and reserve characterized their behavior. In addition, new expectations for behavior and appearance emerged. Members of the new aristocracy were expected to remain aloof from anything the middle-class or "common" people did or said. In the environment of the absolutist court, etiquette and dress became the crucial means by which the aristocractic courtier asserted his privileged position.[13]

The styles and elements of dress that Veblen described as distinguishing the leisure class also identified the ruling class. The attire signified power and authority, which, in the words of Elias, were required for the formation of a "monopoly of force."[14] As Veblen suggested, court attire indicated a system of domination and was intended to elicit a behavioral response—compliance—and not merely feelings of esteem.[15]

Monarchs' attire may be understood as a strategy and tactic they employed in the ceaseless struggles and confrontations they faced. The representation of power in appearance was not merely to repress, to block, or to reject. Monarchs believed that their attire could transform, strengthen, or weaken their hold.

Power, then, must be understood as something that does not exist by itself, apart from other relations. In reality, power implies a more or less organized, hierarchical, coordinated cluster of relations.

11

Commerce and Fashion

Commerce

As previously discussed, the weakened power of the autonomous feudal lords encouraged the development of commercial centers such as Venice, Florence, and Genoa and the establishment of the great northern ports of Bruges and Antwerp. The government at the time controlled the art and fashion worlds, and periodic changes in desired appearance became sources of wealth and prestige. In a study of the court of the Spanish Hapsburgs, J. H. Elliott observed that the lesser rulers were the innovators in matters of display: the fifteenth-century dukes of Burgundy in ceremonial display, and the sixteenth-century Medicis in the art of court spectacle. It was only by compensatory effort of this kind that they could hold their own in a world of great powers. But the great powers followed at their own pace and convenience, conferring their own prestige on practices first developed in the lesser courts.[1]

The Emergence of Fashion

The court of Philip the Good, duke of Burgundy (d. 1467), is considered "the cradle" of fashion.[2] Philip exploited the resources available in the territory he controlled to create new clothing styles. Until this time Paris had been the center of luxurious court dress. As mentioned, the International Gothic Style had been generated in Paris in about 1380, and attire in this style was worn in many of the courts in Europe, which were connected through a complex system of politics and marriage. After the beginning of the fifteenth century, however, Paris was eclipsed as the center of court dress by the court in the northern French duchy of Burgundy. This area lay along the spine of Europe, directly within the Mediterranean trade route for goods being transported to the North Sea and England.[3] People, talent, and commodities flowed into its markets. Members of the court took increased interest in their clothes, adorning themselves with elaborate costumes to display wealth and an awareness of style.

In the painting *Hunting with Falcons at the Court of Philip the Good* (ca. 1442), discussed in Chapter 8, all participants are dressed in white as part of the theme of the festivities. Some wear attire in the International Gothic Style that came out of Paris. Others wear regional garments, including some from Bruges, Ghent, the Netherlands, and Germany. Some of the mantles, gowns, and hairstyles origi-

*The duke of Burgundy, Philip the Good, receiving an illuminated manuscript. Attired completely in black, his appearance was in sharp contrast to the colorful dress worn by members of the nobility. His style was adopted by monarchs in Spain, the Netherlands, and elsewhere in Europe. (*Portrait of Philip the Good, *Dedication Page, Chroniques de Hainault. Bibliotheque Royal Albert I, Brussels, n.d.)*

nated in Italy. The figures of the duke and duchess reveal a new fashion ideal, long and lean. The duke's short gown is belted around the hipline, with carefully arranged pleats in the front; his legs in full-length hose and his pattens, or pointy shoes, are exposed. His sleeves are moderately sized and end with a padded, fur-trimmed cuff. Members of his household, courtiers, retainers, attendants, and musicians wear simpler versions of the same style (nonuniform uniforms). Most of the men wear no hats and their hair is in a bowl cut; the duke wears "a version of the turban."[4] The duchess Isabella wears an ermine-lined long robe and a very sheer veil. A few of the women wear no headcovering at all.

The variety in appearance and the influx of new materials and ideas informed artistic endeavor, helping to develop and support local employment.[5] In addition to its being an international trading center, however, Burgundy also became a fashion center. A sizable Italian community settled around Bruges, formed by Italian merchants who had escaped from Paris along with several Medici bankers during the English occupation. They helped turn the duchy into a cosmopolitan center with exposure to foreign styles and the use of readily available resources (fur and the black cloth manufactured in Flanders). The trade in fashion

Decorated fan and gloves, French, ca. 1885.

had begun. By the middle of the fifteenth century Burgundy had become the center of fashion.[6] Fashion offered a level of prestige to the community that local culture could not. Moreover, aristocrats from the northern countries and other parts of Europe, such as Italy and Spain, copied the Burgundian style and the long, lean, and graceful silhouettes of the court of Philip the Good, thus establishing fashion as a distinct part of elite culture.[7]

Fashion as an Economic Good

A more recent example of a monarch using fashion to stimulate growth of the economy while increasing national prestige is Louis-Napoléon. He used the Great Exhibitions of 1851 and 1855 in London and Paris to show that the French government was behind its fashion industry, encouraging new technology and the export of dress and ornament. The exhibits included the latest cloaks, gloves, hats, fans, and perfumes, which were displayed alongside the crown jewels and the dresses of Napoléon's wife, Empress Eugénie.

The emperor wanted to encourage the well-to-do members of the aristocracy to support the economy by spending money on clothes.[8] There was no doubt that those who frequented the court were expected to dress up and change their costumes often. He also impressed upon Charles Frederick Worth, the court's couturier, that the production of fashion was essential for the well-being of the nation. He encouraged Worth to create a new fashion "each season because everything the Empress wore created a demand first among upper class women and then among the lower classes."[9] He insisted that women who appeared before him be dressed in the latest fashion. Through his efforts, the French fashion

Lord and Taylor's 1874 copies of Charles Fredrick Worth designs.

industry revived, and it continues to be an important source of revenue for the country.

As Simmel ([1904] 1957) observed, openness to social mobility is the social condition necessary for fashion to exist.[10] He explained that there is no fashion in a hierarchical society where the boundaries between social classes are tightly shut and there is no possibility for mobility. The clothing of each class acts as a "uniform" that separates the classes and identifies rank. He noted that in Western society the aristocracy often had to compete with the rising middle class for social rewards, wealth, prestige, and power. To do so successfully the aristocracy had to maintain visual superiority. A new fashion was thus invented by members of the aristocracy as soon as their existing style was adopted by members of the middle class.

Fashion puts a premium on expense. It makes use of novel materials and design innovations, which by their nature are not readily available. Scarcity is the essential element limiting the kinds of fabrics fashionable people are interested in wearing. Fashion often reflects new ideas expressed in art and culture. To determine how to dress, fashionable people monitor what others are wearing so as to "be up to date."

The desire to make what was scarce more readily available encouraged innovation, as John Nef suggested (1958).[11] For example, the demand for calico like that brought to England from India in the eighteenth century stimulated the growth of the cotton industry. The expense and demand for calico, a light, sheer, soft fabric with bright floral patterns, encouraged scientists and practical inventors to concentrate their efforts on finding ways to improve bleaching and dyeing techniques that would facilitate fabric printing and yield washable colors.[12]

Fashion and the Individual

Fashion, Simmel argued, encourages modification and adoption to individual needs. The wearing of fashionable attire enables individuals to separate themselves from their family, to develop a more distinct identity and a more unique sense of self, and yet to maintain an affiliation with the prestigious aggregate. Individuals can extricate themselves from a setting or a situation, scrutinize the image they present, and tailor it to the social response they desire.

Fashion enables individuals to deal with themselves as persons and as social objects. It makes possible both individuation and social connectedness. As Simmel observed: "There is no institution, no law, no estate of life which can uniformly satisfy the opposing principles of uniformity and individuality better than fashion," because it allows individuals to pursue competing desires for group identity and for individual expression.[13] This separation or objectification allows one to correct the image if necessary to achieve the desired response, explained Simmel. By offering the opportunity for "trial and error," fashion encourages social and personal awareness.

12

Beauty as Perfection of Physical Form

PHYSICAL BEAUTY, the harmonious unity of the anatomical form, is often confused with the feminine fashion ideal and viewed as a tool in the oppression of women. Naomi Wolf in *The Beauty Myth* (1991), for example, argued that women in the United States are expected to look pretty, fashionable, thin, and youthful while being enchanting and *submissive*. Through these expectations, society controls what women do with their bodies, reducing women to objects. In this way, society defends the social order but also alienates women from their bodies, voices, and faces. Another purpose of controlling female appearance has to do with pay. Western economies are dependent on the continued underpayment of women. For women to accept underpayment, they must be made to feel "worth less." And having ideal standards of appearance that women cannot meet leads to low self-esteem and low self-worth.[1]

Wolf's observations support those made by Simone de Beauvoir in *The Second Sex*: that beauty, fashion, and cosmetics have been used to force women into a secondary place in society and into a position of an "other." Although the ideal of feminine beauty varies, certain demands remain the same; in particular, to be feminine is to appear weak and docile. However, this appearance gives legitimacy to women's secondary standing in society; they are not as capable as men. The subjugation of women, suggested de Beauvoir, emanates from the expectation that in sexual intercourse a woman must be possessed by a man. Her body must present inert and passive qualities. Costume and style have often been devoted to cutting off the female body from any possible transcendence, de Beauvoir argued. Corsets and long, voluminous dresses hamper physical mobility and personal expression. Makeup and jewelry contribute to the "petrification" expected of women.[2]

In *Face Value: The Politics of Beauty,* R. T. Lakoff and R. L. Scherr confused beauty with the feminine fashion ideal. They recognized that "beauty is power" but contended that the definition of beauty is idiosyncratic: "A choice made by one artist at one time bears no necessary relation to that of another artist. ... Today's essential ingredient is yesterday's irrelevancy." They concluded that "women have given up much of their potential true power to compete in the beauty game."[3]

In contemporary society physical beauty is actually a resource, like wealth or talent.[4] Its importance is appreciated in both genders. Champion boxer Muhammad Ali characterized himself as "the greatest" and "the prettiest." Beauty is found to be a significant attribute in the occupational spheres. There are male movie stars and politicians who are prized for their good looks. At the time of John Kennedy's candidacy for the U.S. president, his youthful good looks were thought by the professionals to be a disadvantage, signifying nothing more than his inexperience. However, after the first televised debate between Kennedy and Richard Nixon, the political appeal of good looks began to be taken seriously, pointed out Arthur Marwick.[5] Today, the good looks of President Clinton and former Vice President Dan Quayle are generally acknowledged.

Desirable personality characteristics are often ascribed to good-looking people. They are seen as more sensitive, kind, sociable, pleasant, likable, and interesting than those who are plain or unattractive.[6] Similarly, a 1981 study by J. Ross and K. R. Ferris of male employees in two large accounting firms found a positive correlation between employees' physical attractiveness and their performance evaluations and salary increases. The authors concluded that good-looking people tend to be viewed as more intelligent and competent. The harmonious attributes of the physical being lead to positive social evaluation and rewards.[7] In the 1970s sociologists began to report that in the United States beauty had achieved a kind of parity with wealth and social position. The importance of being attractive had been promoted by the advertising industry, Diane Barthel suggested in *Gender and Advertising: Putting on Appearances*. Advertisements seduce women and men to recognize their less than ideal appearance and to take advantage of the advertiser's solution.[8]

The Novel and the Beautiful

Veblen distinguished between the feminine fashion ideal, which he called the novel, and the beautiful.[9] According to Veblen, the feminine fashion ideal is specific to a period. It is socially constructed and most often emanates from beliefs about what will enhance a man's image in the eyes of other men. The "novel" is characterized by the norm of conspicuous waste. In the medieval period it was based on the ability of a man to support a woman. Her appearance reflected the fact that the man did not need her labor to provide for her needs.[10] The feminine fashion ideal demanded delicacy of face, diminutiveness of hands and feet, and a slender figure, all characteristic of idleness.

A plump appearance became the feminine fashion ideal during a large part of the nineteenth century, reported L. W. Banner in *American Beauty* (1983).[11] For the many immigrants who associated thinness with poverty, the look of prosperity was chubbiness. "A fat bank account tends to make for a fat man," according to an adage of the day. For people in the middle classes a paunch symbolized economic success. Medical authorities concurred: "No less for a man than for a woman a thin body is unhealthy."[12] It was thought that a woman with plump,

Turn of the century feminine fashion ideal Frankie Haines (left), "one of the bright piquant and buxom beauties of Lester and William's galaxy of talent." (Theater advertisement in The National Police Gazette, *May 28, 1892, New York.) Twiggy (right) 1960s female fashion ideal, modeling (right), a design from her own collection, January 18, 1968. (Reprinted by permission of UPI/Bettmann.)*

rosy cheeks, large breasts, and full hips would have more admirers. As described in *The Laws of Health in Relation to the Human Form:*

> Who can admire hollow eyes, prominent cheek bones, sunken cheeks, angular and shrunken shoulders where the low-necked ball-dress displays at the most inopportune season the sharp collar bones and the edges of the shoulder blades, the flat breast and narrow chest, the skinny arms, the shriveled hands, and thin ankles?[13]

Popular guides to womanly perfection in the nineteenth century included illustrations of buxom women with large derrieres and pudgy forearms.[14] In *The Culture of Beauty* (1877), T. S. Sozinskey commented that to be beautiful a lady should be "of medium stoutness."[15] The *Ladies Home Journal* in 1888 and *Vogue* in 1893 promoted the plump, prosperous ideal. Photographs of society leaders in newspapers and magazines and photos of models in publications devoted to fashion sketches consistently showed women with round faces and ample body proportions.[16]

In the first decades of the twentieth century the literature and art described a new feminine ideal—linear and active. In "Bernice Bobs Her Hair" and *The Great Gatsby*, F. Scott Fitzgerald portrayed young people who were spirited and full of energy. In the novel *Oil!*, Upton Sinclair derided the young who seek "complicated ways of hitting a little ball"—in tennis, golf, and polo matches. A woman was no longer limited to presenting herself as pale, plump, demure, and retiring, as was dictated by nineteenth-century conventions.

The 1922 winner of the Miss America contest lacked the large bosom and hips, the curves, that illustrator Cole Phillips asserted had been definitive of beauty in American women for over a century. The 1921 winner was the curvaceous Margaret Gorman of Washington, D.C., who Samuel Gompers, head of the American Federation of Labor, claimed represented the type of woman America needed—strong, red-blooded, able to take on the responsibilities of "homemaking and motherhood." The 1922 Miss America, Mary Campbell, had broad shoulders, straight lines, and an athletic build. The differences in body characteristics between the 1921 and the 1922 Miss Americas elicited much editorial comment, and the judges were chided for "capriciousness" in deciding on the new ideal of the American beauty. Howard Chandler Christy was the sole judge in the 1921 contest, and the selection represented his taste: the traditional curvy female form. A panel of illustrators was assembled for the 1922 competition, and they chose differently—a streamlined ideal. The judges' distinct view of the feminine ideal led to their choice, observed illustrator Cole Phillips, himself one of the contest judges.[17] The "streamlined" Miss America reflected characteristics of contemporary commercial art and the new expectations for the modern woman—active and healthy. In the summer of 1928 *Vogue* reported that in Paris "narrow hips" were de rigueur and that to tan was fashionable.[18] The boyish look was considered beautiful, for it accommodated the demands of the camera for long legs and a hipless body. Fashion copy described the advantages of the new look, asserting that short skirts allowed a free and swinging walk that showed a graceful length of limb.

Fashion photographers such as Baron Adolph de Meyer, Cecil Beaton, and Edward Streichen helped to style this new ideal of feminine fashion in accordance with the tastes and values of *Vogue* editors. Their photographs of women were composed to reflect an aura of elegance and refinement; they showed women who looked comfortable in their luxurious world. The women's beauty did not reflect perfection of figure and face but "beauty born of refinement and poise," a beauty that required wealth.[19]

Slender of figure, in childlike short dresses that left large expanses of the body exposed, Jean Shrimpton and Twiggy represented the 1960s feminine fashion ideal. At the time, boutiques were actual laboratories. They functioned as hangouts, and ideas sprang from the air as owner-designers sat around chatting with friends. Much of the stock was made in-house with such techniques as rudimen-

Miss America 1921, Margaret Gorman (left), full and curvy. (Reprinted by permission of The Miss America Organization.) Miss America 1922, Mary Campbell (below), streamlined and action oriented. (Reprinted by permission of The Miss America Organization.)

tary sewing, tie-dyeing, batik, lacing together leathers with thongs and applying studs, macramé, crochet, and glue-on appliqué.[20] The styles included "space age abstractions," see-through blouses, and mini dresses with peepholes or inset with clear vinyl strips. The styles were playful, like children playing peekaboo. Jelly bean colors—orange, hot pink, lime green, and purple—and dotted, striped, checkerboard, and other op art patterns in black and white also projected playfulness and fun. Fashion magazines urged their readers to lose their inhibitions, be experimental, and keep up to date.[21]

The 1960s feminine fashion ideal, like that of the nineteenth and early twentieth centuries, was interpreted to be symbolic of wealth, because achieving the look required costly dieting, dressing, and grooming.[22] In earlier eras, however, wealth had been conveyed through luxurious fabrics and styles accentuating expensive detail. The 1960s clothes conveyed youthfulness and innocence. It is more likely that the new feminine fashion ideal reflected the innocence and vulnerability of the United States with its new age structure. President Kennedy, inaugurated on January 20, 1961, was the youngest president ever elected. He personified vigor and campaigned on the theme of "getting the country moving again." He challenged the status quo, proposing new and daring programs: a multibillion-dollar project to land an American on the moon, "where no one had ever dared to go"; a Peace Corps through which an army of idealistic and mostly youthful volunteers would bring American skills to underdeveloped countries; and new frontiers in medicine and education.[23]

The vocabulary of the women's liberation movement was used to style the feminine fashion ideal of the 1970s. Revlon hired Lauren Hutton because she represented the look of naturalness and because she personified the image of the modern woman: energetic, engaged in purposeful action, and able to play many roles. In many ads, Revlon portrayed her as a real woman with a real life. She was shown in different moods, from natural to romantic to glamorous. She looked comfortable and in control in any situation. The implication was that the modern woman was too intelligent to have only one look. She could choose her looks to fit her moods, Lakoff and Scherr pointed out.[24]

The style, model, and photographer lose their prominence when they cease to reflect the ideals of the period. The fashion then acquires the pejorative label "old-fashioned." As suggested by Veblen, a fashion is "beautiful" only because it conveys the present.[25] The feminine fashion ideal is forged by events and sentiments affecting the period.

The *beautiful*, in contrast, maintains its pleasing qualities through time, observed Veblen. It is an autonomous attribute, universal in nature and independent of fashion.[26] Its essence lies in the congruency of the physical features of the biological form; it lies in the natural characteristics of the face and form with which one is born. Aristotle observed that beauty depends upon an orderly arrangement of parts and a size that is not accidental. One derives pleasure from integrity of design, unity, and order, from symmetry, harmony, and perfection. Those who most closely embody these qualities are considered beautiful.[27]

In *Beauty in History* (1988), historian Arthur Marwick observed that we identify objects as beautiful if they are the focus of admiration and give pleasure to the generality of beholders. The development of the appreciation of beauty is not a simple linear one. In preindustrial Europe beauty was perceived as powerful but having a disturbing influence. The beautiful was viewed as the good and was appreciated for the joy it brought; however, as an object of desire and love, it was beheld as superficial, identified with the carnal, and contrasted with the spiritual beauty of the divine. In preindustrial society, the prejudice and confusion about the meaning of beauty, for the most part, resulted in "blindness" to it.[28]

Historical Background of Beauty as a Cultural Value

The proud, courageous heroes glorified in Homer's *Illiad* and *Odyssey* reflected Greek ideals for male behavior. The nude in Greek art expressed social expectations for physically fit, battle-ready youth. A physically fit appearance signified being able to withstand the rigors of battle.[29] In early Greece, a male youth with a supple body and carefully delineated muscles was deemed beautiful and was entitled to social and sexual rewards. An important means of upholding the ideal of physical fitness was gossip. Old men, the heads of leading families, sat by the city gate, where they listened to stories about the performance of each young man and evaluated his skill. Slackers suffered ridicule. Greek youths kept in shape for the deities as well as the state. They emulated the physical perfection of the Greek gods, such as Apollo. Displaying athletic prowess was considered a religious activity; competitions honored sacred and secular authorities. Men competed naked during these events because clothing restricted full action and concealed their superior physiques.

Over the centuries the depiction of the nude in Greek art underwent changes that mirrored changes in desired social conduct. It went "from the physical to the moral sphere," as art historian Kenneth Clark reported. The nude as an art form was invented by the Greeks before the sixth century B.C.[30] The early sculptures presented youths standing alone, proud and naked. Later, the finely tuned muscles of athletes and soldiers in action inspired artists to focus on showing the movement of the body and the idea that the male body should be battle ready. By the fifth century, when democracy became a political and social goal, a new ideal of beauty was evident in Greek art. The harmonious proportions of the nudes emphasized a balanced whole and communicated grace, strength, and gentleness. Poets, philosophers, mathematicians, and dramatists gave voice to the belief that perfection could be sought even though everyday reality was less than perfect.[31]

In ancient Greece, Plato established the enduring value of beauty when he argued that behind its temporal embodiment lay an eternal and absolute form.

Apollo Belvedere, Roman copy of a Greek sculpture from the late fourth century B.C., Vatican Museums, Rome. Apollo Belvedere was considered the supreme example of classical beauty by eighteenth and nineteenth century critics. (Reprinted by permission of Alinari/Art Resource.)

The beautiful, the true, and the good were different manifestations of one eternal divine perfection. To reach it, one must progress from bodily beauty to beauty of mind, to beauty of institutions, laws, and sciences, and finally to absolute beauty itself. Direct acquaintance with beauty could most easily be achieved through an inner, contemplative process, one that occurs beyond the eyes. The Greeks, thus, drew no distinction between the aesthetic and ethical spheres; the beautiful and the good were identical. Excesses in one's life were viewed as aesthetically offensive; physical fitness implied moral behavior. In ancient Greece, the beautiful were believed "blessed" and were less likely than others to be considered as having done wrong.[32]

The moral and intellectual worth attributed to beauty in ancient Greece has been carried into contemporary life. In casting roles in movies and plays, directors have taken literally Plato's view that the beautiful is good and the good, by definition, is beautiful. The "good guy" is portrayed with pleasing harmonious features; the "bad guy" has jagged, distorted, if not grotesque, features.[33]

Studies examining the effects of the attractiveness of offenders on juridical judgment have found that good-looking defendants usually tend to be treated generously in contrast to unattractive defendants; they are seen as less dangerous and more virtuous. The tendency to leniency was explained in this manner: We like attractive people more, and those who are better liked are usually punished less than those who are less liked, the unattractive.

Examining this finding in a laboratory situation, researchers found that for crimes unrelated to attractiveness (burglary, for example), more lenient sentences were assigned to the attractive defendant than to the unattractive one. However, for offenses related to attractiveness (swindle, for example), the attractive defendant received the harsher treatment. The researchers concluded that when crimes are attractiveness-related, the advantages held by good-looking defendants are lost.[34] It is as if beauty is a gift, the malevolent manipulation of which is condemned.

The Modern Emergence of Physical Beauty as a Value

Physical beauty began to emerge as a cultural value in the early nineteenth century, a period scholars identify as neoclassical. Enlightenment ideas encouraged the development of beauty as a cultural value, as did the philosophy, literature, and art of ancient Greece and Rome. These were used to show that among educated men the spirit of *rational* inquiry prevailed. These scholars also encouraged the rejection of religion as a theoretical framework for explaining social and natural phenomena, insisting that observation, measurement, and comparison were the rational means for scientific inquiry.[35] In their early studies some Enlightenment scholars compared animals and people to identify similarities and differences. They next classified people according to race. For example, they

compared the face and body measurements of Pygmies in Africa and other
hunting and gathering societies with ancient Greek sculpture, which by then
was regarded as the standard of perfection.[36]

In *The Rise and Fall of the Victorian Servant* Pamela Horn wrote: "Personal appearance was very important for any boy aspiring to a position of a footman or
page in a large household, for only the tall and well-built were considered." This
requirement marked a change from the late eighteenth century, when servants
were not intended for display.[37] Similarly, in a standard history of the English
country house, which he wrote in the mid-nineteenth century, Merlin Waterson
observed that at the grander country houses the first requirement of a footman,
groom, or coachman was a physique to show his livery off "to advantage," that is,
to present a physically beautiful appearance.[38]

Courtesans, artists' models, and actresses came from different ethnic backgrounds and had different features, but as Marwick observed they were similar
in that their features were well proportioned and conveyed a harmonious unity.
Many of them used their beauty to develop careers. Actress Sarah Bernhardt and
fashion designer Chanel, for example, achieved international fame for their
beauty as well as their talent. The fathers and lovers of such women, Marwick
pointed out, made them aware of their special impact on men. They left home
searching for their individual destinies.[39]

Neither in body shape nor attire did the courtesans conform to the fashion
ideal.[40] In an era of voluptuousness Sarah Bernhardt was thin. "Audiences at first
thought she was ridiculous because she was so skinny. ... When she raised her
arms, people would boo because her arms were not fleshy enough," her
biographer Robert Fizdale related.[41] Moreover, many of her acting roles required
the concealment of her looks rather than their projection. Nevertheless she developed an international reputation as both an actress and a beauty. With dark
hair and eyes, she has been described as a "profoundly appealing, unorthodox
Jewish beauty [with] the faintest suspicion of [a] too long nose (though highly
enticing)."[42] The desire to be close to beauty led men to compete with one another. Beautiful women became status symbols, objects that enhanced a man's
stature in the eyes of other men.[43]

Learning to Recognize Beauty

There is little agreement among people as to who is actually beautiful because
physical realities evoke emotional responses that may be based on personal exposure and experience. In the United States in the nineteenth century, fairs
boasted beauty contests as well as sideshows at which human beings with physical anomalies were exhibited.[44] Together these events helped clarify characteristics of desired and undesired appearance. Dwarfs, microcephalics, armless and
limbless people, and non-Western people were exhibited at carnivals, state fairs,
and at the Barnum and Bailey Circus. In these sideshows, identified as "freak
shows," people with alleged and real anomalies were formally organized to ex-

Actress Sarah Bernhardt, for whom the purpose of acting was "the creation of that elusive, indefinable quality of beauty." (Quote from E. Salmon [1977] Bernhardt and the Theater of Her Time [Westport, Conn.: Greenwood Press], p. 5. Photo by Felix Nadar, 1862, reprinted by permission of The Bettmann Archive.)

hibit themselves for amusement and profit. They achieved their greatest popularity between 1840 and 1940, as Robert Bogdan (1988) noted.[45]

Wendy Chapkis, in *Beauty Secrets: Women and the Politics of Appearance*, related how strangers on buses and trains in the United States and Europe go out of their way to make her feel ugly. Because she is a "bearded lady," they touch her face and pull on her facial hair to see if the moustache and beard are really hers, all the while laughing and making jokes. They insist that her hairy face is an aberration that must be suppressed. Their unwelcome attention in public

Ella Harper, "the Camel Girl," a pretty thirteen-year-old with severe orthopedic problems. She wrote, "I am called the Camel Girl because my knees turn backward. I can walk best on my hands and knees." (Quote from R. Bogdan [1988] Freak Shows [Chicago: University of Chicago Press]. Photo by Charles Eisenman, 1886, Ron Becker Collection, Syracuse University Library, Special Collections Department; reprinted by permission.)

causes her humiliation and pain. Though she is lonely, she welcomes the safety of her home. Many other women, to escape feeling ugly, actively engage in disguising unacceptable features, Chapkis pointed out.[46]

Restoring Symmetry

War-related disfigurements, caused by accidents and injuries, began to challenge the imagination and creativity of physicians in the period between the two world wars. Plastic surgery focused on reconstruction—for example, replacing a missing jaw or restoring facial contours to re-create a sense of unity. It later became the means to correct birth deformities and malformations caused by cancer. It seems that reconstructive surgery, the attempt to reestablish a sense of harmony by reconstructing a nose or an ear, for example, was also practiced in Renaissance Italy. There, taking umbrage to a person's words or actions often took the form of wielding one's sword. Although at that time surgery was not even taught in medical schools in Europe, a professor of anatomy at the University of Bologna, Gaspare Tagliacozzi (1545–1599), developed procedures to restore mutilated noses, lips, and ears. Few attempts were made after his death to systematize the procedures and make them an integral part of medical care.[47]

Data collected in the 1960s by the National Health Examination Survey involving fourteen thousand children six to seventeen years old found that tall children score slightly higher on intelligence tests and perform somewhat better academically than their shorter classmates, perhaps because more is expected of them. The findings were interpreted as suggesting that the shorter students were thought of as younger or less intellectually mature. To enable children to attain a normal adult height and to correct dwarfism, injections of growth hormone were offered in the 1970s. A *New York Times* editorial, however, warned parents that growth hormones can turn people into giants more than eight feet tall. It continued with, "While no parent would wish giant children, some might seek to add a few inches to the height of children who are below the average stature." According to the editorial, that can be accomplished by an essentially cosmetic use of the growth hormone. However, parents and pediatricians who elect to make cosmetic use of the growth hormone take on a heavy responsibility, the editorial warned. Smallness is not a disease; however, tallness secures privilege.[48]

Attaining Physical Harmony

Seeking to realize the fashionable ideal is different from desiring to correct an imperfect body part, most plastic surgeons will point out. In the 1950s plastic surgery was requested to change a hooked nose to an Irish snub; in the 1990s women have been calling on plastic surgeons to plump up thin lips, and men have been doing so to correct cleft chins. Others, however, seek to realize the ideal form. Men and women from thirty-five to forty-five have been asking for brow lifts, ear tucks, chin restructuring, and nose resculpting. Contemporary plastic surgeons are expected to combine the discipline of surgery with a sense for aesthetics, "to put the right nose on the right face."[49]

Patients, moreover, are requesting implants: to camouflage skinny calves, balance the contours of the face, and increase chest and buttocks size. Patients generally work with their surgeons before the operation to express their preferences about the size and shape of a reconstructed body part; however, as Elizabeth Rosenthal reported, these are "hopes that the surgeons find they frequently dash" in the desire to achieve a natural look and good balance.[50]

Preserving Ethnic Identity

"Patients do not want to change their ethnicity, they just want something improved," stated a *New York Times* article in 1991. The article went on to say that doctors are making efforts to preserve ethnic features while enhancing beauty.[51] Since the aesthetics of surgery has historically been tailored for Caucasian faces, surgeons now face a "two pronged challenge": First, they need to define beautiful features for African-Americans, Hispanics, and Asian-Americans, and, second, they must determine how to modify standard operations to achieve those

The bathing suit competition of the Miss America Pageant attests to the importance of self-restraint (through not overeating) and to the principle of universalism (all persons are judged by the same standards). (Photo by Eve Arnold.)

goals. The ideal nose or shape of face is subject to ethnic variation, and the concept of beauty varies among people of different ethnic groups. Orientals, for example, strive for "a softer, rounder" look than the sculpted appearance admired by Europeans. Moreover, experts have warned that the different skin qualities of different groups create both advantages and problems in terms of elasticity and scarring. Hence, patients must choose physicians experienced in operating on their specific ethnic group. Improved surgical techniques and a better understanding of the anatomical differences among people of different races have greatly aided surgeons' attempts to preserve ethnicity.[52]

Cosmetics

Modern culture's emphasis on beauty and the use of cosmetics has led to much criticism. As Harry C. Bredemeier and Jackson Toby (1960) explained, the existence of a sociocultural standard implies that some people are found wanting. Social standards are internalized even by persons who are "substandard." Social rejection goes hand in hand with self-rejection.[53]

Cosmetics make it possible to hide imperfections and to impart a sense of symmetry and harmony to the face. The use of cosmetics, however, has been condemned as objectifying women and oppressing them. What is real is not the exterior form but the essence of the being. Makeup is artifice, a mask, unnatural and immoral. In open debate, male Marxists argued that big cosmetic companies manipulate women's insecurities and fears to rake in massive profits.[54] Female Marxists, however, countered that the use of cosmetics is a basic economic and emotional necessity. To become part of society, to get a job, and to keep a man, a woman needs to look her best. Cosmetics are an important tool in the struggle of lower-class women to emancipate themselves from the status of household drudges.[55]

In their study of female college students, Lakoff and Scherr found that in contrast to the older generation of feminists who argued that cosmetics reinforce women's passivity, dependence on male approval, and dependence on superficial appearance for self-esteem, some feminists now feel that looking good is their birthright—"something that we owe ourselves and others to take advantage of."[56] Putting one's best face forward in dress and makeup was seen not only as a boost to one's ego and a means of enhancing self-confidence and productivity in work and other social settings, but also as providing a subtle compliment to those with whom one interacts, a way of making them feel better and, as such, a gesture of politeness. Careless appearance or the unwillingness to take pains to enhance one's appearance was felt to be rude. These young undergraduate women claimed that they relied on the type of cosmetics that brings out "what is hidden," "enhancing what was already there."[57]

The Utility of Beauty

Contemporary beauty contests go well beyond the construction of desired female appearance. They represent neither the "women's condition," their sexual submission to men, nor the "feminine fashion ideal"—the latter reflecting the "spirit" of the period. The Miss America Pageant makes visible certain cultural values considered essential for interaction in the public place. The ceremony dramatizes the desirability of winning; it attests to the principle of universalism, because all persons are treated according to the same standards rather than according to special relationships. The basic criterion for winning is achievement. The rituals delineate structural-interactional preferences: that conformity to rules prevails, that individual attributes and idiosyncracies be submerged. Uniformity and efficiency are ensured through the ministrations of pageant directors, hairdressers, and makeup people.

Rather than acting demure, shy, and retiring, contestants are required to put forth energy, perform, dance, sing, and demonstrate intelligence. The swimsuit competition proclaims the importance of self-restraint (not overeating). It also affirms that beauty today lies in the fitness of the body, its readiness for action, and its agility and flexibility. The evening gown event proclaims the desirability of knowledge and wealth; the selection of an elaborate, flattering gown requires both attributes. The spoils go to the person who most meets the desired criteria.

For people working in the service industries, in particular, beauty enhances the chances for economic success, or winning. These industries depend upon interpersonal communication and interaction. Good-looking employees are nonthreatening and often pleasing. Such employees can help smooth the way toward a successful conclusion of a sale or interaction. The preference for good-looking employees is thus understandable.

13

The Youth Ideal

IN AN ESSAY on the Op-Ed page of the *New York Times*, Patricia Bradshaw complained that "today's grannies are likely to look 50"; the reality of age is obscured. Women work hard at being *not* old and proving it. They jog, diet, stretch, lift weights, and "have some of their parts patched. ... We have lopped off old age as if it were a double chin," she protested. Women in the United States are free to dress and act as they wish.[1]

Through much of the nineteenth century, however, older women's lives were circumscribed and constrained, observed historian Lois W. Banner (1983). Older women occupied a special sphere. Their clothing, behavior, and physical appearance were designed to set them apart from the young. The feminine fashion ideal was *plump*, providing the older women with a measure of attractiveness.[2] The marital state conferred an identity upon women; when they married, they were eliminated from the category of youth and entered the "old" category. Beauty did not count. Most people disregarded a married woman's physical appearance.[3] By age thirty-five most women donned caps under which they tucked their hair as a mark of a grandmother status, thus symbolically renouncing their sexuality. Whereas husbands in their forties and fifties were social and professional leaders, honored for their accomplishments, most people considered women dull by the age of forty. Thus, at a point when a man was still considered at the prime of his life, a woman was considered old. Bachelor women were expected to stay home and provide some service to the family. The imperfections that accompany old age were accepted, which discouraged attempts at beautification.

In 1851 novelist Caroline Kirkland published an eloquent attack on negative attitudes toward old age, focusing on society's refusal to allow older women to wear bright colors and youthful fashions. At the time, dress indicated age, as much as any other factor. Behind this constraint, Kirkland suggested, lay the fear that older women might try to attract older men. But the constraint resulted in older women becoming crabbed and censorious, exhibiting just the kind of behavior expected of them.[4]

In the post–Civil War years, the boundary between youth and old age began to break down. The separate forces of feminism and the commercial beauty culture were behind the changes in society's perception of older women.[5] Fashion magazines and beauty advice books recommended that women of all ages should be permitted and even encouraged to look as young as they wished. Book after book, pamphlet after pamphlet, rammed home the message "that a woman's *duty* is to be beautiful," observed historian Arthur Marwick (1988). Even scrip-

A leading star of the popular musical stage from the late 1870s through the 1890s, Lillian Russell personified the mature, voluptuous ideal. (Reprinted by permission of The Bettmann Archive.)

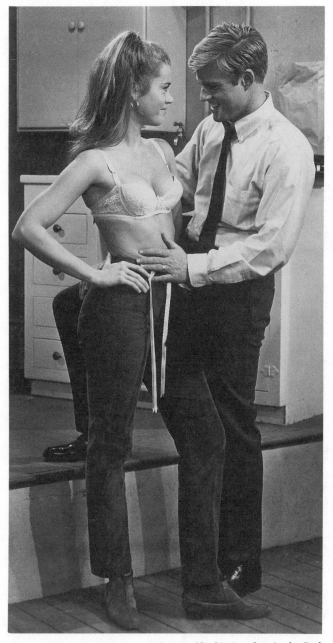

Actress Jane Fonda with actor Robert Redford in Barefoot in the Park,
1967. The photograph shows the youthful, slim ideal of the 1960s.
(Reprinted by permission of The Bettmann Archive.)

tural authority was invoked. The harsh corollary was that no woman has the right to be ugly.[6]

By 1870, the popularity of the old-maid legend had declined. Some older women were independent, dressed well, and did not care whether they married, noted Banner. By 1900, stories about the exciting, independent lives of "bachelor women" affected society's perception of women of older age. The career involvement and reform movement of older women in the post–Civil War years established women's right to age definition similar to that of men. The interests of the commercial beauty industry and those of the women's reform movement intertwined, and their efforts were directed toward a common goal.[7]

Many prominent nineteenth-century actresses not only lived long lives but also remained active on the stage until well into their sixties and seventies. At eighty Sarah Bernhardt became legendary for her ability to play convincingly the part of a young boy. One of the elderly performers in opera, singer Adelina Patti, gave frequent interviews about her ability to retain her youthful beauty. "No tragedy in life is so awful to a woman as the realization that her youth is gone, and in its place are the wrinkles, the dull eyes, and the decrepit figure of age."[8] As the media pointed out, Patti had developed none of these presumed disabilities. She was in her sixties, and her face was unlined, her figure trim, and her step firm.

Discussing in public methods of preserving their looks, older women in the nineteenth century usually stressed diet, exercise, and rest. They also took part in advertising cosmetics. The cultural prohibitions against older women attempting to look youthful declined, and the normal physical attributes of old age—white hair, wrinkles, and sagging muscles—were even more negatively defined than before.

Creating a Social Identity

The denigration of old age reinforced the value of youthfulness, and old age acquired the status of a stigma.[9] In 1927, Upton Sinclair in his novel *Oil!* wrote: "I look at the old women I meet and think which of them do I want to be? And I say, Oh my God! and jump into my car and drive fifty miles an hour to get away."[10] Similarly, in her 1991 book, *The Beauty Myth,* Naomi Wolf told of a fifty-four-year-old woman who lost her job without warning because her boss said that he "wanted to look at a younger woman" so his "spirits would be lifted."[11]

Analyzing the attempts of "over-the-hill" sports superstars such as Jim Palmer, Mark Spitz, George Foreman, and Bjorn Borg to return to competitive sports, a *New York Times* editorial pointed to "the dream of youth." Denying age, the superstars attempt to recapture their glorious past.[12] In an article he wrote that was published in the Sunday *Magazine* section of the *New York Times* entitled "Senior-Circuited," Tom Brokaw, the anchor for "NBC Nightly News," suggested that he had accepted the view of the "20-year-old advertising genius who thinks that 50 is just short of death's door." He confessed that at age fifty he was no longer playing the part of the "brash young man, making the daring moves secure in the knowledge that if they don't work out, there will probably be other chances. At this age, mistakes, however daring, are not easily excused. Achievement is not a cause of praise; it is expected."[13]

Growing old in contemporary society is more than experiencing the progressive decline in body functions.[14] People are placed into a nondesirable social category, and they have to deal with the problem of lack of acceptance by society, suggested Erving Goffman. These people have to play the social game with the cards stacked against them. They try to separate themselves from what the unfavorable identity implies about them. Some assert independence of the identity; others demonstrate mastery over their lives.[15] The basic problem with a "spoiled identity" is that it can become what sociologist Everett Hughes called a "master status."[16] As such, it obscures all other personal and social attributes. When people withdraw their acceptance from a stigmatized individual, they are distorting the person's identity to fit a negative stereotypical expectation. The stigmatized individual may internalize part or all of the negative views of others, consequently diminishing self-esteem and altering the self-concept.

To avoid making the stigma a master status, stigmatized individuals use what Goffman termed "information control." (For example, they may be reluctant to give their age. Recall Jack Benny's perennial "thirty-nine.") They may manipulate their appearance to minimize the extent to which they will feel hurt or suffer a loss of self-esteem. The stigmatized person is thus prone to victimization and vulnerable to advertising claims, in this case for products that supposedly restore youth.[17]

Age Stratification

Biological factors *and* societal beliefs about appropriateness account for a person's ability to perform certain social roles. Few females under the age of twelve or over the age of fifty can have babies. The very young and very old would find it difficult to dig ditches. But most other age limits are culturally and socially defined. Miss America is young because we equate beauty with youth. When airlines first hired flight attendants there was an upper age limit. The reason was not that the job required talents that were age associated but that attendants were expected to be decorative.

The negative definition of age can be seen in the behavior of American executives working outside the United States. According to a recent *New York Times* article, K-mart managers in Eastern Europe believe that the need to change attitudes about selling and buying in that part of the world is the basic challenge they face in generating profits. One problem has been changing the relationship between customer and sales clerk. Many Western companies in Eastern Europe, according to the article, refuse to hire Europeans older than forty on the theory that they will not be able to change their habits. Shaping new customs requires changes in personal attitudes and behavior. K-mart managers were surprised,

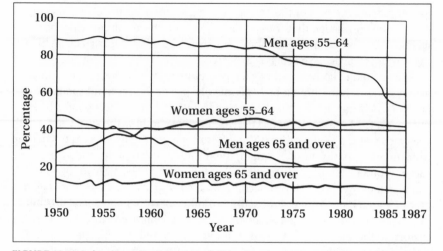

FIGURE 13.1   Labor Force Participation of Older People, 1950–1987, by Sex
At the turn of the twentieth century the majority of employees remained in the workforce
well into their seventies. By 1987 only 16 percent continued to work past the age of sixty-five.
(Source: *U.S. Bureau of Labor Statistics [1988]* Labor Force Statistics Derived from the
Current Population Survey, *Bulletin 2307 [Washington, D.C.: U.S. Department of Labor,*
Bureau of Labor Statistics].)

however, "that as many of the 40-plus age group as in the 30-plus age group
passed psychological tests that screened candidates for leadership qualities, organizational skills and adaptability."[18] (See Figure 13.1.)

Sociocultural Background

The preference for youth was encouraged by the new ways of thinking and working that emerged in the post–Civil War era. In *Old Age in the New Land* (1978),
Andrew Achenbaum suggested that the following factors contributed to the
emergence of a negative attitude toward old age: (1) the rise of professionals who
usurped the elderly's reputation for wisdom; (2) a scientific community influ-
enced by the evolutionary theory, which viewed the elderly as afflicted with dis-
orders and not able to keep pace with the evolving world; and (3) a corporate
structure that had no use for old people.[19]

   In *Captains of Consciousness* Stuart Ewen argued that the economy's production and consumption needs in the post–Civil War years supported the establishment of youthfulness as a cultural value. The requirements of mechanized
production, for instance, helped support the preference for youth. Industry and
assembly-line production depended heavily on consumption but also on the
endurance and reflexes of youth. Once a sign of accumulated productive know-
how, age became a detriment; the need for hands and eyes skilled through time

and practice was suddenly obsolete, replaced by the need for stamina and swiftness, attributes of the young and required by the "cogs and levers of the increasingly versatile machine."[20]

In explaining their decision to manufacture toilet paper in 1879, the Scott brothers, Edward and Clarence, identified the reasons for their choice. The product is (1) indispensable, (2) disposable, and (3) unreusable.[21] The desirability of the product was determined by the potential for profit. In the developing economy mass production and mass consumption were necessary for economic success.[22]

The belief in the opening decades of the twentieth century that the young were free and unfettered by past conventions also encouraged the establishment of youthfulness as a cultural ideal.[23] Aware that adults are cautious to spend their financial resources, advertisers preferred selling to youth directly. By doing so, they did not have to break old habits. Ads often pictured adults as incompetent and unable to cope with modernity, as Ewen pointed out.[24] Advertising devalued parental authority, deeming it "old-fashioned," and conveyed the message that the needs of the child are better understood by industry than by parents. The Pepsodent Company, for example, posed the following question to parents in 1922: "Shall [your children] suffer as you did from film on your teeth?" Parental desire to free children from the limitations suffered by their own generation became a basic theme of advertising.[25]

In his memoirs of American college life at the turn of the twentieth century, Henry Seidel Canby suggested that the orientation of the American executive at that time was shaped by his experience in college. He wrote: "From these campuses came many, if not most, of the two generations of Americans who are now in the executive charge of the country, and the greater part of the codes, ideas, manners, and ideals of living that dominate us."[26]

These were also times when sports solidified their hold in America. The popular sport of football was now played on college campuses, and the most famous football players were college students. By the 1890s Saturday football games assumed major importance as rituals of community cohesion. Sports pages of metropolitan newspapers regularly covered football games, and the articles humanized colleges and made them seem a part of American popular culture with which all Americans could identify. At the same time the frenzy of competitive sports was often duplicated in the intensity of student culture. Students became more involved than ever before in clubs and extracurricular activities, and bouts of drinking and rowdiness were common.[27]

In the prestigious eastern women's colleges modern dance became a new mode of expressing ideas and feelings. It was introduced by individual students inspired by Isadora Duncan, to whom dance was a means of experiencing oneself, a means of being. These students had something to say, something that was contained within them, and they chose movement as a way to express it. They used the body as a means of creating a new art form, making their audiences think and feel. This new mode of expression grew and became appreciated in and out of academia. In 1926–1927 Wellesley College offered two courses in dance composition, and Smith offered three in rhythmic dancing; and in 1928–1929 a student dance group was formed at Smith. The students did their own choreography and performed for fellow students and alumnae groups. Modern dance came to be viewed as a performing art, meant to be presented to spectators. The colleges produced cohorts of performers and audiences reliably following one another. Modern dance and, by extension, the attributes of youthfulness that characterized the dancers acquired greater visibility in American society, and society gained an art form associated with high culture.[28]

Mass Marketing

Geared to youth, mass market production continues to support youthfulness as an ideal by focusing on products that youth feel they need. Clothing is produced that is fitting only for the young. In 1969 an article entitled "The Forgotten Markets" aired the complaint that the fashion industry "is not listening to that vast army of consumers both men and women who aren't going to college, who are over 25, have tremendous quantity of money and taste—and aging wardrobes." It concluded with, "So we wonder whether youth hasn't reigned too long."[29]

Similar sentiments were conveyed in a *New York Times* editorial by James L. Greenfield. He observed that tucked away in the television networks' computers is the fact that half of all spendable income in the United States, $130 billion, is held by people over age fifty. With all that money around, it is logical to suppose that advertisers, particularly those who use television, should be in hot pursuit. Logical but wrong. Most television advertising is still pitched to the eighteen to twenty-five crowd. Not only are the advertisers ignoring the money held by those over fifty, they are also ignoring the fact that those over fifty watch more television than any other age-groups. The reason for the focus on youth is straightforward, according to Greenfield. Most buyers of television time at ad agencies are under thirty, and they buy what they watch. "For them demographics don't count very much"; these are people who essentially think "that at fifty you are brain dead."[30] These young ad executives also seem not to be concerned with the consequences, that is, that their negative view of those over thirty may diminish the self-esteem and alter the self-expectations of those over fifty.

Youthfulness, moreover, is alluded to even when selling to the mature market. In a May 13, 1991, news story in the *New York Times*, Deirdre Carmody described an ad for sweaters in *New Choices*, a magazine for men and women over fifty. A grandmother, flanked by granddaughter and daughter, is portrayed as having fun wearing a baseball helmet and glove and showing off the ball.[31]

Demographic Changes

The idealization of youth, that is, the structuring of the perception and feeling that youth and youthfulness are desirable, has become more problematic and

*Bifocals are identified with aging;
however, Varilux bifocals show no
split in the lens—the lens appears to
be uniform and continuous. Hence,
more youthful appearance is suggested. (Courtesy of Varilux Corp.)*

poignant with the increase in life expectancy. Since 1900 life expectancy has increased from 47 years for white males and 49 years for white females to 72.6 and 74.5 years, respectively. At the same time, pressures have developed to exclude from the labor force the elderly and children in favor of young and middle-aged adults.[32] Assertiveness, competency, self-control, and power are all qualities associated with holding a job. Aging is associated with the loss of a job, the loss of vigor, and the pain and misery lying ahead. Fearful statisticians see the coming aged society as likely to cause a slide "towards inevitable decadency." They fear the implications of "a population of old people ruminating over old ideas."[33]

Baby boomers approaching middle age are courted by marketers who offer them products that enable them to deny their age. In a 1991 news story in the *New York Times,* Peter Kerr reported that as the 78 million Americans of the baby-boom generation begin

> to bulge, sag and squint their way into mid-40's, companies are striking gold with products that offer a bit of youth to these aging yuppies—a group that demographers are calling grumpies, for grown-up, mature professionals. Retailers are ringing out profits with products like wide-seated jeans, frilly girdles, and bifocals without telltale lines in the lenses.[34]

Consumers seem to be willing to pay extra to maintain the image of youthfulness.

Divorce and the hope for remarriage provoke further anxiety about youthful appearance. The proportion of marriages that end in divorce has risen steadily since the 1970s. Current estimates are that fewer than half of all marriages contracted today will remain intact for thirty years or more.[35] The remarriage rate differs by age and sex, with more women than men remaining unmarried and establishing single-person households.

Personal Response to Aging

One's personal response to the preference for youth may depend on inner and outer sources of support, sociologist David Riesman (1954) suggested. His research identified three groups of people. *Autonomous* individuals bear within themselves some psychological sources of self-renewal. For them, aging brings accretions of wisdom with no loss of spontaneity or the ability to enjoy life, and they are relatively independent of the culture's strictures and penalties imposed on the aged.[36] Consider Clint Eastwood in his role as a Secret Service agent in *In the Line of Fire*. As Russell Baker suggested, he provides "an illustrated lecture on the superiority of geezerhood." Eastwood, who is sixty-three, looked it, and was perfectly at ease with it.[37] *Adjusted* individuals, possibly the majority of older people, bear within themselves no such resources but are the beneficiaries of cultural preservative (derived from work, power, or a long-lasting marriage), which sustains them as long as the cultural conditions remain stable and protective. Barbara Bush, the former U.S. president's wife, is an example. *Anomic* individuals make up the third group. Protected neither from within nor from without they lose physiological vitality and decay.[38]

Anomic men and women who read newspapers or magazines or who listen to radio and television talk shows often feel that they can arrest the changes associated with aging. The challenge to *look* young means escaping feeling old. Jogging, dieting, stretching, lifting weights, and undergoing cosmetic surgery make it possible to discard the age benchmarks. A face-lift reduces loose skin and jowls to produce a younger, less tired look.

Practitioners of the new psychologies, those with a holistic view, suggest that one's effort should go instead into developing the inner self. Making oneself whole should be the focus. For thwarting a stigmatized social identity, personal growth and new sources of fulfillment are superior to cosmetic means. The practitioners suggest that "we must get in touch with what we are, to find out what there is in us to become."[39] Only then, it seems, can people enjoy their age.

14

The Health Ideal

HEALTH BEGAN TO EMERGE as a cultural ideal in the second half of the nineteenth century as research-oriented hospital medicine was established and germs were discovered to cause illness. The study of cellular pathology, bacteriology, and asepsis led to the further recognition of distinct diseases. The notion of bacterial infection and the essentials for wound-healing brought about techniques for antiseptic surgery. Analysis and experimentation by Joseph Lister (1827–1912) and Louis Pasteur (1822–1895) revolutionized the practice of medicine. In the United States W. T. Morton (1819–1868) discovered ether in 1846, which made it possible for patients to endure the surgeon's knife.[1]

Once it was found that rats carry the plague and germs cause infections it was possible to control epidemics through sanitation and vaccination. After a debilitating outbreak of cholera that decimated London in the 1830s, authorities campaigned for sanitation facilities in the home, in the workplace, along public streets, and in public parks. Physician John Snow discovered the correlation between cholera and the water supply in the Soho district of London during the epidemic of 1854. To halt further infection he advised the parish vestry to remove the handle from the pump from which the afflicted families were drawing their water. The Public Health Act of 1875 encouraged the construction of urban sanitation systems: Fresh water supplies were brought to cities and sewage plants were established.[2]

The extensive use of vaccinations followed Pasteur's success with anthrax in 1881. Antitoxins against diphtheria and tetanus were discovered in 1891. In 1896 the man considered to have opened up the field of hematology, Paul Ehrlich, began the search for synthetic chemicals effective against infectious diseases. He predicted that specific agents similar to antitoxins would be discovered that would be effective against all bacterial diseases.[3]

All of these developments were taking place at a time when it was generally accepted that the restoration of health entailed medical intervention and heroic measures, such as being bled, blistered, or given poisonous laxatives. These practices had emerged centuries earlier and developed from the belief of both medical practitioners and lay persons that the preservation of health required "taking the cure." They assumed that the body possessed a finite amount of "fixed energy," or a "vital force." Physicians believed that health was achieved through an equitable distribution within the body of this fixed quantity of life force. Illness resulted when one area of the body possessed too little or too much of the needed force. Physiological turning points, periods of climacteric change, for both men and women were potentially dangerous because the body at those times was working toward achieving a new balance, and maintenance of balance constituted health. To aid the body reach that balance all practitioners regulated and altered bodily excretions and secretions through various agents.[4]

Sanitation and Cleanliness

The knowledge that sanitation and cleanliness were means to prevent illness helped upset the fatalism that had characterized medical practice and daily life in Europe since the decline of Rome.[5] Returning Crusaders, however, restored the public bath to Europe, and it became a medieval meeting place where wine and music flowed and the sexes mingled. The bathhouses existed until the fifteenth century, when fear of the bubonic plague caused them to be closed. Bathroom plumbing, which had been refined two thousand years earlier in the courts of Egyptian and Minoan royalty, was negligible or nonexistent even in the grand European palaces. Queen Elizabeth did "bathe herself once a month whether she required it or not."[6] The Reformation and the Counter-Reformation exacerbated the disregard for hygiene. Protestants and Catholics vying to out do each other in shunning temptations of the flesh exposed little skin to soap and water. People did not concern themselves with cleanliness. They simply changed their underwear and perfumed themselves with grimy hands. Chamber pots were emptied into the streets. Disease and epidemics overwhelmed villages and towns.[7]

After a long absence of plague eighteenth-century doctors began to recommend that people wash their hands, face, and neck daily. Washing was done in a basin in the bedroom.[8] The French produced a shoe-shaped running water tub with a drain in the "toe," which Benjamin Franklin introduced to America in 1790. Most Americans, however, did not take to bathing regularly until a hundred years later. When Boston's Tremont Hotel opened in 1829 it featured the nation's first bathrooms. In the basement of the 170-room building were eight water closets (toilets) and eight bathing rooms. America's first private bathrooms were installed in a row of model houses in Philadelphia in 1832. In 1852, to reduce the threat of disease, New York opened baths for the poor, and by the Civil War most of the city's hotels had bathtubs. Private individuals also became more interested in installing toilets, showers, and tubs in their homes.[9] Sylvester Graham, called the "whirlwind" Presbyterian minister, tirelessly championed bathing up and down the east coast.[10]

Diet

Whereas work in the field of bacteriology and in the medical laboratories guided medical practice, individuals who designated themselves as the guardians of health focused on diet. Religious movements in the nineteenth century had a health component; they classified food and recommended temperance, physical education, and dress reform. They thus suggested that the prevention of illness was a "doable goal."

Reducing the threat of disease by proper nutrition was an important component of Sylvester Graham's preaching. He gained many followers as he traveled through the Northeast preaching vegetarianism, bathing, fresh air, sunlight, and sexual hygiene.[11] He recommended that foods should be simple, not concocted from complicated recipes; and he urged the eating of fruits and vegetables and the whole kernel of wheat. Graham developed a wheat cracker that is still eaten today—the graham cracker. Boarding houses were set up to serve these crackers and other foods recommended by Graham. Oberlin College reserved part of its cafeteria for those following the Graham diet. The Seventh-Day Adventists became followers of Graham's edicts. His dietary reforms included allowing time for the proper digestion of different foods, making the thorough mastication of food a necessity, and abandoning the frying pan.[12] Health behavior, or activity taken for the purpose of preventing illness by persons who believe themselves to be healthy, was thus encouraged throughout the nineteenth century.

Utopian Writers

Upsetting fatalism and supporting the institution of health as a cultural ideal were goals that were also promoted by utopian writers. Between 1865 and 1917 at least 120 prescriptions for an ideal society, models for solving the problems of the time, appeared in print. The utopian writers considered what an ideal society would be like and encouraged dreams and visions that questioned the status quo. The fundamental presupposition of utopianism, the belief that human ills are due to bad institutions, suggested that almost anything imaginable was possible; the utopian writers believed that a universal trend of all things is toward improvement. The utopian commitment to progress was driven primarily by the simple feeling that tomorrow would be better.[13]

Reducing Risk

A chilly chamber pot in a freezing bedroom, an old heating stove that burned the face while the rest of the body froze, and a general feeling of helplessness against disease were characteristics of life at the turn of the twentieth century. A new emphasis on therapeutic measures supplanted the emphasis on diagnostic and other medical research that had characterized academic medicine in the United States.[14] Tuberculosis, influenza, and pneumonia were the most common infectious diseases. Antituberculosis associations encouraged the vision that individual behavior can conquer illness and delay death. Reforming personal habits, diet, and hygiene and using drugs less frequently were seen as contributing significantly to averting medical problems. Public health measures supported the belief that mastery over nature was possible.[15]

Preventing Tuberculosis

One of the major killing diseases of the nineteenth century, tuberculosis was seen as a disease against which little action was possible.[16] Its impact was likened to that of a plague. Its symptoms—pallor, emaciation, weakness, and persistent cough—were considered fascinating in the early Victorian era. Slow in its course, it did not produce repulsive lesions. Because it affected both rich and poor, some considered it an act of God. Others who realized that the disease tended to run in families thought it was the result of some obscure hereditary defect. The illness was often kept a family secret because telling others decreased one's eligibility for marriage and for certain occupations and decreased the chances that other family members could obtain life insurance.[17] The hope that tuberculosis could be prevented arose around 1900, after Robert Koch, a German bacteriologist, discovered that a germ was responsible for the disease. Bacteriological studies found that the illness could be prevented if the passage of the tubercle bacilli from person to person was blocked.[18]

The antituberculosis forces issued a general appeal to the population to participate in the fight against the disease. Health departments circulated leaflets titled like the one in New York City, *Rules to Be Observed for the Prevention and Spread of Consumption,* thus attempting to educate the population. Voluntary organizations, such as the Medico-Legal Society of the City of New York, a group composed principally of lawyers, scientists, and physicians interested in social problems, decided in 1899 to organize an American Congress on Tuberculosis at which "the laws of the several states regarding the disease and its treatment" would be considered.[19] The arrest of the disease and the prevention of its spread were the dominant goals. Education and the personal involvement of members of the community were considered essential.

The all-out attempt by the U.S. Public Health Service to monitor potential sources of infection encouraged awareness. On the front page of the September 4, 1920, *Los Angeles Evening Herald* was the edict of Health Commissioner L. M. Powers to his health deputies—those charged with the duty of inspecting ventilation systems in hotels, restaurants, and apartment houses: "Keep your shoes clean."[20] Public participation in the fight against tuberculosis also took another form. In 1907 the first Christmas Stamp sale took place in Delaware. Its success led to the Red Cross Christmas Seal campaign the following year. The appeal for money to support the prevention of illness was now carried out on a national scale.[21]

Bacteriological science made it clear that personal conduct led to the spread of the disease. Individuals who took precautions were less likely to be infected. By the 1920s, tuberculosis yielded its place as the leading cause of death to heart attacks.[22] This new way of thinking about disease was in sharp contrast to the fear of disease and death that shaped seventeenth-century, eighteenth-century, and nineteenth-century attitudes. As the beliefs of the general population and

In the early twentieth century women avidly turned to exercise, dieting, and gadgetry to achieve the new slender ideal. The women in this 1929 photograph attempt to shake off excess weight with reducing machines. (Reprinted by permission of the Division of Photographic History, National Museum of American History, Smithsonian Institution.)

those of medical authorities converged, health as a cultural value became possible.

Adult Height and Weight Tables

The idea that personal effort could protect a person from illness and subsequent death was made visible through height and weight tables. In 1879 Dr. J. J. Mulheron reported that obesity taxes the body and that the fat person has a much more uncertain tenure of life than people of average weight. He went even further, linking obesity to specific diseases.[23] Other physicians at that time viewed obesity as something that violated the integrity of the human organism. Toward the end of the nineteenth century physicians and nutritionists began to examine the relationship between weight and health, and by the beginning of the twentieth century plumpness was seen as a danger to health. Further evidence came from the Medico-Actuarial Mortality Investigation of 1889–1912, which concluded that being overweight was clearly disadvantageous for people over thirty-five years of age. Control of weight was now sought by physicians and insurance companies.

Dr. Louis Dublin, in 1908, studied the impact of weight on life span and linked obesity with decreased longevity. He then calculated average weights desirable for given heights. With significant statistical evidence in hand, the insurance industry was able to demonstrate the link between fatness and mortality. About 1918, as a statistician for Metropolitan Life Insurance Company, Dublin replaced his standard table of average weights with a list of desirable weights, which dictated that after early adulthood men and women should weigh somewhat less than the average for their height. These tables were recommended as the standards to be used by physicians and life insurance companies.[24]

In a September 26, 1992, report in the *New York Times* the Department of Agriculture and the Department of Health and Human Services offered a height and weight table adjusted by age. The report noted that over the years weight charts have varied strikingly, "and there is no significant agreement among health professionals about when a person is overweight or whether it is harmful to gain a little weight as you age." The government's booklet *Nutrition and Your Health: Dietary Guidelines for Americans,* acknowledged that people over thirty-five are likely to weigh more than people between the ages of nineteen and thirty-four. It offered a weight range adjusted by age.

A new genre of books devoted exclusively to weight control and diet appeared on the market after World War I. A book of this genre ranked second on the nonfiction best-seller list of 1924–1925.[25] In her popular beauty guide *Physical Beauty* (1918), Annette Kellerman, the champion swimmer, derided the notion that women were intended by nature to be plump. Women needed to pay attention to their physical appearance, she argued, so they would not grow fat at forty and shrivel up at fifty. "Fat is weakening and in a society where women's weakness was a virtue, fatness in woman may have been desirable. Weakness is no longer a virtue, but a handicap to a woman," she asserted.[26] Eating properly and exercising were seen as the means of maintaining one's ideal weight, and thinness came to reflect the achievement of the new cultural value: health. In *Diet and Health with Key to Calories* (1918), Dr. Lulu Hunt Peters educated her readers about her scientific weight reduction plan. She explained the role of calories, the composition of a balanced diet, and the hazards of violating the laws of nutrition. She noted that it is impossible with exercise alone to reduce weight.[27] The potbelly and the plump look, which had been fashionable among members of the middle class in the nineteenth century, were now considered evidence of sloth and gluttony.

The Well-Child Clinic

A commitment to children's health and to the optimistic view that medical science could prevent much agony, illness, and death was evident in the establishment of well-child clinics and medical and nursing services in the public school

TABLE 14.1   A Comparison of Major Causes of Death in the United States, 1900 and 1990

Causes of Death in 1900	Percent	Causes of Death in 1990	Percent
Influenza and pneumonia	11.8	Heart disease	33.5
Tuberculosis	11.3	Cancer	23.4
Gastroenteritis	8.3	Stroke	6.7
Heart disease	8.0	Accidents	4.3
Stroke	6.2	Pulmonary diseases	4.1
Kidney disease	4.7	Pneumonia and influenza	3.6
Accidents	4.2	Diabetes mellitus	2.3
Cancer	3.7	Suicide	1.4
Infancy diseases	3.6	All others	20.7
All others	38.2		

Source: Adapted from the National Center for Health Statistics, U.S. Department of Health and Human Services, Washington, D.C., 1991.

system in the first half of the twentieth century. Vaccinations and the ingestion of vitamins made it possible for children to avoid some illnesses and also made the growing child aware of the importance of maintaining health.[28] In addition to vaccinations, some schools offered nutrition supplements and medical examinations. The examinations included height and weight measurements, which helped the children become aware that there are criteria of appearance that they must meet.

Prevention of Illness as the Physician's Domain

Since the 1930s medical columns in popular and professional magazines have reflected the fact that the medical profession must broaden its perspective to include preventive health care. Healthy men and women were expected to go to their doctors for routine physical examinations. By the 1980s research had found that degenerative diseases such as heart disease and cancer, rather than infectious diseases, were the leading cause of death (Table 14.1). The medical profession advocated the reform of personal habits, such as smoking, diet, alcohol consumption, and exercise, as means of preventing heart disease and perhaps cancer. Individual responsibility for maintaining health was reaffirmed. Some major medical schools, such as Harvard, Berkeley, and Johns Hopkins, decided to publish "Wellness Letters" to clarify the often conflicting and superficial health information presented in the popular media. The editors claimed that their access to the latest findings regarding threats to health was greater than the mass media's and that they could offer better guidelines on how to reduce the risk of developing chronic diseases. They made it clear that good health depends on lifestyle choices.[29]

The reform of personal habits—for example, adhering to a stringent low fat diet—is viewed as a nonsurgical and nonpharmaceutical means of reversing, not just retarding or preventing, heart disease. The nation's largest provider of health insurance, Mutual of Omaha, announced in 1993 that it would reimburse

184

Today, longevity is a supporting motivation for fitness. (Copyright 1992 by Consumers Union of U.S., Inc., Yonkers, N.Y. 10703-1057. Reprinted by permission from Consumer Reports, *January 1992.)*

patients for participating in programs that offered diet, meditation, exercise, and support groups, thereby acknowledging the value of unconventional forms of therapy.[30] Both individual concerns for staying well and the concerns of the medical establishment reaffirmed the value of health. A trim, fit body with good muscle tone became the symbolic indicator of health.

The Visual Conjoining of Values

A value may have more than one manifestation, and a visual manifestation may reflect more than one cultural value. A physically fit body, for example, may reflect the values of both self-denial and hard work, which are basic to American culture, as sociologist William Graham Sumner suggested.[31] In a 1989 *New York Times* column, "How to Begin an Exercise Program," sports journalist William Stockton wrote: "So you are sedentary and the doctor has scared you with talk of heart disease and a lecture about your weight. Or, a significant other has delivered an ultimatum. Or, you have caught a glimpse of yourself in the bathroom mirror and been unhappy with what you saw."[32] These three statements offer three different motivations for a specific appearance. They demonstrate that the motivation and meaning of the behavior are specific to the individual.

The Suntan

Upton Sinclair in his novel *Oil!* (1927) interpreted the suntan as an example of Veblen's conspicuous consumption and waste.[33] He claimed that society was divided into two groups: those who worked and remained pale, and those who had leisure time, engaged in sports, and acquired tanned faces. Tanned skin, he argued, indicated that one was not a city or office worker and had the time and money to bask in the sunlight. The suntan thus emerged as a status symbol signifying wealth.

Columbia University professor Paul Nystrom, in his book *The Economics of Fashion* (1928), characterized the suntan differently, calling it a "youthful complexion fad."[34] He saw it as an American phenomenon that indicated modernity, separating younger women from older ones. Older women were brought up with the idea that fairness of skin indicated freedom from manual labor. They continued to take special care against the damaging effects of wind, sun, and salt water. "White is beautiful" had been the ideal since the Middle Ages and continued to be the ideal even after World War I. White skin made it possible for the veins to be discerned, helping to support the aristocracy's claim to "blue blood," that is, entitlement to special privilege. Younger women, taught the ideas of a new society, including new energy, opportunity, and freedom, were more likely to expose their body to the sun, wind, and surf.

In the 1920s women were no longer limited to presenting themselves as pale, demure, shy, and retiring, as dictated by puritanical conventions, and these characteristics were no longer requirements for marriage. Women could look tan and "modern," vigorous in appearance and action. Paleness had also been a characteristic of tuberculosis; suntans suggested youth and health.[35]

The suntan continues to be popular. Tanning parlors have appeared in most major U.S. cities. The correlation between skin cancer and exposure to ultraviolet rays of the sun, discovered by physicians in the 1970s, has not dampened the allure. Lotions that screen out ultraviolet rays and big-brimmed straw hats have been adopted by men and women as means of preventing skin damage but still acquiring a tan. The tanned image continues to project energy, youthfulness, and health.

The Lean and Muscular Male Body

Few occupations require a body that is lean and well toned. Yet, since the beginning of the 1990s the beer aesthetic, which had been characterized on MTV by overweight guitar playing men wearing black T-shirts stretched to the limit, has given way to the ideal of the lean, well-toned male body. Superstars, sports celebrities, male models for Calvin Klein, and young men on city streets are displaying this new standard for male appearance. Shirtless, or wearing shirts open to the waist, or wearing vests with no shirts, they show a somewhat skinny but well-toned musculature.

"Athleticism has taken over and shirts have been taken off; across the cultural board from movies to advertisements men are not wearing too many clothes," reported Peter Watrous in the *New York Times* in 1991. He pointed out that pop personalities such as film celebrities are under pressure to fit current notions of what is desirable. For many male rock and roll stars, the choice is simple: "Nautilus or marginal success."[36]

Enlarged pectorals supported by well-defined intercostal muscles and a well-rounded gluteus have emerged as the new status symbols for men. These have acquired prominence over the conventional emphasis on biceps and bulk. Power and militarism were the traditional reasons for athleticism. Command was signified by broad shoulders, chest, and size. Fitness alluded to readiness to engage in physical aggression or to prevent altercation. Today the totally fit body has different meanings and purposes. It proclaims self-discipline (control over the consumption of food and beverage and an abstention from partying; leisure time hours are spent working out). It also indicates control over one's body and the expression of aggression. Breasts in Western culture, however, allude to both nurturing and sensuality, and a tight gluteus intimates superior sexual performance. The ability to contract the muscles in those parts of the body alludes to the ability to give and receive increased sexual pleasure.

The skinny, toned male ideal suggests, in addition to health, a popular desire of men to relate to others beyond the confines of aggression and economics traditionally demanded of them. It may be interpreted as a rebuff to established societal restrictions on the scope of feelings men may experience and express.

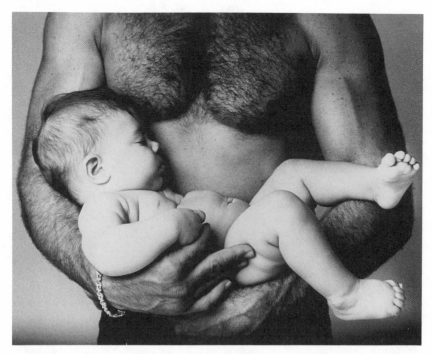

Edward Vitali and his daughter Alexandra, fall 1993. Vitali, manager of a New York health club, displays this picture in his public office. (Reprinted by permission of Edward Vitali.)

Part Five:
Publicspeak

15

Clothing Tie-Signs

 IE-SIGNS IN CLOTHING provide information about a desired social identity. They indicate *membership* in groups outside the boundaries of dominant institutional discourse and interaction with specific others. They provide information about behavior. Attire that is a tie-sign has only one meaning and can be easily "read." It acts to maintain the individual's bond to the group. The ensemble is carefully conceived by the group's decisionmakers to convey an image that counteracts the ideas of the dominant culture; wearing such attire encourages a sense of belonging and supports feelings of worth. Individuals and groups who reject society's hierarchical arrangements, those who resist social change, and those who reject a societal designation of inferiority may develop fellowship with similar persons and with it a distinctive mode of appearance and behavior.

The term "tie-sign" was coined by the sociologist Erving Goffman, who observed that in Western society there is no one-to-one fit between the elements and units of public life and the elements and units of social structure. He suggested that visual indicators that designate a "with among a co-present" be called tie-signs. This term can also be used to describe the clothing of groups whose orientation to social life is in a realm separate from mainstream culture.[1] Tie-signs are markers that provide information about such subsets.[2]

When individuals who share the same sentiments about social conditions form groups to achieve a sense of social and personal significance outside mainstream culture, they may use tie-signs as a means of expression and identity. The wearing of tie-signs enables these individuals to place themselves in a sociocultural category and in a system of rights and obligations. The attire sets members apart from nonmembers, which further discourages participation and interaction in the dominant institutional spheres.[3] The decision to wear attire that is a tie-sign is a conscious one. Individuals adopt the attire to announce commitment to the group and are aware that it places them outside the confines of established structural and institutional order. The audience is thus alerted that the social game will be played under different rules. Members of the audience may associate or interact with group members, but only on their terms.

Three categories of groups wear tie-signs. They are differentiated by the forces that led to their evolution and by the extent of communal life.

The first category involves individuals who *dissent.* They oppose the dominant hierarchical structure and adopt or develop beliefs, values, and lifestyles in opposition to those espoused by the ruling authority. The Hare Krishnas in the United States and the Jains in ancient India are examples. The second category consists of groups that have *resisted* the social and cultural change that came with the individualism and economic success of the Renaissance, the secularization and industrialization of the nineteenth century, and neocolonialism. Interaction and conduct in these groups continues to be guided by traditional forms of connectedness. The Amish, Hasidic Jews, and the Rastafarians are the most prominent examples. The third category involves individuals who develop a bond because of feelings of isolation, alienation, and lowly social definition. The attire enables the individuals to *protest* their designation of inferiority. The zoot suit worn by blacks and Mexican-Americans, and the attire of the Hell's Angels, their "colors," are important examples.

Individuals Who Dissent

The Hare Krishnas

Imported from India in the 1960s, the Hare Krishna society in the United States recruited middle-class whites in their early twenties, many of whom were college dropouts. The sect's charismatic leader, the Indian monk Swami Bhaktivedanta, sought to save Westerners from what he saw as materialism and atheism by converting them to worship the Hindu god Krishna.[4] In addition, he hoped that Western disciples would inspire Indians to rediscover their own religious heritage.

In the United States, the International Society for Krishna Consciousness offers its members complete personal transformation. Through the adoption of new myths and through rituals, such as dancing and chanting, devotees associate with other devotees and that, in turn, encourages a sense of community and belonging. Their saffron robes and shaved heads bespeak asceticism and celibacy. Through begging on city streets and in airports they communicate a collective orientation. To achieve Krishna consciousness they reject the Judeo-Christian belief system and American core values (individual achievement, hard work, and goal-directed behavior). The visual manifestation of this religious sect has attracted much public comment and formal negative response.[5]

The Jains and the Early Buddhists

The imposition of religious beliefs and practices by nomadic Aryan conquerors led to dissent among the indigenous population of ancient India in religious ideas, lifestyles, and attire.[6] The Aryans, who came from central Asia between 2000 and 1500 B.C., designated the local people as inferior and therefore destined for subjugation. They assembled them for religious processions and marched them to the sacrificial grounds, sandwiched between rows of Aryan Brahman priests and warriors. Control was achieved through fear—fear of becoming a human offering, a sacrifice deemed most desirable in Vedic texts, the sacred books of the Aryans. For the Aryans, the images of the two most important Aryan deities acted to support the conquest; Agni, the god of fire, and Indira, who symbolized victorious leadership, embodied the power of the Aryans.

Members of the Hare Krishna sect in the United States. Their distinct lifestyle, hair, and clothing are apparent. (Reprinted by permission of UPI/Bettmann.)

Hunters, gatherers, and herders who had been free to roam the countryside were now forced to settle down and till the land to provide food for the Aryan king, his army, and the Brahman priests. The ideas of the local people regarding sexuality and fertility were integrated into Aryan thinking. Religious worship now included bathing, anointing, and applying cosmetics to visual representations of the gods. The sculptures of gods are shown wearing crowns, earrings, pendants, arm-rings, bracelets, jeweled belts, and rings.

Desired appearance required that one look as beautiful and well groomed as one could, regardless of status. Kings and princes appeared in golden robes, warriors in coats of mail, ordinary people in light-textured cloth. Both men and women enhanced their appearance through luxurious adornment—garlands of lush flowers, decorated cloth, and elaborate jewelry.[7]

By 600 B.C. everyone was assigned a place in a caste system that controlled all aspects of everyday life: whose cooked food one could accept; with whom one could share a meal; whose daughter one could marry; what task one could perform. People were divided into occupationally specialized groups, and no one could shift from one group to another. Everyone was required to request the services and secret rituals of the Brahman priests before proceeding with any endeavor. Taboos were so powerful that a person would rather go hungry and die of starvation than eat food prepared (contaminated) by a person of a lower caste.[8] The stratified social groupings encouraged isolation and narrowed the sphere of possible interaction.

By the sixth century B.C. the religion of Jainism offered a release from the restrictive social and religious ties. The sage of Jainism, Mahavira (599–527 B.C.), taught that being reborn as a Jain enabled one to become free of retribution for the rejection of Brahman sacrifice and the violation of caste norms. Sect members rejected the self-indulgent style of the Aryans in favor of abstinence and asceticism. They repudiated gambling, a favorite pastime of the Aryans, and adopted vegetarianism in reaction to the meat-dependent conquerors, who had even brought their own cattle with them. Jains wore face masks to keep from breathing in and harming the souls of all living particles that they believed floated in the air. They regarded jewelry and ornamented cloth as signs of the social arrangement established by the Aryan leaders and were known as the "space-garmented ones." When Alexander the Great invaded India in 326 B.C., he recognized that the Jains were distinct from the rest of the population and referred to them as "gymnosophists," naked philosophers.[9]

Like Mahavira, Siddhartha Gautama, later known as Buddha, also provided a set of beliefs that made it possible for Indians to escape the compulsion of prescribed obligations. In 535 B.C., at the age of twenty-nine, he renounced his role as a husband and father and his place within the family structure to seek personal salvation and enlightenment. He developed a philosophy and lifestyle based on the idea that suffering would cease if one denied the desire for existing sources of joy and pleasure. Individuals could experience a sense of control by determining what they would allow to affect them.[10]

Buddha advocated cutting one's hair short and giving away one's clothing and other possessions. The monks who followed him were supposed to wear soiled, pieced-together rags. They put on yellow robes and lived like beggars. Through this blatant rejection of conventional clothing, they announced that they no longer subscribed to the dominant system of rights and responsibilities. Their attire was the antithesis of traditional dress, what society considered desirable, and not merely a deviation. It was a powerful visual signifier of the struggle to maintain personal freedom in opposition to the state's domination.[11]

Rejecting the culture of the invaders, these countercultures adopted attire that reflected their contrary sentiments. Through their attire members of the indigenous population were able to express their discontent, lessening the potential for conflict and social and personal upheaval. Their clothing tie-signs also made it possible for those who spurned the system to become recognized as members of new social groups with their own ideas, beliefs, and values.

Individuals Who Resist Sociocultural Change

The term "axial period" refers to a major turning point in the history of human development when invasions from without, or inventions and innovations from within, radically alter the course of life. During such a period a type of human being emerges whose structure of existence differs greatly from the previous norm. The Renaissance, the Protestant Reformation, and the secularization and industrialization of the modern world can be considered consequences of axial periods.

Four cultural ideas assumed prominence in Western society in the nineteenth century and led to a new orientation to social life; a propensity for rational thought; the intention to have a hand in shaping one's own destiny; the contention that the human being is what he or she is, not what he or she was; and a belief in a greater degree of personal freedom. These ideas were signified in a change in the basic style of male dress. The young most easily adapted to the new orientation to social life and the new style of dress. However, during any axial period, members of the old aristocracy and those of older generations who refuse to accept the new orientation sometimes form separate groups that continue to be guided by the old beliefs and ideals. They may adopt a style of dress that is rooted in the past yet reflects a new determination to resist change. Such a group forms a subset within the groups present. The Old Order Amish community (a sect of the Mennonite Church), the male Hasidic Jews, and the Rastafarians are examples of this category.

The Old Order Amish

The Amish who settled in Pennsylvania in the early 1700s formed a hermetically sealed community. They wanted to live without interference from the outside world, which they considered corrupt. They claimed that they were "in the world but not of it."[12] Still today, in their agricultural compounds, continuity of tradition and personal, face-to-face interaction dominate social life. Intense personal relationship encourages dependency on the group. Through praying together, the sharing of food, visiting, and singing every Sunday night, permissible behavior is clarified. In school, intellectual curiosity is discouraged; memorization of facts and differences between right and wrong, good and bad behavior, are emphasized.

Clothing is a major mechanism the Amish use to maintain their distinct identity and to ensure conformity to group norms. Amish dress is uniform; any modification that might suggest individuality is rejected. The homemade attire is void of jewelry, buttons, belts, collars, lapels, neckties, gloves, pockets, zippers, and other modern trimmings. The style has remained unchanged for 250 years. Except for teenage boys who have not yet been baptized who may wear color, much of their clothing is black and loose fitting. Through their attire and lifestyle, the Amish seem to effectively keep outsiders away. In addition, the attire discourages the straying of group members into forbidden places and activities, for it makes them exceptionally visible. Amish women keep their heads covered with a cap or a bonnet at all times; the men wear low-crowned hats with brim widths that vary based on their age and rank.[13]

The Amish, for the most part, do not use or buy products that emerged with the secular state and industrialization, including electric lighting, telephones, machinery, movies, television, novels, comic books, and magazines.[14] Because each Amish community is a closely knit unit, gossip, ridicule, and derision are the mechanisms of social control. Excommunication—social isolation—may be imposed on those who buy a car or marry an outsider. As practiced by the Amish today, the "ban" is an extremely powerful means of eliciting social conformity. When a presiding judge places an errant member under the ban, that person becomes undesirable to all members of the community. No one, including the person's own family, will have anything to do with him or her; even marital relations are forbidden. Informal social control mechanisms thus serve to maintain the Amish people's rejection of modern industrialization and the modern state.

The Hasidic Community

The Hasidim also reject the secular dimension of the modern world. In his study of the Hasidic community, Solomon Poll (1962) found that the clothing Hasidic Jews wear is designed to maintain a distinct religious identity.[15] The men consider their attire, including beard and earlocks, to be the traditional Jewish attire—that which was once worn by all Jews. But because most of today's Jews imitate non-Jews, these garments are now exclusively Hasidic. By "looking like a Jew with the image of God upon one's face," the Hasid creates a barrier against assimilation with non-Jews and a protection against sin. As one Hasid expressed it, "With my appearance I cannot attend a theater, or movie or any other places where a religious Jew is not supposed to go. Thus, my beard and my earlocks and my Hasidic clothing serve as a guard and shield from sin and obscenity."[16]

The extent of a Hasidic Jew's affiliation with Hasidism determines the particular kind of garments worn. The attire and prestige of the Hasid are determined by the frequency and intensity of religious observance, observed Poll. The term "frequency" refers to the number of religious services attended in the course of a day; "intensity" refers to the emotional manifestations observed during public ceremonies. The Hasid may sway back and forth during prayers, may pray longer than others, or may display during prayer certain mannerisms that are known as religious, symbolic gestures. The greater the number of rituals and the more intensely they are observed, the greater the esteem accorded. The most esteemed Hasid is called a Rebbe, and he is distinguished from the others by his large-rimmed beaver hat, long overcoat worn as a jacket, or long silk coat, and slipperlike shoes with white knee socks into which breeches are folded.[17]

Hasidic garments vary from "extremely Hasidic," worn by the most observant, to "modern," worn by persons whose religious performances are of less fre-

A youth from Lancaster County, Pennsylvania. The Amish wear plain clothes, attire that is not machine made and is free of color and ornament. (Reprinted by permission of The Bettmann Archive.)

The degree of religious commitment of a male Hasidic Jew is indicated by his dedication to traditional attire. (Reprinted by permission of Reuters/Bettmann.)

quency and intensity. Although still recognizable as Hasidic, the attire of the latter resembles clothing worn in the secular realm in the Western world. Sometimes outmoded Western clothing is worn: The nineteenth-century double-breasted dark suit that buttons from right to left is a favorite. As Poll reported, the person who wears "extremely Hasidic" clothing would be ridiculed if his behavior were not consistent with his appearance. Religiosity, the major criterion for social stratification, is supported by the Hasidic Jews' attire. The more religious the person, the more traditional is the clothing. The attire supports the group's rejection of secularization in the modern world.

The Rastafarians

Rastafarianism is a way of life designed to promote spiritual resilience in the face of poverty and oppression. It rejects Jamaica's neocolonial reality and draws upon a variety of legacies, among them Hebrew theocracy, African traditions, and to a lesser extent Anglo-Hispanic traditions. The Rastafarians seek to achieve freedom for the self, as well as freedom of speech and expression. In the United States Rastafarianism has been related to black liberation forces. Their ultimate goal is emigration and settlement in Africa.[18]

Each aspect of the Rastafarians' appearance is designed to convey their beliefs. In their wild dreadlocks and unkempt beards, they create distance between themselves and the larger society. The dreadlocks hairdo of Rastafarian men

A Rastafarian with his dreadlocks. (Photo courtesy of Le Roy Woodson.)

simulates the mane of a lion. In its savage appearance it is expected to spur feelings of "dread" in outside communities. Their beards signify their pact with Jah (God) and the fact that the Bible is their major source of knowledge. The Rastafarian elder carries a staff, like Moses, to represent his role as a shepherd leading his flock.

The Rastafarians' clothing is made of plain cloth and is unfitted, simply covering the body. It reflects the belief that in the heart, mind, and spirit of the Rastafarians live wealth and abundance. It is also designed to indicate asceticism, a desire for nothing beyond food and necessities.

Rastafarians are expected to stand fit and feisty, like a lion. The spirit of the lion is also simulated in their emulation of a lion's strut. The image conveys self-reliance and freedom from the rights and obligations imposed by the larger society. The lion is the Rastafarians' most prominent symbol. Its image is found on their houses, flags, and tabernacles, and on objects in their homes. It represents the conquering "Lion of Judah" and Haile Selassie, emperor of Ethiopia, their mighty redeemer.[19] It also represents the dominance of men. Male virility, courage, tenacity, energy, and wisdom are denoted by the lion. The female is Rastafarian only through the male, and the male is the physical and spiritual head of the household. The female must seek his guidance.

To show their commitment to Africa, Rastafarians incorporate the colors red, yellow, and green from the Ethiopian flag into their attire. Other important colors are brown, which signifies the earth from which they believe they have emerged, and black, which signifies pride in their skin color. To enable them to withstand evil forces, Rastafarians wear shield-shaped badges, horseshoes for good luck, and a ship motif, which represents their hope of returning to Africa.

Individuals Who Protest an Inferior Identity

The Zoot-Suiters

In the late 1930s the term "zoot" was used to describe things worn or performed in an extravagant style. It was in common circulation within the urban jazz culture, as Stuart Cosgrove pointed out in *The Zoot Suit and Style Warfare.*[20] The zoot suit was characterized by extremes. It was made as if it were created for a much larger man than its wearer. It was baggy as if to conceal a bad figure, but it had ample room for a holster under the armpit. The "drape shape," as it was called, was associated with American gangsters, and a version of it had even been worn by Danny Kaye and Frank Sinatra.[21]

The zoot suit evoked and provoked feelings. Notably, it was the attire chosen by the pachucos, Mexican-American youths who often formed gangs. The pachucos were a disinherited generation within a disadvantaged sector of North American society, observed Octavio Paz.[22] They were second-generation working-class immigrants. As such, they had been stripped of their old customs, beliefs, and language. But they did not want to be victims. Rejecting the ideologies

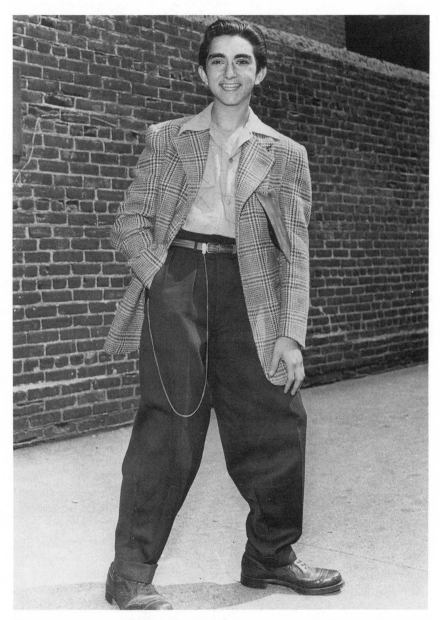

Often worn in protest of a designation of inferiority, a 1943 zoot suit. (Reprinted by permission of UPI/Bettmann.)

of their migrant parents, they rebelled. Rather than disguise their alienation or efface their hostility to the dominant society, the pachucos adopted an arrogant posture.

The pachuco subculture was defined by petty crime, delinquency, drug-taking, and ostentatious fashion. The zoot suit articulated the youths' disdain for establishment definitions and, at the same time, their wish for high social regard. Octavio Paz saw their appropriation of the zoot suit as an admission of the ambivalent place they occupied. "It is the only way [the pachuco] can establish a more vital relationship with the society he is antagonizing which had previously ignored him: as a delinquent, he can become one of its wicked heroes."[23]

The intrusion of the zoot-suiter into the conventions of adult society was met with anger and shock. The zoot-suiter was the antithesis of the World War II serviceman; further, he disrupted the conception of roles assigned to adolescents. Fighting between pachucos and servicemen from military bases broke out on the first weekend of June 1943, and the Los Angeles police arrested over sixty zoot-suiters in order to protect them in the event of further fighting.

The symbolic significance of the zoot suit can be identified in the response of the servicemen. Gangs of marines ambushed zoot-suiters, stripped them down to their underwear, and left them helpless in the streets.[24] In one particularly vicious incident a gang of drunken sailors rampaged through a cinema after sighting two zoot-suiters. They dragged the pachucos onto the stage, stripped them in front of the audience, and urinated on their zoot suits. During the ensuing weeks of "rioting," the ritualistic stripping of zoot-suiters became the major means by which the servicemen established their superiority over the pachucos. The repeated acts of stripping indicated the servicemen's desire to terminate the pachucos' attempt at developing self-regard. Cosgrove concluded that the pachuco was both the victim and the assailant; the zoot suit was simultaneously the garb of "the persecutor and the persecuted, the 'sinister clown' and grotesque dandy."[25]

Hell's Angels

The Hell's Angels occupy a similarly paradoxical position. In everyday life they are victims because they lack what society deems desirable: education and economic success. They are expected to assume the posture of submission. Their contempt for societal definition and expectations is expressed by the menacing attire they wear and by their readiness to pick a fight. Moreover, as Hunter Thompson reported, "Of all their habits and predilections that society finds alarming, the outlaws' disregard for the time-honored concept of an eye for an eye is the one that frightens people most."[26] For example, a man who was marketing Hell's Angels Fan Club T-shirts, on his own, did fairly well until the Angels announced that they would burn all the T-shirts they saw even if they had to rip them off people's backs. Thompson suggested that this belief in total retaliation for any offense or insult is what makes the Angels a problem for police.

Most of the Angels are unskilled and uneducated. In a world increasingly geared to specialists, technicians, and fantastically complicated machinery, the Hell's Angels are obviously losers, and that fact bothers them, Thompson observed. The outlaw motorcyclists see a future with no chance for upward mobility. Their real motivation for joining the club is their certainty that they are out of the ball game. But instead of submitting quietly to their collective fate, they have made it a basis for social vendetta. They do not expect to win anything, but they have nothing to lose. A favorite tatoo among the Angels is "Born to Lose."[27] The occupations they often hold are longshoremen, warehousemen, truck drivers, mechanics, clerks, and casual laborers—any work that pays quick wages and requires no allegiance. Perhaps one in ten has a steady job or a decent income.[28]

Twenty years before the first Hell's Angels chapter was founded, Hollywood created the image of wild men on motorcycles in the movie *Hell's Angels* (1930). That image was later adopted but drastically modified by the real-life Hell's Angels. Hollywood also provided the name for the group. In reality, Hell's Angels originated with ex-GIs, World War II veterans, who rejected the idea of going back to family, job, and school. They wanted privacy, more time to figure things out, and more action. One of the ways to look for action was on a big motorcycle. By late 1947 California was alive with bikes, nearly all of them powerful. Restless veterans founded the first Angel chapter in Fontana, California, in 1950. In 1954 the movie *The Wild Ones* celebrated the motorcycle outlaw.[29]

Politicians, editors, and police, keen on outrage stories of rape, orgies, and senseless destruction, turned the Hell's Angels into a menace in 1965, according to Thompson. Every newspaper in the land denounced the Angels as brutal. The official reports, however, were based on a survey of old police files and the movie *The Wild Ones*. They contained little that was new or startling. In August 1965, *True, The Man's Magazine* reported: "They call themselves Hell's Angels. They ride, rape and raid like marauding cavalry—and they boast that no police force can break up their criminal motorcycle fraternity."[30]

At the beginning of March 1965, there were eighty-five Hell's Angels in California. After the California Attorney General's report on the Angels, "the whole scene changed in a flash. … One day they were a gang of bums, scratching for any hard dollar … and twenty-four hours later they were dealing with reporters, photographers, free-lance writers, and all kinds of showbiz hustlers talking big money."[31] By the middle of 1965 they were firmly established as "all-American bogeymen." Many of the independent bike riders seeking fellowship and status sought to join. The Angels rejected many membership bids, describing those who wished to join as "a plague of locusts."[32]

The California Attorney General described their appearance in this manner: They prefer to ride the large heavy-duty American-made motorcycles (Harley-Davidsons) and have been observed to wear belts made of a length of polished motorcycle drive chain, which can be unhooked and used as a flexible bludgeon.[33]

*Members of the Hell's Angels wearing their "colors." (Reprinted by permission of UPI/
Bettmann.)*

The Angel's "uniform" consists of grease-caked Levis; a sleeveless denim
matching jacket; and tatoos portraying swastikas, daggers, and skulls. Their emblem, termed "colors," is sewn onto the back of the jacket. It must be earned. It
consists of an embroidered patch of a winged skull wearing a motorcycle helmet. Just below the wing of the emblem are the letters "MC" for Motorcycle
Club. Over the wing is a band bearing the words "Hell's Angels." According to
Thompson, "An angel without his 'colors' feels naked and vulnerable—like a
knight without his armor."[34] The only consistent difference between the Hell's
Angels and the other motorcycle clubs is that members of most of the other
clubs wear their insignia only part time. The Angels "play the role seven days a
week." They wear their colors at home, on the street, and sometimes even to
work; they ride their bikes to the neighborhood grocery to buy a quart of milk.[35]

The Angels feel that they are outcasts from society and have to defend one another from attack by "the others"—the "mean squares, enemy gangs or armed
agents of the Main Cop." When somebody punches a lone Angel, every one of
them feels threatened. They are intensely aware of belonging, of being able to
depend on each other. Their motto is "All on One and One on All." As Thompson
stated, "You mess with an Angel and you've got twenty-five of them on your
neck."[36]

In 1966, Hell's Angels clubs existed only in California. Their numbers and clusters increased and spread throughout the country with the widespread publicity

about their altercations with the police. The Hell's Angels themselves, however, believe that their brotherhood is based on love of motorcycles; that their negative image was created in Hollywood, and that it persists because it serves the interests of those who are in charge of law and order. In a benefit held in New York and reported in 1991 they sought to raise funds to pay lawyers to get back their clubhouse on East Third Street in Manhattan. In 1985, the federal government had seized their building under the forfeiture act, claiming that the house was used for dealing drugs. The Angels, however, continue to claim that they are regular guys picked on by the police, that they are hard-working people with children.[37]

⬧   ⬧   ⬧

Groups whose tie-signs developed to show resistance or protest to a social designation of inferiority, like the zoot-suiters and the Hell's Angels, have been loathed by those charged with the maintenance of the social structure. The attire is an attempt to counteract the definition of inferiority. The attire empowers the individual because it affirms the identity he or she desires: for the zoot-suiters, that of mainstream respectability and economic success; for the Hell's Angels, power. The act of wearing the dress was viewed by those in authority as anarchical, the individuals designated dangerous, and the members persecuted.

To conclude, tie-signs in modern society allow for social continuity. They show that people can evaluate their circumstances and the demands made on them by those in authority, and that the shared culture is the source of the image and its meaning. Distress caused by society's moving too fast can be alleviated by holding back and creating communities that preserve more traditional arrangements. Distress caused by social valuation can be lessened by adopting dress and ornament that counteract the imposed identity.

16
Clothing Tie-Symbols

$\mathbf{T}$IE-SYMBOLS are expressions of support, or association, with a particular idea, cause, predicament, or person. For instance, during the Gulf War in January and February 1991, people in the United States took to wearing clothing and accessories emblazoned with the American flag. Wearing the flag was associated with feelings of patriotism and showed support for the men and women in service. Flags could be seen on T-shirts, sweatshirts, swimsuits, beach towels, tote bags, and umbrellas.[1]

A picture of the U.S. Olympic volleyball team printed on the front page of the *New York Times* in summer 1992 showed the teammates with their heads shaven. They shaved their heads as a gesture of solidarity with Bob Samuelson, a team member involved in a dispute with Olympic officials that caused a reversal of the U.S. victory over Japan. Their shaved heads matched his normal "non-do." For them, the shaved head was a tie-symbol; it expressed support for their teammate.[2]

The most visible tie-symbol in 1992–1993 was the inverted red "V" ribbon worn to honor people who have died of acquired immunodeficiency syndrome (AIDS). Since 1991, when the ribbons were designed and worn by a fifteen-member group, Visual AIDS, thousands of the ribbons have been sold. They have become ubiquitous on award shows and on the streets. Their purpose is to display solidarity and sympathy for AIDS victims. A March 1993 report in the *New York Times* pointed out that the AIDS ribbon paved the way for other ribbons—a pink one worn to show breast cancer awareness, and a purple one that calls attention to "the harsh realities of young people growing up in urban neighborhoods."[3]

Tie-symbols are a means of self-association and self-expression, and their adoption is dependent on personal choice. Their term is short and they are ancillary to a person's attire. Concerns, fears, tensions, and hopes within a social aggregate may give rise to tie-symbols. Wearing one announces *sympathy with* a group, a political idea, or a public persona. The tie-symbol can stand for something or against something; it can be pro-social or antisocial. For the wearer, it may or may not have the meaning originally intended.

Advertisers have found that teenagers respond to hero images. These wished-for identities are associated with overcoming obstacles. "Aspirational" has become a marketing buzzword. Aspirational ads are intended to make consumers aspire to, or emulate, the people endorsing the product. Recognizing the benefits of turning clothes into tie-symbols, Levi Strauss hired filmmaker Spike Lee to make the company's commercials. The 1991 ad campaign took viewers to such

*To show support during the Gulf War peo-
ple wore clothing adorned with the American flag. (*New York Times, *February 10,
1991; reprinted by permission of Najah
Feanny/NYT Pictures.)*

sites as East Rutherford, New Jersey, where Joe Hamm, a lighting technician, de-
fied heights to prepare the stage for a Grateful Dead concert; New Braunfels,
Texas, where spelunkers explored mysterious caves; and Las Vegas, Nevada,
where people were making arrangements for a Mike Tyson fight. According to
Levi's marketing director, Daniel M. Chew, the Levi spots were intended to make
the target audience, the fourteen-to-twenty-four age-group, ask: "Gee, if these
guys are doing all this, what could I be doing?" Lee's earlier campaign, "501 Button Fly Report," had been very successful. The ads provided the inspiration for a
line of Levi's T-shirts carrying the slogan "Button your fly" and unauthorized
versions saying "Unbutton my fly." Both slogans demand action.[4]

Tie-symbols are important in the United States because they provide people
with a means of finding out about their own values and goals. In more traditional societies a sense of identity and appropriate goals were handed to the individual by one's religion, family, and community. Such a path is often not easily
available in more complex, contemporary societies. Tie-symbols make it possible for a person to play out different roles and try out different values; they also
enable individuals to associate themselves with a desired persona, such as Madonna. Tie-symbols make it easier for individuals to find out about different
paths and discover ones they might desire; hence, they are popular among the

*The inverted "V" red ribbon that symbolizes
AIDS awareness. (Reprinted by permission of
Ozier Muhammad/NYT Pictures.)*

young and with those with less circumscribed lifestyles. Tie-symbols are used by
individuals to help *define the self, maintain self-definition,* and *express political
values and goals.*

Seeking Self-Definition

The term "reference group" was used by Herbert Hyman in 1942 when he described the phenomenon whereby individuals who do not belong to a particular
group (the reference group) use that group's ideas, beliefs, and values to guide
their behavior.[5] The reference group provides the standard that is referred to in
appropriating an appearance or behavior.

Grade school children are often concerned with *fitting in,* and they prefer
wearing what other children in the school wear. They feel a need to dress "like
the herd," Elizabeth Hurlock (1949) pointed out.[6] They often reject homemade
clothing in favor of store-bought clothes. They sometimes resist wearing what
their parents want them to wear. Convinced that wearing clothes like those of
their classmates will win them acceptance, they explain, "Kids don't want to play
with you unless you wear the same clothing they do." Children in the lower
grades see the attire chosen by the older students as the preferred style.

Since the 1940s the appearance of adolescents in American society has been
remarkably similar to that of their peers and exceptionally different from both

American volleyball players shaved their heads in sympathy for a teammate during the Olympics in Barcelona. (New York Times, *July 29, 1992; reprinted by permission of AP/Wide World Photos.)*

adults and younger children.[7] Gaining the *approval of their peers* becomes paramount to youth during their junior and senior high school years, and their attire comes under close peer scrutiny. They realize that they have several choices and that the choices they make can lead to acceptance or rejection by their peers. Their concern with the questions "Who am I?" and "Who do I want to be?" may lead to periodic changes of style.

In the 1990s, spiked hair and pierced ears have been sources of parental anxiety. To gain information that might allay such feelings, Lawrence Kutner interviewed psychiatrists and developmental psychologists specializing in adolescence. The child development experts pointed out that "fashion statements" by adolescents are a part of the road to adulthood; hence, they are a normal phenomenon. Most people adopt the ideals and beliefs of their families when they become adults. The experts recommended that parents allow their children "to make choices and mistakes in this area. Wardrobes can be changed and hair will grow back."[8]

Through the clothing decisions an individual makes, he or she gains greater awareness of a self that is distinct and separate from the family yet still anchored in society's basic ideas and beliefs. The act of wearing peer- or self-designated attire may make it easier to detach oneself from home and family, preparing the individual for the kind of adult independence required in American society.

*Spiked hair. (*New York Times, *December 8, 1991; reprinted by permission of
Jack Manning/NYT Pictures.)*

Adolescent Peer Culture and Trendy Attire

"Schools are not supposed to be a fashion show, yet the halls of high school
could pass for runways. For it is in these places of learning—and the streets leading to them—that many fashion trends are born," reported the *New York Times*
in 1991.[9] The story noted that the styles of clothing pervasive among rap artists,
such as layered hooded sweatshirts, baseball caps, and cable chains with large
medallions, have appeared in the collections of Karl Lagarfeld, Charlotte
Neuville, and Isaac Mizrahi. Examining attire presently worn in high school may
be of help in predicting future fashion.

Examining current styles in high schools in New York, Connecticut, and New
Jersey, the reporters for the *New York Times* article found that bagginess was a
major trend. Yet although some New York City teenagers insisted on wide-
legged, over-sized jeans that hang at the waist, sag in the back, and in some
cases have two or three inches of cuff, others preferred tight-fitting, straight-
legged jeans. In a high school in the Bronx, wearing leggings with long, loose
sweaters was considered in style. In Westwood High School in New Jersey, button-down shirts in solid colors with baggy jeans were the representative attire.
Students at Greenwich High School in Connecticut liked their jeans tight but
torn; in Bridgeport, Connecticut, they liked the preppy look, corduroy and
denim. The female students wore shorts and shirts with matching tights.

Bagginess also allows an individual to carry or transport implements of self-
protection, such as guns, clubs, or knives; tight-fitting styles do not. High school
attire is thus sensitive to specific needs, such as the current concern with safety,
and it depends on the cultural and socioeconomic background of the wearer.
Students in violence-prone city high schools prefer boots and heavy Bass and
Doc Marten's shoes with thick soles to sneakers.

A retrospective study of the clothing experience of students at the Fashion Institute of Technology during adolescence found that many of the students often
heard their parents object that "kids go to school to learn, not for a fashion

*Baggy pants. Some high school students
wear oversize, wide-legged jeans that
hang below the hips and sag in the
back.* (New York Times, *December 1991;
reprinted by permission of C. M. Hardt/
NYT Pictures.)*

show." Their objections were to no avail, however. Wearing the trendy style enabled the adolescents to "feel at one" with their peers.[10]

A strategy used by many adolescents is described in the following quote by one of the Fashion Institute students: "In the beginning of each year from junior to high school, I would look at what everyone else was wearing, then I would simply imitate. ... I insisted my mother take me shopping each year to remodel my wardrobe. Because if one was seen in last year's fashion, one would be the talk of the town, in a negative way." As another female respondent described the experience: "I can still remember my first pair of designer jeans—Sassoon. Everyone had to have a pair, and everyone who was anyone did. We all looked like clones. But I felt I was a part of a group. It is incredible what a pair of Sassoon jeans could do for one's image. They gave me a sense of security, of being accepted." And another said:

> My best friend had a pair of Nike sneakers, which I wanted very much but [they] were too expensive. Forty dollars was too much at the time. Any kid in school wearing a pair of Nike's was considered "in." I felt "out" because I didn't own a pair. When I finally got the courage to ask Mom to buy me a pair she said "no" and yelled at me for trying to be flashy. I begged and nagged her every day until she couldn't take it anymore. I'll never forget the day she took me to Herman's Sporting Goods Store to purchase my sneakers. I was so happy you couldn't wipe the smile off my face. [But then] in junior high Skippy was the "in" sneaker. All my girlfriends wore them. They were under ten dollars so I bought a few pair. This made my mom real angry, since just the

year before she bought me the Nikes, which I stopped wearing. I told her nobody at school wears them anymore, so I couldn't wear them and look stupid. As usual she could not understand why I had to follow what all the other kids wore. … I guess parents don't understand peer pressure and the need for kids to feel wanted by a certain group of friends.

That mothers are often cost-conscious and teenagers style-conscious is exemplified in the following story:

My mother took me and my sister school clothes shopping, which always turned into a nightmare. I wanted the latest fashion and my mother wanted clothes that would last. Buying them a little big so I could wear them the next year also. We often had screaming matches in the stores. Eventually my father had to take me, which was great because he let me get what I wanted and would spend more.

Some teenagers whose parents cannot or will not buy them the "right" clothes steal, mug, and even murder to get such clothes. Most, however, go to work. A young man whose family had immigrated from Taiwan when he was eight years old described his experience in this manner:

In junior high school I became brand conscious. I started working on the weekend delivering Chinese food [and] earning $200 to $250. This was disposable income. Everything I bought was "brand-labeled." Nike and Puma sneakers, Calvin Klein and Sassoon and Sergio Valente jeans. Members Only jackets. I almost had everything I wanted. During my high school days Japanese fashion became "in" [1982–1983]. The clothing [sic] were layered and loose fitting. They were not cheap. A jacket was $350 to $450 and sweaters $100 to $150. They were not boring and made me feel great. Now I was an American. I belonged.

The desire for peer approval has often incorporated a concern with weight. "The height of the disco period was in my ninth grade [1979]," reported a female student. The movies *Thank God It's Friday* and *Saturday Night Fever* were very popular. As she described it:

The common dress for girls my age were [sic] Danskin bodysuit worn with designer jeans. We competed with one another to lose weight. I was very successful at losing ten pounds and decided to keep on dieting. My anorexia craze ended once I reached a hundred pounds. My menstrual period stopped for six months and was extremely painful when it resumed. I learned my lesson the hard way.

Impact of a Public Persona

At Brooklyn Technical High School, across the street from Spike's Place, Spike Lee's retail shop, many students wear baseball caps with the letter "X," a promotional item for the director's movie on Malcolm X. Some students at Brooklyn Tech and other schools say they wear the hats, Malcolm X buttons, and other accessories because they support the slain leader's more aggressive approach to black civil rights.[11]

Spike Lee (right), director of the film Malcolm X, *talking to reporters during the Cannes Film Festival, 1992. His cap shows a desired association with Malcolm X, his history, or his political agenda. (Reprinted by permission of Reuters/Bettmann.)*

Becoming popular among men in the summer of 1992 was the bandanna handkerchief tied on the head in an urban-gypsy style. It was folded into a triangle, pulled back over the skull, and knotted in back, as Woody Hochswender reported in the *New York Times*. He noted that John McEnroe wore a pink paisley bandanna for the U.S. Open and "was savagely chic." Photographer Bruce Weber was well known for the practice and not just for hacking around in the garden: "He went hanky-on-top to Anna Wintour's [the editor of *Vogue*] little soiree at the Paramount Hotel last week."[12] Weber gave legitimacy to the look by wearing it to Anna Wintour's party.

For teens of the 1980s the movie *Flashdance,* and MTV were important sources of style. Referring to *Flashdance,* one said, "I remember going home and cutting up all my sweatshirts." Another noted, "My mom thought I was crazy cutting up perfectly good shirts and turning them into rags." And another related, "The movie had a big impact on us kids who watched it. Even guys wore cut shirts and sweatshirts that bared their shoulders and belly buttons."[13] A ripped sweatshirt became the desired style.

With the start of MTV in 1981, music and fashion began to go hand in hand for the younger teenage group. Madonna's style had a significant impact. Prior to 1983 and Madonna's impact, the oversized man-tailored shirt and tight jeans were the most visible trend for this age-group. Only a few other trends were seen, such as the short dresses, usually in black, of teens in the Punk movement in the East Village in New York. Madonna's videos *Borderline, Lucky Star,* and *Like a Virgin* showed her first "look": a short black dress, big cross earrings, silver and rubber bracelets, black crosses and many silver chains worn around the neck, and a bare midriff.[14] The short tube skirt, tank tops, cropped leggings, and fingerless gloves that Madonna wore became "required attire" among the younger teenage set. Fashion forecasters predicted these elements would be the rage for girls up to sixteen. Hundreds of young girls showed up at Macy's in New York for a "Desperately Madonna Contest," a look-alike contest held after the movie *Desperately Seeking Susan.* As one respondent described it: "I loved the way Madonna dressed—and I dress like her: lace outfits, spandex leggings, tight miniskirts, and tons of rubber bracelets."[15]

Anticipatory Socialization

Starting high school marks a critical turning point in the lives of most youth in the United States. It often entails a dislocation from the past and feelings of loss. The sense of belonging and established feelings of familiarity are upset. High school students must step out of the life conditions they had earlier experienced, step away from their playmates and friendships, and adjust to new classmates, classrooms, and schedules. Moreover, they must establish an identity. Reference group attire that is associated with a particular type of music often helps to solve the problem of connectedness. A T-shirt with a political message, brightly colored and spiked hair, and metal bracelets and chains are also examples of tie-symbols that announce affinity with a particular set of ideas and beliefs. They enable the student to establish a recognizable identity, which facilitates social participation and interaction.

Music and dress offer growing adolescents a means of self-definition. One of the basic motivations of high school students for seeking a job seems to be to acquire the means to buy the clothes and music they want. Through them teenagers learn to recognize particular values and specific orientations to social life, encouraging self-definition. These representations (clothes and music) may also act to link the young to the adult world, a form of anticipatory socialization. As presented in a recent exhibition, five different reference groups appear to have emerged in American high schools: preppies, greasers, jocks, freaks, and nerds. Each is identified by a well-defined style seen in the foods eaten, level of expected higher education, occupational goals, leisure activity, and, of course, appearance.[16]

Maintaining Self-Definition

College Groups

The Yale School of Drama is "filled with suffering artists dressed in black," reported Alex Witchel in a 1991 article in the *New York Times Magazine*.[17] Entering college freshmen adopt a particular type of sneaker, jacket, or color in vogue in a particular school. It reaffirms and maintains their new association.

A 1982 study by Margaret Rucker and her colleagues at the University of California, Davis, provided information on how the problem of self-definition is worked out in college. The researchers found that students in different majors tended to wear different styles: A long ethnic dress identified female students majoring in art; a suit (blouse, skirt, and jacket) characterized textile and clothing students; jeans and plaid shirts were the choice of engineering and psychology majors; overalls were worn by those studying animal science.[18] Students adopt the appropriate styles to show they are connected to a particular social aggregate. They thus announce that they have a particular identity and a social base within the larger university population. Here, reference group attire acts to *deindividuate*. It helps to create a social entity within a context of ongoing interaction.

Homosexual Subculture

Until the 1980s most gay men felt pressured to remain invisible to the world outside the gay community. Many did, however, come up with subtle ways to let each other know who they were, as Michelangelo Signorile reported in *Outweek*.[19] Often they adopted what is now called the Old Clone look. They wore jeans, lumber shirts, jackets, and heavy boots and sported a moustache and sunglasses. Instantly recognizable by other gay men, the look would not offend at work, for most nongay colleagues would miss its significance. It gave the wearer the feeling that he was in one sense openly gay, even if most straights did not realize it. The masculine clone look also helped to prevent violence from "queer bashers."

As a means of denouncing the strategy of hiding, some gay men adopted another style. These men believed they were free-spirited rebels, and they chose innovative attire "with heavy sexual innuendo": close-cropped hair, small drop earring, "Read My Lips" T-shirt, leather motorcycle jacket, silver whistle, leather wristband, wide black leather belt, tight-fitting, cut-off gray Levi's 501 jeans, white sweat socks, and black Doc Marten's boots.

These factions, the "invisible," the "clone," and the "rebel," provide gay men today with distinct modes of dress, allowing for a greater sense of affiliation. The author of the *Outweek* article, a gay man himself, observed that the choice of style offers a means of belonging.

216

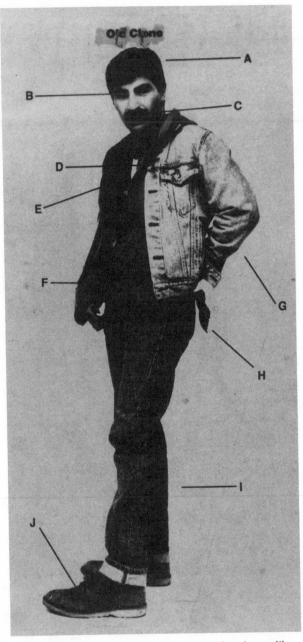

*The "Old Clone" style worn by homosexuals before the gay liberation era. By adopting this look, homosexuals could hide their sexual orientation from nonhomosexuals but announce it to other gay men. (*Outweek, *November 28, 1990.)*

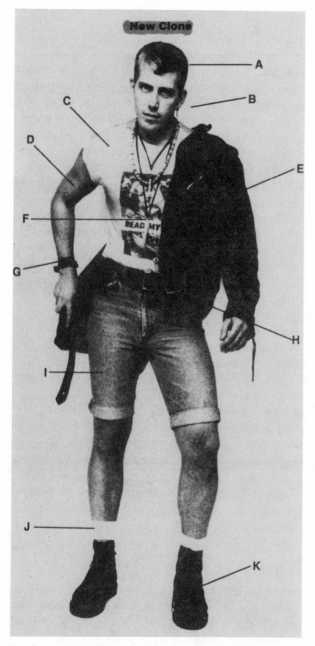

Overtly sexual, the "New Clone" look is postliberation appearance. Ornament and tight-fitting clothing make sexual orientation visible. (Outweek, November 28, 1990.)

Tattoos

Robert B. Edgerton and Harvey F. Dingman found that of the 2,282 residents in a residential school for the mentally retarded (ages twelve to twenty) 90 percent had acquired tattoos shortly after their arrival, and most of the tattoos were self-inflicted.[20] The tattoos fell into four different categories: 30 percent were associated with powerful gangs outside the institution; 40 percent referred to a love object, such as "mother" or the name of a boyfriend or girlfriend; 10 percent proclaimed the individual's personal attributes—as a fighter or a lover, for example; and the last 20 percent consisted of circles, squares, parallel lines, question marks, and other symbols that had no conventional meaning and therefore could not be understood by others. The tattoos in the latter group presumably communicated something about the self to the self in a private system of meaning. Here, in a new and unfamiliar environment that they were not allowed to leave, the residents connected themselves symbolically to an outside source of support, one that was most meaningful to them. The tattoos helped them cope with a sense of institutional isolation.

The style of a tattoo may be a form of symbolic affiliation also for those outside the institutional setting, as Clinton R. Saunders reported in his study of commercial tattoo settings. He noted that proprietors pride themselves on having a large selection of designs, although only 10 percent of these are chosen by clients with any degree of regularity. According to Saunders, tattooists emphasize that they are involved in a "business" activity in which "the customer is always right." They stress that they are involved in popular culture production rather than creator-oriented fine art.[21]

The wearing of tattoo tie-symbols can also help an individual overcome a sense of alienation, as noted by Goffman in his discussion of the meaning of tattoos for sailors.[22] Sailors with tattoos are often expressing their "life experience solidarity," Goffman pointed out. The tattoo marks the individual as a sailor and, thus, distinct from the "land society." By adopting the tattoo the sailor acquires a social base, a group of peers. The tattoo enables the sailor to protect himself from feelings of alienation and isolation. He shows that he is not alone, that his behavior is not idiosyncratic or deviant, that he operates within the safety zone of a group of peers.

Imitating a President's Wife

Copying the personal preferences of the president's wife, that is, the color and style of her clothing, has often been a means of creating a sense of connectedness to the established social order and the mythic "First Family." When U.S. President Theodore Roosevelt was in office, his daughter Alice was looked upon as "Princess Alice." Light blue was her favorite color, and it soon cropped up in clothing throughout the country under the name "Alice Blue." A popular song of the time, "My Sweet Little Alice Blue Gown," reinforced the style that she wore.[23]

The predominant color of Florence Harding's wardrobe when she came to the White House in spring 1921 was a darker shade of blue. It became the newly desired color. When Grace Coolidge displayed a preference for red, there were few women around the country who did not possess a red garment of some sort.[24] Jackie Kennedy's fondness for bouffant hair and her adoption of the pillbox hat spread throughout the country.[25] Nancy Reagan's passion for red led to the acceptance of bright-colored clothing among the general population. It also caused White House correspondents to start donning red dresses or red ties as a way of catching Ronald Reagan's eye at news conferences.[26] The color took on a regal significance when Reagan staged formal news conferences at the end of a long, red-carpeted hall. Once the vivid emblem of the Russian Revolution, red became "Reagan red," a new and very different tie-symbol from that used during the Russian Revolution.

Expressing Political Values and Goals

Groups and aggregates desiring, protesting, or rejecting a political agenda may signify their sentiments in their dress. In the United States such expressions vary. They may involve (1) identifying the side one is on, (2) taking a stand and dressing the part, and, sometimes, (3) hiding one's identity.

The most familiar, popular, and least tumultuous example of political attire is the slogan T-shirt, which came into being in the 1960s. Many artists were involved in such projects, the best known being British designer Katharine Hamnett. She received so many requests for her T-shirts that she had to stop making them in 1987.[27]

In 1991 T-shirts were used as a means of environmental education and a form of fund-raising for environmental causes. James Brooks reported in the *New York Times* that T-shirts were being sold to adults to raise funds for research on how to protect sea turtles and were being given free to schoolchildren as a means of educating them about the endangered species.[28]

Benetton, an Italian-based company that produces and distributes colorful sportswear for men, women, and children, has been portraying itself as antiracist. The company's trademark, "The United Colors of Benetton," depicts people of all ages and different races holding hands and being visibly happy about it. Since its initial advertising campaign in 1983, the company has used the themes of racial equality and civil rights to appeal to the consumer rather than pictures of actual garments. Its ads, the company claims, are intended as a hymn to global understanding, racial and multicultural harmony. They often carry more than one message. To promote AIDS awareness, for example, condoms, in pastel colors and out of their wrappers, were placed horizontally next to one another on a white background. In one sense, the multicolor emphasis suggested global unity; at the same time the ad championed social responsibility.[29]

Revolutionary Tie-Symbols

Rejecting the Vietnam War and the draft, hippies adopted an appearance and clothing that reflected their "revolution" against rationality, self-restraint, and goal-directed behavior, the values underlying institutional discourse. In contrast to the conformity of the gray flannel suit and the impeccable, modest mien required by the establishment, they looked disheveled and unkempt. They wore their hair long, and jeans and work shirts became their "uniform." Young men often wore Indian headbands, amulets, shell necklaces, beads, and embroidered vests instead of shirts. See-through outfits flaunted sexuality.[30]

The hippies of the 1960s demanded the right to full self-expression. In a study of hippie communities, D. L. Wieder and D. H. Zimmerman found that immediacy, spontaneity, and hedonism were favored over sobriety and industry. Property was rejected by the hippies because it identified privilege, and they had no qualms about receiving welfare or panhandling.[31]

As a cohort, a group of people born during the same time period, this generational unit was critically aware of inequality and the mindless pursuit of affluence. Rejecting traditional concepts of career, education, and morality, they produced a culture in opposition to technocracy. They searched for alternatives to the prevalent traditions of lifestyle and occupationally linked identity. Their disaffiliation took different forms. For some it was militant and political; for others it was mystical and religious.[32]

Other groups, long before the hippies, also wore revolutionary tie-symbols. The Protestant reformers, who rejected the morality of the official church and searched for a new connectedness to God, are an example. They refused to accept the church's contention that to commune with God elaborate ritual was necessary. They regarded as false the need for sumptuous vestments. The name "Puritan" was first used in 1566 because this group of reformers sought to "purify" the church in England. Puritans campaigned against clerical attire, religious statues, stained-glass windows, and sacred music, which were seen as impediments to spirituality. The Puritans felt that spirituality emanated only from a direct relationship with God. Self-direction and conscience, not simple submission to those in authority, became the new determinants of behavior. Adopting dark and plain clothing made of wool or cotton was in keeping with the Puritans' ideal of religious simplicity and directness.[33]

In eighteenth-century Paris, the name "sansculottes" was used for the attire worn by urban workers at the time of the French Revolution. Instead of wearing the fitted breeches (culottes) worn by the aristocracy, the workers wore long trousers striped in red and blue. In addition, they wore white shirts open at the neck, short, loose jackets, wooden shoes, and the red Phrygian cap, a symbol of revolution. The antiaristocratic attire indicated their desire for complete social equality.[34]

Worn to frighten blacks and avoid personal responsibility, Ku Klux Klan attire is a reactionary clothing tie-symbol. (Reprinted by permission of AP/Wide World Photos.)

Reactionary Tie-Symbols

Members of the Ku Klux Klan, the notorious white supremacist group, hide behind a white pointed hood, mask, and gown. Their attire is more precisely a costume; it is worn only at group gatherings. On such occasions it acts more as a tie-sign than a symbol, since it is required attire and has only one meaning. The original Klan appeared after the Civil War and sought a return to the racial caste system. White people in the South, particularly middle-class whites, were impoverished as a result of the war. Many were deprived of the right to vote because of their participation in the war against the Union. The Ku Klux Klan, with its strange rituals and ghostly costumes, provided a means for frightening the local black population into a servile demeanor. The activity of the Klan continued until it had accomplished its racist goals of empowering white people and reducing the black vote. By 1877 the original Klan had been officially disbanded.[35]

The twentieth-century Klan was formed in 1915 by William Joseph Simmons at Stone Mountain, near Atlanta, Georgia. Klan activities were now directed against Roman Catholics, Jews, and the foreign-born as well as blacks. This Klan claimed to protect the racial "purity" and moral values of the native-born, white, Anglo-Saxon Americans and claimed a higher morality and dedication to religious fundamentalism. Because the Klan was not strictly regional in its appeal, its influence spread to other parts of the country such as Colorado, Indiana, New Jersey, Oklahoma, and Oregon. Its tactics for inculcating fear and intimidation included whipping, tarring and feathering, branding, mutilating and lynching. The Klan reached the height of its power in the early 1920s when it probably had between four and six million members. As a political force the Klan was effective, and it prompted the election of many pro-Klan officials on the local level. In 1924, after the Klan helped split the Democratic presidential convention, its influence began to wane.

The Klan was again revived in Georgia after World War II. In addition, other white supremacist organizations arose in the South as the movement for increased civil rights for blacks spread, particularly after the Supreme Court decision on school desegregation in 1954 and the Civil Rights Act of 1964. Many bombings and murders were attributed to the Klan.[36]

Similar angry feelings fuel the hatred that Skinheads feel toward African-Americans and other minorities. Beatings, stabbings, and killings in the defense of "white power" have occurred in cities as diverse as Portland, Oregon; Denver, Colorado; and New York City. Skinhead attire is their everyday dress; unlike the Klan, their attire is not limited to special occasions. It also incorporates more variety than the Klan costume. Their heads are almost completely shaved and they wear caricatured working-class attire: old-fashioned shirts, suspenders with shrunken trousers, and heavy, oversized shoes or military jackboots.

17

The Presidency and Contemporary Fashion

A CLOTHING FASHION can be described as a period's desired appearance. It is a cultural construct consisting of an image that tells a story. The source of the story, the theme conveyed by the fashion, emanates from the interplay between political and economic forces and the dynamic movement of intellectual, artistic, and moral constraints. Designers sensitive to the story or theme interpret it in visual representations, producing a seemingly eclectic array of simultaneously fashionable styles. The basic theme, its meaning and message, is conveyed by most of these styles. The vocabulary of images that has accumulated in the course of human history is the source for the image and its meaning.

In contemporary society, for example, the "grunge" fashion has its roots in the attire worn by teenagers on the streets of Seattle. Tattered garments, flimsy floral print dresses in a 1930s style, ripped jeans, and untucked flannel shirts are worn with heavy stomping boots. The style is thrift-shop inspired and speaks of dressing in what is on hand, suggesting poverty.[1] Youth who are pessimistic about the future are responsible for the style, as Tom Julian, fashion director of the Men's Fashion Association, observed.[2] The perception that no significant economic recovery is at hand may explain why the teenagers' style was adopted into fashion. The high-priced version of the grunge style consists of a layered, unkempt look. It includes shirts with unbuttoned sleeves, transparent or see-through flimsy fabrics, and clunky shoes or boots. Designer Marc Jacobs sent his beautiful models down the runway in grunge attire, appearing as if they had not slept or washed their hair for a week.

The fashion also includes jewelry and accessories that call forth the intervention and protection of supernatural powers: Christian crosses, Judaic Stars of David, pendants of mystical, spiritual origins, such as Egyptian ankhs, New Age angels, traditional beads, Ethiopian tribal talismans, and Chinese good-luck shields.[3] The crochet-and-lace sleeveless coats, vests, sweaters, and skirts go back to the Edwardian era and the crocheting grandma. It is as if the sense of malaise that grunge fashion reflects is ameliorated through the use of superhuman and human popular and traditional sources of support.

Prior to the nineteenth century the desired style of appearance, the fashion, was designated by those in authority and often developed with a particular *political* message and a system of feelings and beliefs in mind. Francis I used his

223

The New York Times *included this photograph in an early article on the grunge look. (*New York Times, *November 15, 1992; reprinted by permission of Kim Garnick/NYT Pictures.)*

*Interpreting the grunge look into fashion: white shirt hanging below a cropped black vest, loosely knotted tie, and unbuttoned shirt sleeves. Designed by Joan & David. (*Women's Wear Daily, *August 18, 1993; photo by George Chinsee; reprinted by permission of Fairchild Syndication.)*

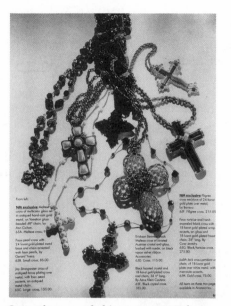

Crosses become a fashion accessory. (Advertisement by Neiman Marcus, September 5, 1993; reprinted by permission of NYT Pictures.)

jewels not merely to demonstrate his wealth but to create a beautiful image. Moreover, Francis I insisted that the style of dress adopted by his wife and the other women of the court complement that of the male. He was the first to realize that coordinating the color and texture of the attire of the members of the court would create a mass that is overwhelming in its magnificence and would assert preeminence.[4]

Louis XIV, in his quest for supremacy, dressed in gold. The goal of Jean-Baptiste Colbert, one of the most important of Louis XIV's ministers, was that France dominate the luxury textile and ornament trade; fashion for France should be what the gold mines of Peru were to Spain. For this goal to be achieved France had to establish itself as the arbiter of European fashion.[5] Baroque, a style characterized by exuberant decorative richness and first introduced by the Counter-Reformation movement in the sixteenth century, was introduced nearly a century later into Louis XIV's court, creating what fashion historians consider the most magnificent court in the history of the Western world. To demonstrate his dominance, Louis XIV's attire was emblazoned with gold fleurs-de-lis and completely lined in ermine. France began to export costly and prestigious items including tapestries, silk brocades, lace, ribbons, wigs, and feather accessories to the rest of Europe.[6] It is reputed that Louis XIV had his subjects melt down furniture that was made of precious metals "in order to keep his ladies adorned." He insisted upon appropriately sumptuous dress for all those who participated in the ritual of court life. François La Rochefoucauld, a seventeenth-century French writer, observed that during that period clothes became a "national fixation." In his writings he commented: "In all professions one affects a particular look and exterior in order to appear what he wishes to be thought ... so it may be said that the world is made out of appearances."[7]

Physical imperfection was unacceptable to a ruler whose reign was based on Divine Right, and fashions often developed as a result of a monarch's effort to conceal physical flaws. When at the age of twenty-three Louis XIII of France became bald, for example, he adopted a curly wig to hide the imperfection and mitigate his feelings of inferiority.[8] As a result, wigs became an important element of male fashion in France, England, and even in the Puritan Bay Colony of Massachusetts.[9]

In Western society the institution of beliefs, expectations for behavior, and the assuaging of negative feelings were often indicated in dress. Those in authority often became visual models to emulate, and desired ideals and goals were reflected in the prevailing fashionable style.

The U.S. Presidency and Male Fashion

The U.S. presidency is intended as an office of great power. The successful operation of the American constitutional system requires that this power be used. Presidents who do not use their power vigorously are condemned as weak and as failures in office.[10] Probably more than the monarchs of the past, the president of the United States is a figure who draws together the people's hopes and fears for their future. A president is the human symbol of national unity, the only official who can speak for "the United States" and who has ready access to the media.[11]

A president's personal preferences in dress, like those of the monarchs of the past, are often emulated. In his memoirs Russell Baker, a senior columnist for the *New York Times,* reported that Herbert Hoover's preference for a detachable collar made that style popular among men in the early 1930s.[12] In 1937, during Franklin D. Roosevelt's presidency, *Esquire* championed the "command look" for men. It consisted of a padded, fitted jacket with broad shoulders. Until then a loose-fitting jacket with natural shoulders was the preferred style. Roosevelt himself is described as "magisterial," having the look of a leader.[13]

John F. Kennedy's preference for a two-button suit (because it better accommodated his back brace) became popular in the 1960s. His rejection of the bowler hat (homburg), some say because he had a full head of hair and was proud of it, led to the demise of hats even for formal occasions.[14]

The U.S. Presidency and Female Fashion

The impact of the American president on the female fashion ideal is more difficult to discern. Prior to World War II, most fashions for U.S. women originated in

Paris, the city usually viewed as the capital of fashion. The fashion industry in Paris has behind it tradition, resources, and governmental support. In fact, to become known, to acquire an international reputation, a designer must show his or her collection there.[15] Paris fashion is an entrepreneurial enterprise designed to generate profit. Since the 1970s, many of the top Paris designers have turned to clothing that is mass produced for the ready-to-wear market. The styles presented on runways are conceived to demonstrate the talent and ability of the designer and to show that he or she understands, moreover, what is going on in art and society. The *couture shows* present what designers think is happening here and now; however, since many of the consumers of the French ready-to-wear industry live in the United States, Parisian designers have to be sensitive to American society, its culture, and its changing values and mood.[16]

Another reason it is difficult to accept the notion that a U.S. president can have an impact on female appearance is that female fashion is viewed as a "frivolous phenomenon." It seems preposterous that a male president could have an impact on such an insignificant manifestation, and especially one that affects the opposite gender. In addition, presidents vary in their effect on culture and society.

But the vision or agenda a president brings to the office, his desire and ability to pursue it, and the level of his activity (the degree of energy he expends in the office) are the variables that some political scientists believe are related to a president's impact on the nation. That is, success at making policy and degree of energy expended in office may be significant in appraising the impact of a presidency on fashion.[17] The questions that emerge are: Is contemporary fashion related to the president's *agenda?* And how does the president's level of *activity* affect the fashion trend?

The Reagan Presidency

Ronald Reagan's presidency (1981–1989) is considered strong and passive. He had a definite agenda and was able to get it through. Hence, he has been judged as a strong president. His political discourse centered on the state of the domestic economy. His goal, he claimed, was to restrain the power of an increasingly intrusive government. Reagan established the priorities for his presidency and gave substance to the ideas of the conservative branch of the Republican party. He set the national priorities that conferred power and respectability to the modern conservative movement.[18] At the same time, Ronald Reagan was less than active. Virtually every report illustrates that he was the most inattentive and indifferent of presidents, largely following "scripts" that led him through his eight years in the White House, as Lou Cannon, a *Washington Post* reporter who covered Reagan's entire political career, observed. He commented that Reagan "may have been the one president in the history of the republic who saw his election as a chance to get some rest."[19]

Chanel's rendition of the Doc Marten's work shoe supports the idea that American taste influences high fashion abroad. The boots reflect a desire for empowerment. (New York Times, February 28, 1993; reprinted by permission of Bill Cunningham/NYT Pictures and Naum Kazhdan/N.Y. Times Studio.)

The Reagan style. President Ronald Reagan and Nancy Reagan leave the White House in January 1981 for a round of inaugural balls. The cost of Nancy Reagan's inaugural wardrobe was said to be about $25,000. (Reprinted by permission of UPI/Bettmann.)

The 1980s were characterized not only by a glorification of capitalism, free markets, and finance, but also by an ostentatious celebration of wealth. Political analyst Kevin P. Phillips noted that as the decade ended there were too many stretch limousines in Manhattan, too many yachts off Newport Beach, and too many fur coats in Aspen.[20] It was the very wealthy, more than anyone else, who flourished under Reagan. Greed and ostentation pervaded the culture.

Throughout her tenancy in the White House Nancy Reagan's delight in clothes, balanced for color and ornament, extravagant and luxurious, was consistently reported in the news. It is thus suggested that through her use of clothing, she offered visual support to her husband's political and personal agenda and helped to make up for his passivity in office.

In an Op-Ed column in the National Weekly Edition of the *Washington Post*, William Raspberry wrote: "My favorite Reagan has disappointed me. After promising in 1982 that she ... would list her borrowed designer frocks on financial dis-

Nancy Reagan in a red dress that hugged her body and delineated its contours, characteristics that ancient church authorities defined as seductive. The dress was designed by Bill Blass.

closure forms—Nancy Reagan changed her mind."[21] Since 1982 she had borrowed scores of gowns and items of jewelry and had reported none of them, in violation of the 1978 Ethics in Government Act. Greed and ostentation characterized Nancy Reagan's presentation of self. Upon the Reagans' impending departure from the White House, Mrs. Reagan remarked in an interview that she hoped that despite the "terrible press" she had received over her fondness for designer gowns throughout her tenure in the White House, history would remember her for her efforts to solve the drug problem.[22]

The Public Wife

On November 17, 1987, the headline of a *New York Times* article by fashion reporter Bernadine Morris asked, "The Sexy Look: Why Now?" Fashion in the 1980s had become increasingly form-fitting, slinky, and slithering, accentuating the female curves. It focused on what Flugel described as "the interplay of concealments and half transparencies."[23] Exposed backs, low necklines, side and front slits, and the pouf were designed to create sexual allure. The attire was colorful and often in fabrics that shimmered or glittered. The display of wealth and sexiness characterized the fashion of the 1980s. It reflected President Reagan's vision of burgeoning economic success and women in traditional female roles. The notion of the "public wife" explains how the ideals of a passive president became visible, and the term "nouveau riche" helps to explain why pride in economic success was expressed in sexually alluring and showy fashion.

The notion that a wife's attire supports the rank claimed by her husband and can come to support his policies is rooted in the history and experience of Western society. Martin Luther had carried the idea further when he suggested that the wife of a minister is a public figure who must in dress and action be exemplary. People look to her to represent her husband. To affirm his position, the conduct and attire of the public wife must convey his ideas and values.[24] Veblen called such attire *vicarious consumption*.[25] (Today, in the corporate world, the wife of a candidate for an executive position is often scrutinized before he is offered the job. She is an additional source of information about him).

A president's wife has a choice about whether she will become a public figure and how she will participate in public life. Whereas Nancy Reagan did play an active public role, Pat Nixon refused. In 1972, the fashion industry sought Pat Nixon's support in introducing the midiskirt, a below-the-calf-length skirt. The industry hoped that the miniskirt fashion trend had run its course and that it was time for a change. When Pat Nixon publicly announced that neither she nor her daughters would adopt the new length, the midi died on the vine.

Because of her social distance, the passage of time, and the momentous events that took place during the Nixon presidency, it is difficult to determine exactly why Pat Nixon rejected the longer length skirt. But not only did the midi lack political support, it also lacked popular support. For the consumer the early 1970s was still a time of rebellion and youthful exuberance, which the miniskirt signified.

A similar attempt by designers on Seventh Avenue in 1987 to introduce a different length skirt, short this time, was supported by Nancy Reagan, who appeared in public wearing an above-the-knee hemline. But the style was rejected by working women. In a report on the Style page of the *New York Times* on July 17, 1987, Michael Gross stated that the short skirt calls attention to the person, is provocative, and is inappropriate for work. Women seeking to build a career rejected the style, which led to weakness in sales. Two months later, in another *New York Times* story titled "Knees and Even More: Hems Are Up, Sort Of," Georgia Dullea reported that women were holding fast to their hemlines, waiting to see if the storm on Seventh Avenue would blow over. "It is nothing like the 60's, when the mini blew in on the hips of the young, in a glut of sex and rebellion. For today's women it was one more calculation, as they sized up the 21-inch length versus the 19-inch." Their attitude, the reporter observed, was affecting the consumption of this fashion trend: "For the city's retailers, the reservations have

translated into uneven sales." The failure of the short skirt, signifying youthfulness, to become fashion after being endorsed by Nancy Reagan suggests that a
wife can only support her husband's vision; she cannot introduce her own.

The Notion of Nouveau Riche

The term "nouveau riche" describes people of modest means who have acquired
new wealth and use dress, ornament, and other material objects to show off
their newly found success. In the United States between 1830 and 1860 and again
after 1865, there were periods marked by a rapid urban and industrial growth.
During those times, a person of "humble means was brought into contact with
those of vast wealth, and a temptation to imitate the customs and to strive for
the enjoyments of those who possess larger means rose," as Catherine Beecher
wrote. L. W. Banner reported that after the Civil War, at least 10 percent of New
York's financial elite were individuals who had risen from poverty to riches.
Members of the upper class such as Charles Astor Bristed, Nathaniel Parker
Willis, and Anna Cora Mowat unmercifully criticized the newly rich for their
coarse faces, loud voices, and vulgar display of wealth.[26] Recent observations on
the consumption of fashion among "old blood and old money" also support the
contention that the newly rich are more likely to engage in what Veblen called
conspicuous consumption. Proud of their personal success, they are more likely
to flaunt it.[27]

The Reagans were born to families of modest means. Hollywood was a place
of wealth and glamour. While they lived in Hollywood, Nancy Reagan sought to
capture the spotlight on formal occasions and wore glittering evening dresses
that she borrowed. The female fashion ideal of the 1980s stemmed from a newly
rich family proud of its achievement and success, its *stardom.*

The Bush Presidency

In his inaugural address George Bush set himself apart from the Reagan presidency and its concern for display. His intention was "to celebrate the quieter
deeper successes that are not made of gold and silk."[28] Moreover, Bush came
from a social class characterized by sociologists as "old blood and old money," a
class that underplays the possession of wealth. These two personal factors alone
suggest that a change in fashion would occur.

The president's principal sphere of interest was foreign policy. He is described
as having approached politics with a more pragmatic rather than ideological
view of the world. His domestic policy was in a holding pattern. A cartoon by Jeff
Danziger in the *Christian Science Monitor* portrayed a planning session to re-
elect Bush in 1992. His ten advisers were seated around a table searching for an
appropriate slogan. The one they agreed on was "The nothing president."[29]
Rather than make law, the president used his veto power. "Two years into his
first term, and having vetoed 20 public bills, President Bush is emerging as a Veto
President," observed Ruti Teitel, an associate professor of constitutional law. In

contrast, in the entire eight years of his office Ronald Reagan vetoed sixty-five bills, twenty-nine in his first term of office and thirty-six in his second.[30] In an editorial entitled "The Energetic Naysayer" the *New York Times* editors supported her conclusions.[31]

Conservative Republicans have considered George Bush an inadequate heir to Ronald Reagan. Only at times did he cater to their politics on issues like abortion and, for a time, taxes, as *New York Times* reporter Andrew Rosenthal pointed out. Rather than propelling their ideology, conservative leaders claim that Bush went his own way.[32] Bush is thus perceived as having had no agenda, and his activities as having been unrelated to domestic economic needs. His presidency can be considered weak and passive. Popular sentiments were, therefore, more likely than political sentiments to determine fashion themes during his administration.

Although the glittery, body-hugging, sexy attire that characterized the Reagan era continued into the Bush era, in 1989–1990 a new feminine fashion ideal came into being. The short skirt became the new fashion story. It was worn with a form-following jacket that covered the hips. Also new were the lingerie dress and tights with an oversized shirt. All three outfits left the legs exposed; the breast, waistline, and hips, the traditional means of anchoring women in society, were thus deemphasized.[33]

Meaning of the Image

If Halbwachs's notion of public memory is valid, fashion's meaning and significance must be found in this vocabulary of images available to a society. Power and powerlessness, authority and lack of authority, are some of the earliest constructs that inhabit public memory. In the *Palette of Narmer,* commemorating the unification of Egypt in 3300 B.C., and in stelae celebrating victory in ancient Mesopotamia, those holding power and authority are more completely clothed and protected than those who are poor or vanquished. The female fashion during the Bush presidency, with its flattening of the breast, long stretches of revealed body, and easy access to the torso, conveyed *vulnerability.*

The validity of this interpretation can be supported by examining the accessories worn. They spoke of self-empowerment and self-protection. Jewelry consisted of crystals and richly colored stones; they were used on hair, belts, and pocketbooks. Earrings were long and jackets had fringes. Gloves and coats were full and in bold, natural colors—pigments that are a part of nature. In tribal societies an extra measure of energy is acquired by tapping into forces that power the universe. The accessories worn in the Bush years, together with their style and color, were ones believed to capture the power of the universe, making the wearer feel less vulnerable.[34] The 1989–1990 fashion thus told of anxieties and fears and attempts to conquer them.

Behind the 1989–1990 styles lay a crisis in leadership: The national deficit and the Savings and Loan banking scandal were threatening the economy, the problems of homelessness, AIDS, and environmental pollution continued, and there

Expressing the need for comfort and nurturing, paci-
fiers made in bright colors and hard plastic became a
fashion accessory among teenagers during the Bush
*years. (*New York Times, *December 2, 1992;*
Newsweek, *December 28, 1992; reprinted by permis-*
sion of NYT Pictures.)

was a growing feeling that the president might be unable to solve any or all of
these problems.

The Evolving Fashion Trend

If the interpretation given in the previous section is accurate, then a change in
the perception of the president, as well as changes in political and economic
conditions, should be reflected in the further evolution of the trend. With the
Gulf War the sense of powerlessness receded. By the end of January 1991 consumer confidence in the president's leadership was manifested in a surge of
stock prices as well as in a newly desired style of dress. Raincoats that gleamed
like sunshine in the rain suddenly appeared. Baby-doll dresses in pink, the color
of innocence, and in floral prints graced the advertising pages. Rather than the
empowerment offered by crystals and colored stones dug from the earth, jewelry
consisted of flower buds, blossoms, and petals. It spoke of the fragility of bloom,
rebirth, and hope.

More important, perhaps, was the new fashion style: The waist was now
cinched, the hips accentuated, and the breasts emphasized. Examples included
a flaring skirt, a fitted jacket over a bell-shaped skirt, and the sleek scuba dress.
The new femininity may have come as a counterpoint to the military uniforms
traditionally worn by men.[35]

In the March 1991 fashion shows, themes of vulnerability, protection, and empowerment merged. Leggings were in color. The cat suit—a one-piece body-
hugging garment made of stretch fabric—delineated the body, making the person wearing it seem more susceptible to harm. In all ways imaginable the attire
was further elaborated by adding fake jewels and swirled metal stitching. Body

jewelry, heavy bracelets, macramé dresses and vests, jackets over rubberized leg-gings, and blasts of color all signified empowerment and protection. In addition, ethnic group culture and the traditional home were important sources of style. In Paris, Oscar de la Renta showed plaids. In New York, Christian Francis Roth re-produced Amish quilt patterns, and Isaac Mizrahi, with beaded leathers and fringe, evoked the American Indian culture. The language of the Aztecs was rep-resented in a multicolor patchwork coat by Christian Lacroix. Baseball-style caps, bringing to mind a game associated with childhood and father, acquired new popularity. They also offered a degree of physical and emotional shelter.

The origins of the 1991 image also lay in the streets of New York City and in the notion of *role strain*. Role strain occurs when the roles one occupies demand more than one can fulfill. Women in 1991 had to deftly juggle marriage, career, family, school, home, and an exercise program. Overextended and with tight schedules, they often left the health club wearing tights or bicycle shorts and a jacket. Sexy, and a symbol of "being with it," the look was imitated by the young and became prominent on the streets of New York, inspiring Seventh Avenue and later Paris fashion houses.

The Contemporary Fashion Process

The fashion process, the process by which a new fashion emerges and grows to become popularly accepted by the consumer, is different in the United States than in European countries. In Europe, the traditional elite decides on the fash-ion, and the same mode is found in most stores. In the United States, a new fash-ion is the result of "collective selection," as Herbert Blumer (1969) observed. A designer offers about thirty styles on the runway. About six to eight designs are chosen by the buyers—"a highly competitive and secretive lot," Blumer ob-served. Their choices are made independently, without knowledge of the other buyers' selections. Yet their choices converge because the buyers are immersed in the common world of what is happening to women. By means of their fervent reading of fashion publications and close observation of one another's lines of products, buyers develop common sensitivities and similar appreciations.[36]

Designers also develop an "intimate familiarity" with the most recent expres-sions of modernity as they appear in the fine arts, current literature, political de-bates, and general "discourse in the sophisticated world," observed Blumer. They translate themes from these areas and from the media into dress designs. Thus, it is not surprising that designers working apart from one another in a large number of different fashion houses independently create remarkably simi-lar designs. They "pick up ideas of the past but always through the filter of the present," explained Blumer.

The fashion is thus set through a process of free selection from a large number of competing but similar models. The creators of the models seek to catch and give expression to what Blumer called "the direction of modernity."

*By 1993, the vulnerable look replaced the opulent image of the 1980s. Waiflike Kate Moss (left) sports the vulnerable look; supermodel Christy Turlington (right) sports the opulent look. (*Women's Wear Daily, *February 5, 1993; photos by George Chinsee; reprinted by permission of Fairchild Syndication.)*

In the 1970s, however, consumers' choices from among the styles offered by store buyers and boutique owners were the ones that were reordered and became the fashion. Since then, moreover, through "market research" the industry has become even more geared to producing styles that are emotionally relevant. The new thrust in production is to anticipate a demand and be able to furnish the "right" product. "The consumer-is-king" philosophy has become the newest practice among manufacturers and retailers. The profitable way of doing business, they insist, is to study the customers, find out what they want, and make and market it.[37]

The production of fashion has thus shifted away from the artist, manufacturer, and specialist to the consumer. The perception of a social dynamic leads to a joint selection of a particular fashion theme. Often the perception of a social dynamic is made by people with artistic sensibility "who put their ear to the ground and hear the rumble long before the train appears." Competing themes may emerge, but the one most selected by youth in urban centers usually wins out. Because of the different traditions, and climactic conditions, however, fashionable attire in New York may have a slightly different manifestation than that in Paris, London, or Milan. But the image and its meaning are likely to remain essentially the same.

Historical Perspective

The fact that two distinct visual images were seen in the presidencies of Reagan and Bush—the former presidency characterized by personal convictions and political agenda and the latter by the population's fears, anxieties, and attempts at empowerment—raises questions about earlier presidencies and their relative influences on fashion. Do the ideas of the strong and active president help determine desired female appearance? And what are the stylistic sources of fashion during presidencies considered weak and passive?

Presidents Woodrow Wilson and Harry Truman are viewed by some political scientists as strong and active. Presidents Warren Harding, Calvin Coolidge, and Dwight Eisenhower have been described as weak and passive.[38] If there is a patterned impact it is likely to appear in a comparison of fashion in these two groups.

The Wilson Presidency and the Harding and Coolidge Presidencies

Woodrow Wilson, a president described as strong and active, initiated policies that empowered women. He was president from 1913 to 1921. During World War I women were asked to abandon the steel corset for the war effort; they were admitted to the army, the navy, and the Marine Corps; they could also join the workforce and acquire independent economic means. When World War I was officially declared in 1917, the fashionable ideal was a matronly figure. The skirt was long and flared, and the bosom and hips were emphasized. By 1919, however, the flared skirt was replaced by a tunic-style dress that hung from the shoulders. Loose fitting, the clothing denied the traditional elements that anchor the female identity to the womanly role—that is, the breasts and the hips. Requiring no fastenings the dress was simply pulled over the head.[39]

The highest possible compliment during the 1920s was, "My dear, you have got absolutely nothing," where "nothing" meant that the woman was flat "behind and before," as fashion historian Doris Langley Moore (1949) reported.[40] "Audacious decorations in contrasting lines and colors" completed the look. Hairstyles and hemlines became short, and the vogue was considered boyish. By 1924, the naked neck appeared longer, and women played nervously with their necklaces, flourishing long cigarette holders. The fashion was popular enough to evoke both admiration and rebuke.[41]

The presidents of the era, Warren G. Harding, elected in 1921, and Calvin Coolidge, who assumed the office upon Harding's death in 1923, had no particular agenda; both are considered weak and passive presidents.[42] These characteristics made it possible for the other, more diffuse cultural forces to take over and visually define the period. The "flapper" fashion of the Roaring Twenties was an American invention made possible by these weak and passive presidents.

The origin and popularity of flapper fashion have been attributed variously to people's desire to seek mindless fun and their despair in response to the consequences of World War I; to the fact that young women were now employed and could "call the tune"; and to the fact that the fashion embodied the dynamism of the new technology and energy.

Frederick Lewis Allan's *Only Yesterday* (1931) described a revolution in manners and morals that took place in the 1920s. The 1920 census found that the great majority of Americans were living in urban areas, where greater freedom from traditional "gatekeepers" existed and the possibility of wearing "outrageous" fashion became viable.[43] Another influence that supported the consumption of the flapper fashion was the shift of the economy from a capital-goods to a consumer-goods base. In fashion as in the other artistic expressions, such as jazz and literature, the fashionable ideal reflected the activism, dynamism, and speed of new technology—trains, planes, telegraph, and telephone. When a president is weak and passive, has *no* domestic agenda, and has a low level of activity, he has little direct impact on fashion. Sentiments existing within the population at large, the dreams, fears, and hopes of the people, can be expressed and are reflected in fashion.

The Truman and Eisenhower Presidencies

In April 1945 the mantle of the presidency of the United States fell on Harry Truman. World War II continued, but a victory over Hitler was in sight. Truman's most pressing task was to follow through and win both the war and the peace. He was active in all three aspects of his presidential role: chief executive (domestic policy), head of state (foreign policy), and commander in chief (the military arena).[44]

*With flapper fashion, women were freed from the constraints of the corset. This 1924
Chanel dress was designed to be hipless and bosomless.*

The 1950s were seen as a time for families, babies, and the home. (Photo by Eve Arnold.)

On the home front millions of men who had been in the armed forces, men capable of using force, had to be dispersed and rapidly transformed into civilians. Providing them with educational benefits and housing loans became a priority. A "new look" for women, a tight waistline that emphasized the size of the bust and the hips, traditional maternal attributes, was introduced into fashion by Christian Dior in 1947.[45] The president's *domestic* agenda gave the style legitimacy, and despite much protest the "new look" was established as a full-scale fashion.

The Truman presidency was characterized by executive assertiveness (The buck stops here). Political scientists have evaluated his performance in the office as strong and active. That is, he had a definite agenda, setting the presidency as central to national debate, and was for the most part successful. He expended much personal energy in office.[46]

The Eisenhower presidency, which began in 1953 and ended in 1961, has been evaluated as weak and passive. Fashion during the Eisenhower years continued the theme of the female in the maternal social role. Styles varied, but the emphasis on hips and bust remained.[47] The increase in the birthrate that began in 1947 continued until the beginning of the Kennedy era, leading to "the baby-boom generation."

                  *   *   *

Fashion is a visual image that tells a story about the important ideas, events, developments, and core tensions of a given period. The ideas and values of a strong and active president seem to be reflected in female fashion and behavior. In the case of President Wilson, this impact led to clothing that allowed greater physical and social freedom. In the case of President Truman, it led to a new emphasis on family and on women in maternal and nurturing roles.

President Eisenhower, in contrast, cultivated a leadership style that projected an image of sincerity, fairness, and optimism. He enjoyed harmonizing the efforts of potentially quarrelsome allies. In the White House he struck the pose of an "unpolitical" president and is considered to have "soothed the anxieties of his troubled countrymen much as a distinguished and well-loved grandfather brings stability to his family."[48] These characteristics made it possible for the style trend initiated in the Truman era to continue.

The economic recession that began under President Bush, a president considered weak and inactive, has continued into the presidency of Bill Clinton. The state of the economy has *not* yet improved, and the sense of pessimism about the future continues to be exhibited in fashion. The fabrics and styles of fall 1993 indicated a pervasive sense of vulnerability, and the accessories seemed to act as a means of protection.

Contemporary fashion, then, is a visual representation that informs one of the need to reorient personal wishes and goals because of changing conditions and unpredicted events. It speaks to the necessity to redirect energies and reorder social priorities.

18

The Personal Self

THE TERM "PERSONAL SELF" refers to the "I" component that invariably influences individuals when dressing the public self.[1] Elements of dress and styles of appearance that individuals choose to represent the personal self are part of a dialogue between self and society. The clothing allows the individual to integrate personal self with the public one. The personal self is both the author and the audience of one's appearance.

English anthropologist E. R. Leach suggested that there is a difference between public-sociological symbols, which identify social persona, are a part of the "collective representations," and are readily available to interpretation, and private-psychological symbols, whose meanings may lie in the individual's unconcious. Private-psychological symbols are, however, expressed as public behavior. They affect the emotional state of the performer.[2]

Legitimacy of an Individuated Self

Courts in recent years have supported the distinction between the public and the personal self. Judges have ruled in favor of school boards trying to implement dress codes for teachers, but they have distinguished between work attire and an individual's choice of personal appearance. They have maintained that long hair, a beard, or a moustache is an aspect of a teacher's personal self. To try to regulate these elements of appearance represents a violation of individual rights.[3]

On November 11, 1986, New York State's highest court ruled that a Rastafarian inmate who had not cut his hair for twenty years "cannot be compelled to shed his four foot long dreadlocks." The court struck down a state prison regulation that required inmates entering state prisons to get haircuts and a shave for purposes of security and identification, ruling that the regulation "needlessly infringes" on the prisoner's beliefs.[4]

In Boston, the court ruled otherwise on June 30, 1992. Six "mustachioed" members of the police force claimed that they had a constitutional right to maintain their appearance. The State of Massachusetts insisted that they "bare their upper lips" because a clean-shaven face is part of the State Police identity.[5] Not only for police but for all men facial hair alters the individual's appearance and how he is perceived by others. Such alteration can be cosmetic, such as growing a beard to cover up a weak chin or jowl or growing a mustache to provide a horizontal element in a long, angular face, as noted in *Man at His Best: Es-*

*Two of the six mustachioed members of the Massachusetts Metropolitan, Capitol, and Registry Police who sued the police department rather than shave. (*New York Times, *July 1, 1992; reprinted by permission of by Evan Richmond/NYT Pictures.)*

quire's Guide to Style. A beard can also be a political statement, as it was for many activists of the late 1960s.[6]

Analogous to male facial hair is the use of cosmetics by women. They are free to wear makeup or not, as they see fit; however, much pressure does exist. A ticket-counter agent at Logan International Airport was dismissed by Continental Airlines in 1991 because she refused to wear makeup on the job.[7] The agent had spoken to the Civil Liberties Union of Massachusetts and was ready to sue. A spokesman for the airline claimed that cosmetics were in keeping with the company's attempt to improve its image in terms of its aircraft, its facilities, and its service to its customers. In line with the new image, the airline adopted a personal appearance code that required female ground workers to wear makeup. Within a week, after much public outcry, Continental had retracted its mandate and the agent was back at her job.[8]

Continuant Identity

The particular emphasis, nuance, or innuendo of the "I" component can emanate from individual history, memory, and experience. It may be a *continuant* mode of dress, lasting throughout life—a personal hallmark. Or it may be *temporary,* in response to a particular situation, a mood or event. In the latter case the particular emphasis reflects the present rather than the past.

A news story in the *New York Times* about the author Norman Mailer provides an example of how the personal self, or the "I," is reflected in the attire worn for a front-stage performance. Describing the author's choice of dress, the reporter noted that "Mr. Mailer himself is still appearing in public in his usual ensemble of a slightly rumpled blue blazer, with tan pants." The image, according to our vocabulary of images, conveys approachability and defiance.[9] Norman Mailer's attire was continuant and reflected his personal self. It was informal in a formal situation and somewhat unkempt when neatness was the norm. Power and the limits of coerciveness are issues that inform much of Mailer's writing. They are most evident in his novel about World War II, *The Naked and the Dead.*

Patterns of socialization, family interaction, communication with significant others, and biological characteristics help to form the distinct way in which each individual interprets the world and relates to it. The diversity and individualism of American society, as well as lack of knowledge about expected attire, make it possible for adults to modify the dress they wear for front-stage performance, reflecting the "I," and incur minimal disapproval for such modification.

Temporary Identity

Attire that reflects the "I" may also be worn in response to a special place, situation, or event. In the early 1970s, before disco became popular, whatever one wore during the day would be just as good at night, noted fashion designer Bob Mackie.[10] With disco, however, young women and men discovered that there were places for dancing where reality was suspended, where "fantasy had a chance to thrive," where rules of everyday dressing were thrown out. People could indulge in wearing any clothes they wished to the disco.[11] However, gatekeepers ensured that those dressed in attire that would ruin the fantasy, attire that was associated with the workplace, were kept out.

The attire chosen for disco was determined by personal imagination and dreams. The disco was a highly visual environment, and clothing became an integral part of the milieu. In a disco environment, soft lighting mixed with shadows away from the dance floor, and bright flashing lights created a stage-show atmosphere around the dancers. Special clothes were essential to a charged environment that brought together personal fantasy, music, lights, and dancing.

Seven general disco "looks" developed: The Basic Disco Look, Bodywear, Futuristic, Thrift-Shop, Jock/Roller, Rock and Roll, and Prep-Collegiate. They could be put together any which way, but the attire had to have glitter and shine. Men got down on the dance floor wearing silk shirts or shiny imitations, gold chains, and decorative rings or wrist jewelry. For women, entire makeup lines with sparkle and glitter were available, along with books on how to use them. Things that shine are nice to look at; they provide pleasure and a release from the day, explained Terry Melville of Macy's.[12] He related that in the past only in the period before Christmas did retail stores feature "dressed up" clothes that people could wear for the holidays. But with disco such merchandise was available year round. The new category of nightlife led to using fabrics like Lurex and velvet and anything that had trimmings on it, such as rhinestones or beads. A whole segment of the fashion industry was geared to outfitting discoers.[13]

The rock 'n' roll disco look. (Photo by Mike Kuentz.)

Motives for Personal Dress

News stories and observations by psychologists suggest that in the dialogue with society, dress is used for four personal motives: (1) to validate personal identity; (2) to protect the personal self; (3) to portray a wished-for identity; and (4) to proclaim one's personal values.

Validation of Personal Identity

Attire used to validate personal identity reflects the self-image. Public memory, the vocabulary of images that exists in American society, is the core source for self-image. Images from the past are often updated. The nineteenth-century ideal of ruggedness and masculine self-reliance, for example, was updated in 1991 and 1992 ads that portrayed Ralph Lauren in a well-worn work shirt, jeans, a jean jacket, a belt with a large buckle, and boots. The mass media are the vehicle through which ideas and images materialize. Stereotypes are often used because they are familiar, easily understood, and likely to be unquestioned; for example, nearly everyone associates eyeglasses with learning and a large body with brawn. Public memory and the media offer options, possibilities, and parameters for the personal self. The following sections describe different aspects of self-identity that are validated through attire.

Meeting the Challenges of Nature   At the beginning of the twentieth century, social critics argued that the new emphasis on clothing symbolized the vice and immorality of the city, the corruption that had increased with the advent of industrialization and urbanization. Urban newspapers advertised that "the goodness of America lies in the small town where life and nature meet to make for genuine living."[14] Durable overalls, blue denim pants, and cotton work shirts signified the high "moral fiber" and productivity of rural life. These attributes were personified by the farmer, the hunter, and the woodsman: strong, self-reliant, and capable of meeting the challenges of nature. In the contemporary television show "Northern Exposure," for example, the ensemble of a pair of jeans or overalls, work boots, a flannel shirt or a work shirt, a leather belt with an ornamented metal buckle, and a sleeveless jacket or vest, worn by men and women, continues to be seen as an image of independence and self-reliance.[15]

Practicality   Attire that requires little upkeep and is durable and roomy is considered practical. Clothes in dark colors often do not show dirt; housedresses do not restrict the body; and clothes developed for backpacking, hunting, and fishing typically have both of these characteristics. A down vest, for example, keeps the body warm and accommodates additional layers of clothing both under and over itself; and it can be shoved into a backpack or shoulder bag when the noonday sun is shining. Equally practical are oversized heavy wool shirts that can be worn as jackets and shirts of wool flannel and chamois cloth. Worn for activities outside the realm for which they were designed, they suggest that pragmatism and efficiency may be essential elements of self-definition.[16]

Encouraging Approach   The word "casual" signifies both a category of dress and an attitude of openness to interaction, as the editors of *Esquire* noted. T-shirts and parkas, open-neck shirts, $6.00 gray sweatshirts with the sleeves cut off, and $50.00 white dress shirts with sleeves rolled up are components of dress that encourage approach.[17] The wearing of soft collars and bright colors also facilitates communication. Flugel observed that such attire signifies a freer play of emotions. He noted, moreover, that the readiness with which a woman removes her cloak or coat when she enters a public place such as the theater or a party suggests her degree of friendliness and willingness to invite sexual admiration.[18]

Corporate Self-Importance   Within the corporate world, personal taste is judged by the attention given to the proportion and fit of clothing. For men, the goal is to create a sense of solidity and a unified whole. The shirt collar, in combination with a knot in the necktie and the lapels of a suit, serves to frame a man's face, directing attention toward his face and providing support. The suit, the rock upon which the professional man's wardrobe is founded, constructs the public persona. It asserts status, establishes identity, and announces intentions. Choosing the right suit is of paramount importance. Personal preferences are secondary. Basic features such as cut, color, and fabric must be pertinent to the profession, office culture, and body type.[19]

Despite such prescriptions, or maybe because of them, many older, more mature men come to view the "correct" suit, shirt, and tie as reflecting a "personal" self. Paradoxically, the corporate prescription becomes a personal self.

Female Personality Types   In their research, S. Sweat and M. Zentner examined the notion that women actively choose among appearance alternatives and attempt to select styles that will communicate desired impressions. They identified four female personality types associated with clothing styles and with a distinct orientation to interaction.[20] These were *dramatic,* characterized by clothing with bold or severe lines; *natural,* characterized by informal clothing with minimal ornamentation; *romantic,* characterized by clothing incorporating gently curved lines to convey a feminine air; and *classic,* characterized by clothing employing simple, tailored lines.

Sweat and Zentner also found that observers distinguished among the four but construed the images differently than the researchers intended. Dramatic attire was read as very unconventional, approachable, somewhat sophisticated, and somewhat dominant; natural, as very conventional, somewhat approachable, somewhat unsophisticated, and slightly dominant; romantic, as unconventional, very approachable, sophisticated, and somewhat submissive; and classic, as conventional, somewhat approachable, very sophisticated, and very dominant. The researchers concluded that although sender and receiver do not necessarily share in the meaning of the image, four distinct styles of appearance with relatively consistent characteristics do exist.

Immunity from Frivolous Distraction   Inconspicuous appearance, as Flugel observed, may be a standard internalized by the self and designed to demonstrate seriousness of mood and devotion to duty.[21] He explained that a preference for clothing that is unprovocative in color, ample in size, thick, and stiff indicates immunity from frivolous distraction. Referring to nineteenth-century attire, he pointed out that preference for physical stiffness has been symbolically associated with moral probity and firmness; the real protective value of thick clothing is to guard against moral dangers because the body is perceived as a source of evil passions.[22]

The norm of modesty is so powerful that the people adhering to this norm consider certain styles of dress to be, in themselves, immodest. A décolleté dress is censured by those holding the norm of modesty. A puritanically minded person, Flugel noted, often does not change out of formal modest attire even in the privacy of the home. Although husbands may appreciate the bold appearance of other women, they often prefer their wives not to attract attention. As a result, married women tend to wear more conventional clothes, more layers of clothing, and darker colors than unmarried women.[23] A beautiful woman is more likely to focus on her appearance because it is easy for her to derive pleasure from adorning physical beauty. By contrast, Flugel observed, "the impulse of modesty has an easier task when a woman possesses an aesthetically inferior body." She is less likely to beautify and display herself because the pleasure derived from doing so is inherently more limited.[24]

Artwear   Some artistically minded people prefer to dress themselves in original works of art. Since the 1970s this style of dress has become more available. A number of American artists have decided that rather than create art that hangs on the wall they will make "wearable" art. The fact that it is worn is secondary to its being art. They transform static two-dimensional surfaces into one-of-a-kind works of art in motion. This clothing and jewelry is sold in special galleries.[25]

American popular culture has inspired the work of French artist Jean Charles de Castalbajac. His dresses are shapeless canvases with sleeves. They bear images of Coke bottles, Campbell's soup cans, the dial faces of telephones, and cartoon characters, such as Woody Woodpecker. His unisex jackets and coats are cut from blankets to evoke the comfort and warmth of the security blanket immortalized by Linus. Castalbajac translated the Jack Kerouac classic *On the Road* into a practical design to be worn or mounted like a sculpture. The modern nomad is depicted in a one-piece hooded coverall with many deep pockets. The coverall is made of tent cloth, creating the image of a kind of movable house; the pockets are the rooms and the hood is the roof.[26]

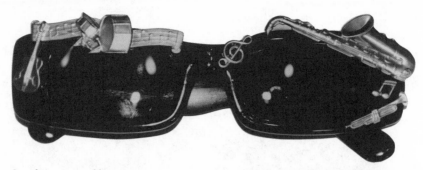

Sunglasses created by Mercura New York, Fine Art to Wear. (Reprinted by permission.)

Lattice Work, *Woman's eveningwear-kimono by Darlene Kay Riggins. (*Wearable Art: Art in Motion, *1985, Indianapolis Museum of Art; reprinted by permission of Darlene Riggins.)*

Rain poncho created by Jean Charles de Castelbajac. Blown up, it can be used as a buoy. It is a protective and playful garment. (Reprinted by permission of Jean-Charles Castelbajac.)

Energy and Physical Prowess   Vigor and athletic prowess are suggested when one wears the attire adopted by "jocks," young athletes in their prime. With the widespread promotion of health and exercise centers, physical conditioning became possible for people of all ages, not just the young. Clothes once worn exclusively by athletes such as running shoes, sweat suits, "muscle shirts," tank tops, and side-vented shorts are now worn outside the gym. Bicycle messengers in New York adopted the sweatband and the knee-length spandex shorts worn by competitors in the Tour de France.[27] Athletic gear was appropriated for street use by such diverse figures as Elvis Presley, Andy Warhol, and New York's working women before and after the April 1980 subway strike.[28]

Richard K. Donahue, president and chief operating officer of Nike Inc., commented that to grow, the sporting goods industry must go "beyond the sock and jocks image: It must appeal to women by offering them what they would like. Only about 10 percent of the women's market consists of committed athletes who buy solely for function. The other 90 percent consider both function and style." He noted that women do not respond to the same sales messages as men. Women will not buy a product just because a superstar, Michael Jordan, for example, wears it. Nike, Reeboks, and L.A. Gear Inc. all scheduled new advertising campaigns in the early 1990s that focused on women acquiring greater "command" over their lives and their emotions.[29]

"Nerds"   Although women may be "nerds," the term is used mostly to describe men. In contrast to the muscular grace of a star athlete, the nerd is bookish, physically underdeveloped, and often wears glasses. In focusing on intellectual development and study (particularly engineering), he seems to ignore matters of appearance and style. In the media he is often depicted as ineffectual, unsophisticated, and oblivious to physical comfort. His shirt is buttoned to the collar, but he wears no tie. The "nerdpack," a plastic pocket protector, is the distinctive element of his dress. It allows a pocket to be stuffed with pens, pencils, rulers, and slide rules or calculators. His pants are often too short.

The nerd is also described as compassionate and vulnerable. In the comic strips, Clark Kent, wearing dark-rimmed glasses, can step into a telephone booth and emerge as Superman. In the film *Revenge of the Nerds* (1984), a young woman commends one of the characters for his sexual performance. He reminds her that nerds don't spend their spare time in self-centered exercising to keep themselves muscular; they think about sex. The character of the nerd emerges as a sexual creature, vulnerable and feeling, a perfect partner because he is not concerned only with himself.

The preeminent nerd exemplar is filmmaker and actor Woody Allen. The traditional garments Allen has appropriated, among them the oxford cloth shirt with button-down collar, are sought after. As art historian Richard Martin suggested, they have come to characterize the nerd image, making it a more desirable social category.[30]

Protecting the Personal Self

When people find themselves among others who are unsympathetic, or among people they feel superior to, have nothing in common with, or fear, they adopt mechanisms to protect the self, Flugel observed.[31] They manipulate style and color to become invisible, to create distance, or to turn their clothing into shelter, thus shielding the self.

Becoming Invisible "Fade into the woodwork" to elude the street thief, advised Enid Remy in a *New York Times* article.[32] Robbers and muggers are unable to distinguish between the real and the fake, be it jewelry, handbag, or fur. Defensive dressing is the smart choice. There are some women who no longer carry handbags. Lipstick and keys go in one pocket, money and a credit card in another; they carry nothing else. Afraid to draw unwanted attention, a young career woman with long blond hair will tuck every last strand under a beret before leaving home in the morning. She takes the beret off only when she reaches her office building.

Fear of sexual harassment is often a reason for choosing attire that enables the individual to be "invisible." Some female graduate students seeking to escape undesired attention wear shabby jeans and oversized work shirts, and their faces are half covered by unkempt stringy hair.

Creating Distance Creating distance is another method of protecting the personal self. Sunglasses may be used to create distance. Like a mask, they keep the person's eyes concealed and intruders remain uninformed. Mirrored lenses, the kind that make the wearer look like a state trooper, are most effective in turning back the intruding looks of others.[33]

A man in a dress suit will often wear an overcoat while walking in the street, even in warm weather, observed Flugel. He feels he needs to wear the overcoat because most of the other people in the street are not in formal dress and are likely to regard his dress suit with a degree of suspicion and hostility.[34]

Flugel also noted that women sometimes keep their outer wrap on at the theater or other public functions to preserve distance. They may be bashful, or they may feel out of harmony with their surroundings and not wish to invite intimacy from those around them.[35]

When in an unfriendly environment, whether human or natural, people tend to button up and to draw their garments closely around their bodies. On a chilly day, when people leave their warm houses and enter into an inhospitable street, they turn up their collars and settle as snugly as possible into their coats. General unfriendliness prompts people to withdraw their inner selves into the protection of their clothes, much as the tortoise withdraws its head into its shell, Flugel pointed out. Sensitivity to cold is heightened under conditions of unfriendliness. A student from the United States studying in London wrote: "It may be that homesickness calls for more clothes."[36]

Covering the eyes makes one inscrutable. Wearing sunglasses has the added effect of keeping other people at bay. (Advertisement entitled "Wire Rims for the '90s," Esquire Gentleman, *Spring 1993; reprinted by permission of Alexis Rodriguez-Duarte.)*

Coldness is a universal metaphor for lack of love. Individuals who feel unloved are more likely to feel cold. They use clothing to protect themselves from both the cold and the unfriendliness of the environment. They are less ready to make the body visible and may keep a coat on indoors for warmth and to preserve a certain aloofness.[37]

Empowering the Self In a *New York Times* article entitled "The Flip Side of Jackets," Ruth La Ferla wrote: "In a season when what a man wears beneath his suit can say as much about him as the suit itself, linings are more than just insulation. ... How else to explain the proliferation of crests, crowns, elks, hunting scenes and other upper class insignia on the flip side of everything from suits to coats to collars?"[38] The wearing of finery and symbols of the upper class where they cannot be publicly discerned offers a degree of personal support. Under precarious economic conditions, men in pagan and nonliterate societies often adorned themselves with elements that they believed would empower the self.

Colorful vests that draw upon nature's color harmonies similarly empower. An April 28, 1991, *New York Times* article reported: "A new generation of men has discovered the vest. But forget about the timid designs that once accompanied the three buttoned suit to the office." New vests come printed with floral designs, have flash and dash, and are often worn without a jacket. When temperatures soar, young men wear vests over bare chests or over short-sleeved T-shirts.[39]

Portraying Wished-For Identities

Images that enable a person to feel as if he or she personifies a desired social ideal fall into the category of images that portray a wished-for identity. Societal prescriptions for gender appearance and behavior are often represented in idealized images by the media. Individuals appropriate goods and services to claim a desired identity. When failure to achieve the ideal ensues and rationality prevails, vicarious consumption may result. The pursuit of thinness by women and the longing of men to look and "feel like women" (cross-dressing) are two prime examples of wished-for identities.

Thinness, a Female Ideal   The female physical ideal celebrated by the media is different from the national norm. In 1980, the average Miss America contestant was five feet, eight inches tall and weighed 117 pounds; the average North American woman was five feet, four inches tall and weighed 144 pounds. A large advertising team will expend hours and hours of collective effort in the manufacture of a single high-fashion image of beauty. What emerges is an illusion.

In her film *Famine Within,* a documentary about the American woman's obsession with body weight, filmmaker Kathrine Gilday observed that much energy and intelligence are absorbed by the desire to lose weight. Although thinness signifies the triumph of willpower over nature, and has less to do with beauty than with a deep cultural meaning, many women are adamant about becoming thin. Weight loss, in fact, has taken on the power of a religious conviction, Gilday observed. About 80 percent of fourth grade girls have already dieted.

A *Vogue* survey of its readers in 1988 revealed that 20 percent wore clothes of size 16 or larger, and 49 percent wore at least size 12. But the magazine's contents focused on sizes 4 and 6. The disparity between the actual reader and the ideal image suggests that reading the magazine enabled women to identify with the desired ideals as if these images personified them.

Cross-Dressing   Trying out female attributes is the dream of cross-dressers, males who periodically dress in female attire. Self-gratification, rather than social deception, underlies their behavior, as John Talamini pointed out in his book, *And Boys Will Be Girls.* He found that cross-dressers come from all socioeconomic backgrounds and hold conventional jobs. Many have children and have served in the military.[40]

Because cross-dressing violates social norms, confusion and guilt may accompany such behavior. Since the liberation movements of the 1970s, at least two societies, The Society for the Second Self and the International Alliance for Male Feminism, have been formed to offer men a means of meeting other cross-dressers and forming a subculture and support system. Through attending their weekly meetings, one researcher found that members referred to one another as sisters when they cross-dressed. Their meetings included discussions on buying wigs, clothes, and makeup. Members frequently joked in a good-natured way about their bizarre outfits. They were careful to avoid "dirty" or erotic language.[41] Their ability to acquire clothes at retail stores is hampered by fear of exposure. They worry that salespeople will know that the desired item is actually for them, so they often use the excuse that they are preparing for a masquerade party or purchasing for a woman who is "about their size."

Unaccustomed to the feminine world of dress and makeup, cross-dressers have a tendency to overdo "femininity." Those who feel they can pass as a woman often venture forth in public. They shop, go to the movies or restaurants, ride buses and trains; however, they usually avoid bars because of the possibility of being approached by another man who is fooled by the feminine disguise.

Proclaiming Personal Values

Personal values consist of ideas and goals that are reflected in personal conduct as well as ideas and goals that underlie societal behavior. Two alignments seem to exist. The first consists of an orientation that justifies social class hierarchy, that is, the "rightness" and desirability of the unequal distribution of resources as well as pride in personal success. Accumulating and demonstrating one's wealth is expected social conduct. The second is an orientation toward egalitarianism and equality. Emotional growth and the actualization of personal talents underlie social conduct.

Conspicuous Consumption and the "Good Life"   Economic success at the turn of the twentieth century was often accompanied by a lavish display of the ability to consume. As economist and social critic Thorstein Veblen pointed out in 1899, the goal of such consumption was simply to impress others, to show off one's success by engaging in wasteful behavior. Veblen argued that this conduct violated the tradition of Puritanism and the ideal of democracy.[42] Public discussion of conspicuous consumption reemerged with Nancy Reagan's reported $46,000 inaugural wardrobe and her $200,000 china for the White House dinner table. Her pattern of consumption contributed to the depiction of the 1980s as the "greed decade."

The yuppies, the young urban professionals of the affluent 1980s, provide another example. They were groomed by their parents in all manners of taste and tact and indoctrinated into a prescribed style of life that included college. Once graduated, they sought to enjoy the "good life." They rejected the homogeneity of the suburbs, where many of them grew up, and sought the excitement of city life. Their "swinging singles and mingles" lifestyle stimulated the development of urban condominiums, small luxury apartments, two-bedroom townhouses, and converted lofts. Long forgotten neighborhoods were rediscovered and revi-

Cross-dressing. "Empress Razor Sharp," a man dressed in female attire for Night of a Thousand Gowns, a benefit for New York City Gay and Lesbian Community Services. (Members of the Imperial Court of New York, Program Notes, March 16, 1991.)

talized with "upscale" services. The yuppies were devoted to consuming the best that money could buy. Bespoke tailoring, which was popular among movie stars in the 1930s and 1940s, was again being sought after by those that could afford it. Yuppies were obtaining shirts and suits custom made in London.[43]

"The New Guilt" "Opulence is on the wane," reported Susan Slesin in January 1992. Her comment was based on the observation at the Winter Antique Show in Manhattan. Despite the recession, waves of layoffs in architectural and interior design offices, and sluggish sales, some people where still renovating, decorating, and buying; but they were affecting a very low profile, "a definite slink. In the decorating world mum's the word right now. Call it the new guilt," Slesin observed. "Those with buying sickness might still make purchases but keep quieter about it." Fixing up what one has rather than moving and starting over assuages a lot of people's decorating guilt, she concluded.[44]

Restraint currently characterizes the consumption of new attire, too. "Fixing up" what one has and wearing old things in new ways have become a trend. Buttons and costume jewelry are used to perk up one's dress. In a 1992 issue of *Antiques Today*, Lita Solis-Cohen reported that costume jewelry was being worn in new ways. "It is now stylish to wear multiple pins. Bugs are worn on shoulders, on sleeves, even crawling up the back of a blouse."[45]

Egalitarianism Among the youth of the 1960s, debate about inequality, injustice, and the Vietnam War led to the view that one's personal vision for society may be expressed in dress. In contrast to those for whom economic success and expensive attire were major goals, there were others who sought deeper meanings in life and rejected symbols of economic achievement. Jeans, painter's coveralls, and work shirts indicated egalitarianism. The attire symbolized the rejection of hierarchy, injustice, and privilege.[46]

This symbolic embodiment of ideology underlies the consumer typology developed in 1978 by the Stanford Research Institute in Menlo Park, California. The typology was created to provide American producers of clothing with a better understanding of the market and a means for projecting trends. Different categories of consumers were defined according to their wealth, education, emotional needs, values, and lifestyle: *Need-directed consumers* have low education and are caught up in the struggle for survival. *Outer-directed consumers* are driven by the psychological need for approval. They buy with an eye toward appearances; what other people think is more important to them than their own inner satisfaction. *Inner-directed consumers* feel that self-approval is more important than the approval of others. Well-educated, their lifestyle and buying habits are diverse. The researchers concluded that the higher the individual is in the social class hierarchy (education, occupation, and income), and the greater his or her psychological maturity, the more his or her clothing is likely to reflect personal values.[47]

Alternatives and Ambiguity

"Rob Morrow was looking nothing like a petulant small-town doctor as he padded in to dinner in a *baggy blue suit* that could have been fairly cheap or very expensive," wrote Sarah Lyall, reporting about her interview with the actor.[48] The nonpadded jacket contains none of the protection provided by the structured rigidity of the traditional male suit. It reflects the postmodern questioning of the nineteenth-century belief in rationality and the conviction that reality is ordered according to laws that the human intelligence can grasp. The "sack suit," a loose-fitting nontailored jacket worn over a shirt that is buttoned all the way up, no tie, and loose-fitting pants, emerged in the mid-1980s as a new aesthetic expression. In its lack of clear harmony and balance it articulates the view that reality is unordered and ultimately unknowable.

In the television series "Miami Vice," Sonny Crockett, the undercover police officer played by Don Johnson, glamorized the wearing of the sack suit. Rather than conveying occupational responsibility, symbolized by the uniform or the traditional suit, the sack suit reflects the postmodern sensibility of discontinuity with the past, skepticism, and uncertainty.[49]

In the beginning of the 1990s the sack suit became a viable alternative for young men whose occupations were associated with media and the arts, where creative imagination is desired. Two styles of male suits have since come to reflect the two distinct orientations to structure—discipline and self-expression. A news report on the field of advertising had the following headline: "By Design, Deutch Chooses a Non-Madcap President."[50] To clarify, the reporter, Stuart Elliot, asked a rhetorical question: Can an account executive who works for "straightlaced packaged-goods clients like Unilever and dresses like an investment banker" find happiness in the "most aggressively creative and controversial advertising agency?" The photograph that accompanied the story showed Steve Dworin, the new president of "Madcap" agency, in a traditional-style jacket, pants, and a tie. The creative director of the agency, Donny Deutch, was wearing a sack suit—a loose-fitting jacket and pants with the shirt buttoned up and no tie. Management, the exercise of authority, is signified by structure and constraint, and awareness of the latest intellectual and artistic trends is intimated by the informally structured attire.

The sack suit worn by the man on the right obliterates a barrier to interaction. Without the padded "shield," the suit suggests a greater ability to respond to specific situations and needs. (Reprinted by permission of Garry Rosso/NYT Pictures and Steve Dworin.)

Conclusion

THERE HAS ALWAYS BEEN some awareness of the role clothing plays in social life. But the ways in which visual images direct, affect, and reflect societal, cultural, and personal discourse have not been fully appreciated.

Although thrones, crowns, and pageantry are mostly gone, and the structure and expression of social life have changed, the inner necessities that animate social life have not. *Clothing signs* enable a political authority, such as the police, to define itself and advance its claims. In the form of a visual image that transmits meaning, a clothing sign provides the cultural frame within which the political authority can function. Required attire, clothing signs specify a range of feelings and behaviors that are expected. They allow only certain kinds of response, linking the individual to a particular social order. Their meaning is generally shared; when the meaning is clear, the message is concrete and direct.

Familiarity with these images makes the existence of clothing signs inconspicuous, often too mundane to be consciously noted. More likely to be noticed are changes, increases or decreases, in the use of clothing signs. These are likely to have repercussions in other spheres of social life as well as for the definition of the self. The existence of clothing signs, however, is impossible to censor; hence, they can become a valuable source of information about a society's patterns of interaction.

When images mean different things to the persons who wear them and to their intended audience, misunderstandings may result. Both participants and observers are left wondering why a person or a group is dressed in a certain way. Often it is concluded that the appearance is merely "a style," an innocuous expression, although that conclusion may trivialize an important social phenomenon.

Clothing symbols may also be misinterpreted and their meaning trivialized. Clothing symbols are an important component of a people's cultural heritage. Their use depends on the wearer's knowledge and mood. For example, at the signing of the peace accord between Israel and the Palestine Liberation Organization, President Clinton wore a jewel-toned blue and yellow tie with a design of little trumpets. For the president the colors symbolized the dawning of a new political day. He chose the trumpets to suggest the hope that the "walls" that separate the two groups will come down, just as the walls of Jericho once did.[1]

However, lack of familiarity with the meaning of clothing symbols may lead to misinterpretation. For example, a fall 1993 promotional newsletter by *Forbes*

Magazine inquired, "Do you know that necktie styles forecast the economy? ... Wild and whimsical ties are in fashion when the economy is cool, and conservative ties are worn when business is booming." *Forbes Magazine* thus formally recognized that the socially constructed categories of ties that spoke of status and class in the past—the diagonally striped "rep" tie, the patterned "club" tie, the paisley, solid, or monogrammed tie—have been replaced, and two distinct configurations characterize the new trend in ties. The first consists of styles and colors that are inspired by nature, such as earth tones, muted oranges, rust, soft gold with touches of pale blue, forming flowers, leaves, and pinecones, and the plumage of tropical birds. In traditional societies spirits were embodied in the sun, rivers, stones, and trees, and wearing such elements was thought to renew the spirit. The second configuration consists of jewel tones and a regularity of pattern, such as little boxes, larger squares, diamonds, and ovals. The pattern is reminiscent of the gemstones placed at regular intervals that characterize the attire, crown, and sword of royalty, decorative elements that indicated a desire to stay politically alive. They spoke of access to cosmic powers and an orderly universe.

The new styles in ties are an expression of the current uneasy times. They reveal the continued belief that by incorporating into dress elements whose powers lie outside the human domain one may empower the self. The ties represent the current reality, the decline of the economy. They represent an attempt to reverse it emotionally, much like good-luck charms that reduce anxiety and increase the likelihood of success. *Forbes Magazine* had it backwards. Rather than forecasting a downturn, the new trend is the *result* of the decline in the economy, which began in 1988. As Bronislaw Malinowski pointed out, we do not find magic where the pursuit is certain. Where the outcome of an enterprise cannot be predicted, however, such as when one takes a trip, goes to battle, or makes a movie, the help of superhuman forces continues to be sought.[2]

In addition to an awareness of images and meanings, the valid interpretation of an image requires an understanding of the sociocultural context within which the image appears. Designers respond to the period's ideas and tensions with styles they believe are relevant. Like other artists and authors, they may not be completely aware of the meanings of the images they create. Their comments about a fashion can only be informative or indicative of a direction; they are not the full meaning. The media, called upon to analyze and interpret meaning, are often concerned with the promotion of a new style. Moreover, they may be ignorant of the many images that inhabit our cultural universe. They seize upon one element and proclaim it as the fashion's full meaning.

Media analysis of fall 1993 fashion is an example. Since religious themes characterized the clothing and jewelry, media observers concluded that the "bona fide message" was that of "spirituality" or "piety."[3] Reminiscent of religious habit, crosses were worn on filmy, often see-through black robes. These were presented together with the grunge style, the untidy, unkempt look. The sociocultural context was that of continuing economic recession. The reduced buying

*A design by Donna Karan said to signify spirituality. (*Womens Wear Daily, *August 29, 1993; reprinted by permission of Marilyn K. Yee/NYT Pictures.)*

power of the public and the loss of talent to AIDS could not have gone unnoticed. The new U.S. president, young and untried, could not offer a full measure of security or comfort. Within Western culture crosses and other religious jewelry have always offered a protective measure; they make the individual feel less accessible to harm. Like the new trend in ties, the "spiritual" theme in fashion is more likely an attempt to overcome the sense of vulnerability discernible in much of contemporary sociocultural discourse—in health care, for example.

The valid interpretation of clothing images, then, depends on awareness of the vocabulary of images and understanding of the sociocultural context within which the images appear. Knowledge of the accumulated basic signs and symbols is important not only as a means for consciously discerning the ongoing drama of social reality; it may also be useful in tracking social and cultural shifts in order to better understand possible future trends.

Notes

Chapter 1

1. R. Sennett (1974) *The Fall of Public Man* (New York: Knopf).

2. T. Veblen (1953) *The Theory of the Leisure Class* (New York: Mentor Books). Originally published 1899.

3. G. Simmel (1957) "Fashion," *American Journal of Sociology* 62. Originally published in 1904 in *International Quarterly* 10: 294–295.

4. Ibid., 308–309.

5. M. and A. Batterberry (1977) *Fashion: The Mirror of History* (New York: Greenwich House); E. Wilson (1987) *Adorned in Dreams* (Berkeley: University of California Press); A. Hollander (1978) *Seeing Through Clothes* (New York: Viking).

6. L. Malvano (1988) *Fascismo e politica dell'immagine* (Torino: Bollati Boringhieri), pp. 77–140. Trans. for author by J. Cascaito.

7. D. Hebdige (1979) *Subculture: The Meaning of Style* (New York: Methuen).

8. M. Halbwachs (1980) *The Collective Memory,* trans. F. J. Ditter, Jr., and Vida Yazdi Ditter (New York: Harper and Row).

9. Ibid., pp. 20–24, 40–41, 152–157.

10. U. Apolonio, ed. (1973) *Futurist Manifestos: Documents of Twentieth Century Art* (New York: Viking Press), pp. 132–133. Published in two parts in Lacerba, Florence, March 15, 1914, and April 1, 1914, with two different titles, and as a leaflet by Direzione del Movimento Futurista, March 18, 1914.

11. F. de Saussure (1974) *A Course in General Linguistics* (Huntington, N.Y.: Fontana).

12. E. Cassirer (1961) "Ideational Content of the Sign," in *Theories of Society: Foundations of Modern Sociology,* vol. 2, ed. T. Parsons, E. Shils, K. D. Naegele, and J. R. Pitts (New York: Free Press), pp. 1004–1008. Also E. Goffman (1951) "Symbols of Class Status," *British Journal of Sociology* A (4): 294–303, quoted in P. I. Rose, ed. (1972) *Seeing Ourselves, Readings in Sociology and Society* (New York: Knopf). Also see G. P. Stone (1962) "Appearance and the Self," in *Human Behavior and Social Process,* ed. A. Rose (Boston: Houghton Mifflin, pp. 86–118.

13. J. C. Flugel (1966) *The Psychology of Clothes* (London: Hogarth Press), p. 157. Originally published 1930.

14. Ibid., p. 34.

15. Ibid., pp. 36–37.

16. T. Carlyle (1967) *Sartor Resartus* (New York: Dutton), p. 26. Originally published 1838.

17. Stone (1962), op. cit., pp. 107–110.

18. M. Gottdiener (1977) "Unisex Fashions and Gender-Role Change," *Semiotic Scene* 1 (3): 13–37.

19. Flugel, op. cit., p. 106.

20. Goffman (1951), op. cit., pp. 259–261.

21. Veblen, op. cit., pp. 118–130.

22. See also H. Spencer (1969) *The Principles of Sociology,* ed. S. Andreseki (Hamden, Conn.: Archon Books), pp. 160–161. In contrast to status symbols, attire that exhibits a departure or deviation from cultural values has been termed "stigma symbols." E. Goffman (1963b) *Stigma: Notes on the Management of Spoiled Identity* (Englewood Cliffs, N.J.: Prentice-Hall), p. 45.

23. Veblen, op. cit. The idea of social superiority and entitlement is discussed in Veblen's chapter entitled "Conspicuous Leisure," pp. 51–60.

24. G. Stone (1962) "Appearance and the Self," in *Dress Adornment and the Social Order,* ed. M. E. Roach and J. B. Eicher (New York: John Wiley and Sons), pp. 226–227.

25. The concept of "publicspeak" has its roots in the work of C. Wright Mills and Herbert Gans. Mills pointed to a distinction between "personal troubles," which are a private matter, and "public issues," where factors outside one's personal control affect daily life. Gans used the term "culture publics" to suggest that a great variety of "taste cultures" exist in the United States. See C. W. Mills (1959) *The Sociological Imagination* (New York: Oxford University Press) and H. J. Gans (1974) *Popular Culture and High Culture* (New York: Basic Books).

26. A. Rockford and E. Burke (1985) *Hare Krishna in America* (New Brunswick, N.J.: Rutgers University Press); H. B. Thompson (1967) *Hell's Angels* (New York: Ballantine Books).

27. *New York Times,* September 17, 1989.

28. Flugel, op. cit., p. 160.

29. H. Blumer (1969) "Fashion: From Class Differentiation to Collective Selection," *Sociology Quarterly* 10: 275–291.

30. Carlyle, op. cit., p. 25.

Chapter 2

1. P. Stubbs (1583) *Anatomy of Abuses.* Quoted in J. Laver (1969) *Modesty in Dress* (Boston: Houghton Mifflin), p. 22.

2. T. Veblen (1953) *The Theory of the Leisure Class* (New York: Mentor Books). Originally published 1899. Also G. Simmel (1957) "Fashion," *American Journal of Sociology* 62. Originally published in 1904 in *International Quarterly* 10: 294–295. Both examined social class distinctions, clothing, and their impact on the self and society.

3. J. Laver (1969) *Modesty in Dress* (Boston: Houghton Mifflin), pp. 9–11.

4. In S. Lyman (1978) *The Seven Deadly Sins: Society and Evil* (New York: St. Martin's), pp. 54–57; also Laver, op. cit., p. 17.

5. Lyman, op. cit., p. 56.

6. Laver, op. cit., p. 9.

7. Ibid., pp. 20–25.

8. L. H. Newburgh, ed. (1968) *The Physiology of Heat Regulation and the Science of Clothing* (New York: Stretchet Haffner).

9. F. R. Wulsin (1968) "Adaptations to Climate Among Non-European Peoples," in Newburgh, op. cit., pp. 26–30.

10. Quoted in Wulsin, op. cit., p. 31.

11. D. Hardy (1968) "Heat Transfer," in Newburgh, op. cit., pp. 65–83; also H. C. Bazett (1968) "The Regulation of Body Temperature," in Newburgh, op. cit., pp. 109–117.

12. Wulsin, op. cit., pp. 4–25.

13. W. H. Forbes (1968) "Laboratory Field Studies: General Principles," in Newburgh, op. cit., pp. 320–329.

14. Wulsin, op. cit., pp. 4–11; also Forbes, op. cit., pp. 323–324.

15. Wulsin, op. cit., pp. 47–53.

16. Ibid., pp. 38–47.

17. Forbes, op. cit.

18. T. Carlyle (1967) *Sartor Resartus* (New York: Dutton), p. 2. Originally published 1838.

19. Ibid., pp. 1–47.

20. R. P. Rubinstein (1985) "Color, Circumcision, Tatoos and Scars," in *The Psychology of Fashion,* ed. M. R. Solomon (Lexington, Mass.: D. C. Heath), pp. 243–254.

21. R. Brain (1979) *The Decorated Body* (New York: Harper and Row), p. 86; V. Ebin (1979) *The Body Decorated* (London: Thames and Hudson), pp. 42–44; J. C. Faris (1972) *Nuba Personal Art* (London: Duckworth).

22. Brain, op. cit., p. 70.

23. Faris, op. cit., p. 8.

24. A. Seeger (1975) "The Meaning of Body Ornament," *Ethnology* 14: 218.

25. T. S. Turner (1979) "Social Structure and Political Organization of Northern Kayapop," Ph.D. diss., Harvard University.

26. Brain, op. cit., p. 86.

27. Ibid., pp. 50, 78.

28. B. Malinowski (1948) *Magic Science and Religion and Other Essays* (Garden City, N.Y.: Doubleday/Anchor). Originally published 1925.

29. A. and M. Strathern (1971) *Self Decoration in Mount Hagen* (Toronto: University of Toronto Press).

30. Brain, op. cit., p. 140.

31. Ibid., p. 42; J. G. Frazer (1959) *The New Golden Bough,* ed. T. H. Gaster (New York: Criterion Books), p. 17.

32. W.E.A. Budge and W. Thompson (1961) *Amulets and Talismans* (New Hyde Park, N.Y.: University Books), pp. 14, 19, 27.

33. Frazer, op. cit., pp. 401–466; R. Benedict (1933) "Magic," in *Encyclopedia of Social Sciences,* vol. 10 (New York: Macmillan), pp. 39–44.

34. L. M. Gurel (1979) "Eskimos' Clothing and Culture," in *Dimensions of Dress and Adornment: A Book of Readings,* ed. L. M. Gurel and M. S. Beeson (Dubuque, Iowa: Kendall/Hunt Publishing), p. 41.

35. Frazer, op. cit., pp. 9–11; also Gurel, op. cit., p. 42.

36. M. H. Kahlenberg and A. Berlant (1972) *The Navajo Blanket* (New York: Praeger); also G. Witherspoon (1977) *Language and Art in the Navajo Universe* (Ann Arbor: University of Michigan Press).

37. Laver, op. cit., p. 3.

Chapter 3

1. In "The Body Versus the Social Body in the Works of Thomas Malthus and Henry Mayhew," Catherine Gallagher observed that a two-millennia tradition sees the individual body as a sign of the health or infirmity of the larger social body. In C. Gallagher and T. Lacquer, eds. (1987) *The Making of the Modern Body: Sexuality and Society in the Nineteenth Century* (Berkeley: University of California Press), p. 83.

2. P. Hughes (1948) *A History of the Church* (London: Sheed & Ward).

3. P. Brown (1988) *The Body and Society: Men, Women, and Sexual Renunciation in Early Christianity* (New York: Columbia University Press), p. 51.

4. Ibid., p. 149.

5. Ibid., p. 443.

6. Ibid., pp. 272–273; also M. Chambers et al. (1974) *The Western Experience* (New York: Knopf), p. 406; C. F. Lawrence (1981) *The German "Bauernkrieg" of 1525: Organization and Action of Peasant Revolt* (Ann Arbor: University of Michigan Microfilm International).

7. M. and A. Batterberry (1977) *Fashion: The Mirror of History* (New York: Greenwich House), p. 73; F. Boucher (1965) *Twenty Thousand Years of Fashion* (New York: Harry N. Abrams), p. 164.

8. Boucher, op. cit., pp. 162–163; A. Hollander (1978) *Seeing Through Clothes* (New York: Viking), p. 363.

9. L. G. Deruisseau (1939) "Dress Fashions of the Italian Renaissance," *CIBA Review* (January): 589–594; also M. and A. Batterberry, op. cit., pp. 94–95.

10. A. Ribeiro (1986) *Dress and Morality* (London: Batsford). In "Visual Art as Social Data: The Renaissance Codpiece," G. Q. Vicary argued that the hardened construction of the sixteenth-century codpiece served as a container for medicine. Syphilis had struck Europe.

She suggested that the codpiece may have been used for protection, but it was probably also used as a container for mercury salts and unrefined yellow animal grease, which were used to treat an infected penis. See G. Q. Vicary (1989) "Visual Art as Social Data: The Renaissance Codpiece," *Cultural Anthropology* 4 (1): 3–25.

11. Cited in M. and A. Batterberry, op. cit., p. 98.

12. Hollander, op. cit., pp. 214–216.

13. E. Eisenstein (1979) *The Printing Press as an Agent of Change* (New York: Cambridge University Press).

14. C. Mukerji (1983) *From Graven Images: Patterns of Modern Materialism* (New York: Columbia University Press), pp. 98, 142–164.

15. J. Laver (1963) *Costume* (New York: Hawthorne Books), pp. 67–81; also R. König (1973) *A La Mode* (New York: Seabury Press), pp. 84–85; J. C. Flugel (1966) *The Psychology of Clothes* (London: Hogarth Press), p. 111.

16. Flugel, op. cit., pp. 110–111.

17. König, op. cit., p. 157.

18. Ibid.

19. Hollander, op. cit., p. 385.

20. N. Elias (1978) *The Civilizing Process: The Development of Manners* (New York: Urizon Books), p. 235.

Chapter 4

1. R. Sennett (1974) *The Fall of Public Man* (New York: Knopf), pp. 3–27; W. H. Form and G. P. Stone, (1957) "Urbanism, Anonimity and Status Symbolism," *American Journal of Sociology* 62 (5): 504–514.

2. M. and A. Batterberry (1977) *Fashion: The Mirror of History* (New York: Greenwich House), p. 139; A. Hollander (1978) *Seeing Through Clothes* (New York: Viking), p. 385.

3. T. Carlyle (1967) *Sartor Resartus* (New York: Dutton), pp. 139–147. Originally published 1838.

4. E. Moers (1960) *The Dandy: Brummel to Beerbohm* (New York: Viking), pp. 147–163. For a more contemporary view see L. H. Lofland (1973) *A World of Strangers. Order and Action in Urban Public Space* (New York: Basic Books). Lofland argued that the appearence of the preindustrial city did not survive the chaos and confusion of early industrialization. The economic and social revolution made it virtually impossible to retain the traditional expressions of identities. The spatial ordering of the modern city makes it a place for living among strangers. City living requires learning the skills for moving in a world of strangers.

5. Moers, op. cit., pp. 287–330; V. Steele (1985) *Fashion and Eroticism* (New York: Oxford University Press), pp. 151–152.

6. V. Steele (1988) *Paris Fashion* (New York: Oxford University Press), pp. 143–144.

7. F. W. Taylor (1911) *The Principles of Scientific Management* (New York: Harper Brothers).

8. *New York Times Magazine,* December 16, 1990.

9. M. and A. Batterberry, op. cit., p. 216; also Steele (1988), op. cit.

10. *New York Times,* September 19, 1989.

11. *New York Times,* September 29, 1989.

12. *New York Times,* May 13, 1990.

13. *New York Times,* June 13, 1987.

14. Sennett, op. cit., pp. 17–20, 165.

15. C. W. Mills (1951) *White Collar* (New York: Oxford University Press), p. 65.

16. W. H. Form and G. P. Stone (1955) "The Social Significance of Clothing in Occupational Life," *Michigan State University Agricultural Experiment Technical Bulletin,* no. 247.

17. Form and Stone (1957), op. cit.; also J. Thompson, ed. (1983) *Image Impact for Men* (New York: A & W Publishers).

18. E. Goffman (1959) *The Presentation of Self in Everyday Life* (Garden City, N.Y.: Doubleday), pp. 1–30; E. Goffman (1963a) *Behavior in Public Places* (New York: Free Press); E. Goffman (1967) *Interaction Ritual* (Garden City, N.Y.: Doubleday/Anchor Books), pp. 16, 55; also M. Wood (1990) "Consumer Behavior: Impression Management by Professional Servers" (Paper delivered at the 85th Annual Meeting of the American Sociological Association, Washington, D.C., August 11–15).

19. E. Goffman (1961a) *Asylums: Essays on the Social Situation of Mental Patients and Other Inmates* (Chicago: Aldine), p. 27; also E. Goffman (1961b) *Encounters* (Indianapolis: Bobbs-Merrill), pp. 99–115. See also R. M. Barker (1968) *Ecological Psychology: Concepts and Methods for Studying the Environment of Human Behavior* (Stanford: Stanford University Press); R. E. Turner and C. Edgley (1976) "Death as Theater: A Dramaturgical Analysis of the American Funeral," *Sociology and Social Research* 60 (4): 377–392.

20. *New York Times*, April 28, 1987.

21. E. Goffman (1961a), op. cit., pp. 20–21.

22. "Schooling of Boy, 4, Snarled by Long Hair," *New York Times*, March 9, 1991.

23. J. Curry, "Mattingly Chooses Seat on Yank Bench over Barber's Chair," *New York Times*, August 16, 1991. A similar point is made by Dennis B. Levin (1992) in *Inside Out: A True Story of Greed, Scandal and Redemption* (New York: Berkley Books), p. 86. Levin reported that a team of three men from Smith, Barney, the Wall Street investment firm, went to Hawaii to do a presentation to the board of a corporation based in Honolulu that was contemplating a major investment. They were wearing suits. They met with the chief executive officer, Henry Walker, the day before the presentation. He told them, "I would appreciate it if you would not wear the pin striped suits for the board meeting tomorrow." Levin, the head of the team, responded, "All we brought with us is our work clothes." Walker replied, "You are in Hawaii now and you have to wear aloha attire—flowered shirts and the like." He directed them to a store that carried the appropriate attire.

24. "At the Bar," *New York Times*, Law page, June 5, 1992.

25. *New York Times*, May 2, 1991.

26. M. J. Horn and L. M. Gurel (1981) *The Second Skin: An Interdisciplinary Study of Clothing*, 3d ed. (Boston: Houghton Mifflin), pp. 181–182, 187–188.

27. E. Goffman (1963b) *Stigma: Notes on the Management of Spoiled Identity* (Englewood Cliffs, N.J.: Prentice-Hall).

28. "Where the Hat Is the Man," *New York Times*, May 27, 1973.

29. Goffman (1963b), op. cit., pp. 3–5.

Chapter 5

1. M. Weber (1947) *The Theory of Social and Economic Organization*, trans. A. M. Henderson and T. Parsons (New York: Free Press), p. 152; C. W. Mills (1959) *The Sociological Imagination* (New York: Oxford University Press). In his May 29, 1993, essay in the *New York Times*, Russell Baker observed: "The British Empire was almost surely destroyed by the swagger stick. It made imperial Britain's military men look so hatefully arrogant to the rest of the world that the empire was doomed." It is important to note that a swagger stick extends the person's reach; and when employed, it inflicts pain.

2. M. Weber (1993) "Power, Domination and Legitimacy," in *Power in Modern Societies*, ed. M. E. Olsen and M. N. Martin (Boulder: Westview Press), pp. 37–47; M. Weber (1978) *Economy and Society: An Outline of Interpretive Sociology*, ed. G. Roth and C. Wittich (Berkeley: University of California Press), chap. 3.

3. M. Chambers et al. (1974) *The Western Experience* (New York: Knopf), pp. 435–454, 581; F. L. Ganshof (1964) *Feudalism* (New York: Harper and Row); M. and A. Batterberry (1977) *Fashion: The Mirror of History* (New York: Greenwich House), p. 110.

4. A. Hollander (1978) *Seeing Through Clothes* (New York: Viking), p. 371.

5. *The New Golden Bough: A New Abridgement of Sir James George Frazer's Classic Work*, edited, with Notes and Foreword by T. H. Gaster (New York: Criterion Books), pp. 3–142.

6. M. Foucault (1978) *The History of Sexuality: Volume 1, An Introduction* (New York: Random House), pp. 135–143.

7. The 1804 coronation of Napoléon I, for example, which was commemorated by David in *Le Sacre*, was a spectacle that consisted of traditional signs of power—ecclesiastical and secular. In *Le Sacre*, the pope, seated high, is wearing a gold-edged miter and an elaborately decorated crimson and gold embroidered orphrey and is holding a cross staff. Invoking Imperial Rome, Napoléon is wearing the laurel wreath of the Roman emperor and his vestments, including the ankle-length gold embroidered satin gown and crimson velvet mantle. He holds high the customary gold crown. Velvet and silk, crimson and gold, fabrics and colors restricted in Europe to holders of power, are also used for the attire of his wife Josephine. The women in Josephine's court are clad in Grecian-style dresses and hairdos, women's latest fashion, which contributes to the grandeur.

8. M. Mann (1986) *The Sources of Social Power*, vol. 1 (Cambridge: Cambridge University Press), pp. 456–457.

9. G. Ferguson (1977) *Signs and Symbols in Christian Art* (New York: Oxford University Press). Also J. Mayo (1984) *A History of Ecclesiastical Dress* (New York: Holmes and Meier), p. 171.

10. N. Elias (1978) *The Civilizing Process: The Development of Manners* (New York: Urizon Books).

11. C. D. Bowen (1966) *Miracle at Philadelphia* (Boston: Little, Brown).

12. Ibid., pp. 54–67.

13. Ibid., pp. 47–51.

14. M. Weber called the exercise of power within such a structure "legal-rational authority." In M. Weber (1968) *Economy and Society* (New York: Bedminster Press). Originally published 1922.

15. B. Schlenker (1980) *Impression Management: The Self-Concept, Social Identity, and Interpersonal Relations* (Monterey, Calif.: Brooks-Cole), p. 243.

16. H. Frankfort (1951) *The Birth of Civilization in the Near East* (Garden City, N.Y.: Doubleday/Anchor Books), pp. 111–113; also H. Frankfort (1961) *Ancient Egyptian Religion* (New York: Harper and Row), pp. 33–43.

17. M. Lurker (1980) *The Gods and Symbols of Ancient Egypt* (London: Thames and Hudson), pp. 44, 124, 127; W.E.A. Budge and W. Thompson (1961) *Amulets and Talismans* (New Hyde Park, N.Y.: University Books), p. 150; Frankfort (1961), op. cit.

18. A. Erman (1971) *Life in Ancient Egypt* (New York: Dover Publications), pp. 228–229. Originally published 1894.

19. Ibid., pp. 200–280.

20. Ferguson, op. cit.

21. Ibid., pp. 166, 182.

22. Ibid., p. 180.

23. Ibid., pp. 99–100.

24. Ibid., p. 38; also Budge and Thompson, op. cit., pp. 350–352.

25. C. Morris (1972) *The Discovery of the Individual: 1050–1200* (New York: Harper Torchbooks), pp. 23–24.

Chapter 6

1. R. Sennett (1980) *Authority* (New York: Random House), pp. 18–20, 126.

2. J. C. Flugel (1966) *The Psychology of Clothes* (London: Hogarth Press), p. 36.

3. N. Joseph (1986) *Uniforms and Nonuniforms: Communication Through Clothing* (Westport, Conn.: Greenwood Press), pp. 21–27.

4. N. Joseph and N. Alex (1972) "The Uniform: A Sociological Perspective," *American Journal of Sociology*, 77 (4): 719–730.

5. Joseph, op. cit., pp. 37–38.

6. In a study that reviews the literature on the wearing of uniforms, Michael Wood pointed out that in a novice the quality of one's appearance affects judgments of competency and technical efficiency. M. Wood (1990) "Consumer Behavior: Impression Management by Professional Servers" (Paper delivered at the 85th Annual Meeting of the American Sociological Association, Washington, D.C., August 11–15).

7. N. Elias (1950) "Studies in the Genesis of the Naval Profession," *British Journal of Sociology* 1 (4): 291–309.

8. J. Roth (1957) "Ritual and Magic in the Control of Contagion," *American Sociological Review* (22): 310–314; also E. Goffman (1963b) *Stigma: Notes on the Management of Spoiled Identity* (Englewood Cliffs, N.J.: Prentice-Hall), p. 141.

9. J. Laver (1969) *Modesty in Dress* (Boston: Houghton Mifflin), pp. 56–58.

10. R. La Ferla, "Tales that Ties Tell," *New York Times Magazine*, June 8, 1986, p. 66.

11. The Tie Rack U.S. (1989) *The Book of Ties* (New York: Ruder & Fin). The Tie Rack U.S. is Britain's specialty designer and retailer of ties.

12. J. Molloy (1978) *Dress for Success* (New York: Warner Books).

13. A. M. Earle (1971) *Two Centuries of Costume in America, 1620–1820* (Rutland, Vt.: Charles E. Tuttle), pp. 725–728. Originally published 1903.

14. E. Warwick, H. C. Pitz, and A. Wycoff (1965) *Early American Dress* (New York: Benjamin Bloom), pp. 105–109.

15. Earle, op. cit., p. 726.

16. Ibid., pp. 729–730.

17. R. La Ferla, *New York Times*, April 30, 1989. In a similar vein, rather than conforming to traditional executive style, President Reagan, and earlier President Kennedy, availed himself of custom tailoring for the purpose of projecting an image. In "Live Men Do Wear Plaid" (*Time*, June 28, 1982, p. 39), journalist Hugh Sidey, reporting on the attire President Reagan wore to Europe, observed: "Not since John Kennedy posed boldly in a two button coat, defying decades of three button tradition, has a suit of clothes gained so much attention as the blue-and-grey glen plaid outfit that Ronald Reagan wore to Europe." The other functionaries, all swathed in plain blue and gray, were pained when they saw "Reagan's cheery plaid." "Reagan's glen plaid" has good lineage, the reporter continued. The fabric was manufactured by the British firm of Illingworth, Morris & Co. A bolt was sent to Beverly Hills tailor Frank Mariani, who made all of Reagan's suits. Sidey noted that "men in the executive suite rejected President Reagan's choice."

Jack Haber of *GQ* insisted that President Kennedy, by refusing to wear the traditional headgear to his inauguration, put the last nail in the coffin of the men's hat industry, as reported in H. Sidey, "Live Men Do Wear Plaid." Kennedy was proud of his bushy hair and refused to wear a hat, despite the pleading of the industry. In contrast to those before him, President Carter sought to project an image of a "less imperial presidency." He abandoned the limousine for the mile and a half walk from the Capitol to the White House for his inauguration and was photographed wearing jeans in the White House and to Cabinet meetings. See G. M. Boyd (1989) "Bush Inaugural Will Signal Open, Accessible President," *New York Times*, January 13, 1989.

18. H. Frankfort (1951) *The Birth of Civilization in the Near East* (Garden City, N.Y.: Doubleday/Anchor Books), pp. 56, 63.

19. Ibid.

20. J. Campbell (1974) *The Mythic Image* (Princeton: Princeton University Press), pp. 71–87.

21. F. Boucher (1965) *Twenty Thousand Years of Fashion* (New York: Harry N. Abrams), pp. 119–120.

22. Because the toga was held together by draping, Tertullian, one of the church fathers, argued that it was "a burden, not a garment." M. and A. Batterberry (1977) *Fashion: The Mirror of History* (New York: Greenwich House), pp. 57–69.

23. M. Johnson (1972) "What Will Happen to the Gray Flannel Suit," *Journal of Home Economics* 64 (8): 5–12.

24. D. W. Blumhagen (1979) "The Doctor's White Coat," *Annals of Internal Medicine* 91 (1): 111—116.

25. C. H. Krueger (1966) "Economic Aspects of Expanding Europe," in *Twelfth-Century Europe and the Foundations of Modern Society,* ed. M. Clagett, G. Post, and R. Reynolds (Westport, Conn.: Greenwood Press), pp. 59–75.

26. M. Mann (1986) *The Sources of Social Power* (Cambridge: Cambridge University Press), pp. 376–377; also C. Mukerji (1983) *From Graven Images: Patterns of Modern Materialism* (New York: Columbia University Press), pp. 39–46; J. M. Vincent (1935) *Costume and Conduct in the Laws of Basel, Bern and Zurich 1370–1800* (Baltimore, Md.: Johns Hopkins University Press), pp. 44–45.

27. R. H. Bainton (1962) *Early and Medieval Christianity* (Boston: Beacon Hill); D. Knowles (1969) *Christian Monasticism* (New York: McGraw-Hill).

28. A. B. Cobban (1975) *The Medieval University: Their Development and Organization* (London: Methuen); D. Knowles (1962) *The Evolution of Medieval Thought* (London: Methuen).

29. Guibert of Nogent (1970) *Self and Society in Medieval France,* ed. J. F. Benton (New York: Harper Torchbooks), pp. 40–41. Originally published 1064?–1125.

30. C. Brooke (1947) *The Monastic World* (New York: Random House); J. Mayo (1984) *A History of Ecclesiastical Dress* (New York: Holmes and Meier), pp. 11–37; I. V. Duchenne (1976) "The Development of Religious Habit of the Faithful Companions of Jesus," *Costume: The Journal of Costume Society,* no. 6.

31. Mayo, op. cit., p. 36.

32. G. Ferguson (1977) *Signs and Symbols in Christian Art* (New York: Oxford University Press), pp. 151–153; Mayo, op. cit., pp. 38–61.

33. M. S. Enslin (1956) *Christian Beginnings* (New York: Harper Torchbooks); Ferguson, op. cit., p. 157; Mayo, op. cit., pp. 123, 167.

34. Mayo, op. cit., p. 40.

35. Ferguson, op. cit., pp. 155–159; Mayo, op. cit., p. 110.

36. P. Cunnington, C. Lucas, and A. Mansfield (1967) *Occupational Costume in England from the 11th Century to 1914* (London: Adam & Charles Black), pp. 371–377.

37. E. Wilson (1974) *History of Shoe Fashions* (London: Pitman), pp. 68, 70, 91, 142.

38. T. Wright (1922) *Romance of the Shoe* (London: C. J. Forncomb), pp. 163, 170, 181.

39. J. O'Faolain and L. Martines, eds. (1973) *Not in God's Image* (New York: Harper Colophone Books), pp. 155, 157, 163; M. Richmond-Abbott (1979) *The American Woman: Her Past, Her Present, Her Future* (New York: Holt, Rinehart and Winston), p. 637.

40. M. Chaytor and J. Lewis (1982) "Introduction," in *Working Life of Women in the Seventeenth Century,* ed. A. Clark (London: Routledge and Kegan Paul), pp. ix–xxxxviii.

41. O'Faolain and Martines, op. cit., p. 154.

42. M. Bloch (1961) *Feudal Society,* trans. L. A. Manyon (Chicago: University of Chicago Press), pp. 359–374; E. H. Kantrowicz (1966) "Kingship Under the Impact of Scientific Jurisprudence," in *Twelfth-Century Europe and the Foundations of Modern Society,* ed. M. Clagett, G. Post, and R. Reynolds (Westport, Conn.: Greenwood Press), pp. 89–105.

43. W. N. Hargreaves-Mawdsley (1963b) *A History of Legal Dress in Europe* (Oxford: Clarendon Press).

44. Ibid., pp. 31–58.

45. E. McClellan (1904) *Historic Dress in America* (Philadelphia: George W. Jacobs), pp. 148, 335.

46. Ibid., pp. 114–115.

47. Ibid., p. 340.

48. Bloch, op. cit., pp. 312–319; P. Cunnington (1974) *Costume of Household Servants from the Middle Ages to 1900* (New York: Barnes and Noble), pp. 156–160.

49. L. Twining (1967) *European Regalia* (London: B. T. Batsford), pp. 4–19.

50. W. Y. Carman (1957) *British Military Uniforms from Contemporary Pictures: Henry VII to the Present Day* (London: Leonard Hall).

51. Earle, op. cit., pp. 697–698.

52. Elias, op. cit., pp. 291–309.

53. Cunnington, Lucas, and Mansfield, op. cit., pp. 254–260.

Chapter 7

1. G. P. Stone (1962) "Appearance and the Self," *Human Behavior and Social Processes*, ed. A. Rose (Boston: Houghton Mifflin).

2. S. M. Levin, J. Balistieri, and M. Schukit (1972) "The Development of Sexual Discrimination in Children," *Journal of Social Psychology and Psychiatry* 13: 47–53.

3. E. Goffman (1979) *Advertisements* (New York: Harper and Row).

4. J. C. Flugel (1966) *The Psychology of Clothes* (London: Hogarth Press), pp. 25–30.

5. J. Laver (1969) *Modesty in Dress* (Boston: Houghton Mifflin), pp. 1–44.

6. Stone, op. cit., pp. 107–110.

7. E. Gross and G. P. Stone (1964), in "Embarrassment and the Analysis of Role Requirements," *American Journal of Sociology* 57: 1–15, also argued that male attire acts to initiate and mobilize interaction; as an identity document it presents a man's social title.

8. R. L. Coser (1986) "Cognitive Structure and the Use of Social Space," *Sociological Forum* 1: 1–26.

9. "She Is No Barbie, Nor Does She Care to Be," *New York Times*, August 15, 1991. In this article the 1991 Santa's list included a "Happy to Be Me Doll" that had bendable arms and legs, making it easier to dress it and to pose it in action "like active women who enjoy and get involved in life." Her wardrobe consisted of only nine outfits—easier on parents' pocketbooks in a time of recession. "Shaped more like an average woman," she was designed to be "a wholesome alternative for little girls who like to dress up dolls." The "Happy to Be Me" measurements of 36-27-38 were more realistic than Barbie's 36-18-33.

10. "Seeking a Place on Santa's List," *New York Times*, February 11, 1991. In the 1980s, Barbie was joined by Cabbage Patch Dolls, the Magic Nursery Doll, and My Pretty Ballerina.

11. T. Carlyle (1967) *Sartor Resartus* (New York: Dutton), p. 23. Originally published 1838. Also P. Cunnington, C. Lucas, and A. Mansfield (1967), in *Occupational Costume in England from the 11th Century to 1914* (London: Adam & Charles Black), pp. 32–36, reported that for many centuries, aprons of different colors and patterns were worn in England by different occupational groups: blue for gardeners; black for cobblers; checks for barbers. Those who wanted to be recognized as skilled rather than menial laborers wore white aprons, which they starched and pressed. Since aprons were used by those performing menial tasks, in time an "aproned person" denoted an individual deemed of lesser value. The "aproned person" continued as a social category in the new land. In his first article published in *The New England Courant* on April 2, 1722, Benjamin Franklin wrote: "And since it observed, that the Generality of People, now a days, are unwilling either to commend or dispraise what they read, until they are in some measure informed who or what the author of it is, whether he is poor or rich, old or young, a Scollar or a Leather Apron Man ... and give Opinion on the Performance according to the Knowledge they have of the author's cir-

cumstances" (C. M. Picket [1977] *Voices of the Past: Key Documents in the History of American Journalism* [New York: John Wiley and Sons], p. 26).

12. A. A. Albert and J. R. Porter (1988) "Children's Gender-Role Stereotypes," *Sociological Forum* 3: 184–210.

13. S. B. Kaiser, M. Ruddy, and P. Byfield (1982) "The Role of Clothing in Sex-Role Socialization: Persons' Perception Versus Overt Behavior," in *Proceedings of the Regional Meetings,* Association of College Professors of Textiles and Clothing, pp. 288–289. Reported in S. B. Kaiser (1985) *The Social Psychology of Clothing* (New York: Macmillan), pp. 288–289.

14. A. L. Rowse (1971) *The Elizabethan Renaissance: The Life of the Society* (New York: Scribner's), p. 161.

15. 1 Cor. 11:4–10.

16. 1 Cor. 14:34–35.

17. 1 Tim. 2:11–15.

18. B. P. Prusak (1974) "Women: Seductive Siren and Source of Sin," in *Religion and Sexism: Images of Women in Jewish and Christian Traditions,* ed. R. R. Reuther (New York: Simon and Schuster), p. 101.

19. S. Lyman (1978) *The Seven Deadly Sins: Society and Evil* (New York: St. Martin's), pp. 23, 110–117.

20. Ibid., p. 23.

21. Ibid., p. 22.

22. Ibid., pp. 110–111.

23. *Altarpiece of St. John the Baptist and St. John the Evangelist, 1479,* in St. John's Hospital, the Memlingmuseum in Bruges. In the nineteenth century the cult of the "femme fatale" spread throughout the West, affecting not only painting and sculpture but also illustration, the decorative arts, performing arts, and literature—both popular and esoteric—and probably affected male attitudes and behavior toward women, as Patrick Bade pointed out in *Femme Fatale* (1979) (New York: Mayflower Books).

24. H. Lobelle-Caluwe (n.d.) The *Memlingmuseum* in St. John Hospital (Bruges: Die Keure), pp. 66–82.

25. Metropolitan Museum of Art (1982) *The Art of Chivalry* (New York: American Federation of Arts).

26. A. Marwick (1988) *Beauty in History* (London: Thames and Hudson), p. 68.

27. R. Pistolese and R. Horsting (1970) *History of Fashions* (New York: John Wiley and Sons), pp. 118–121.

28. B. Payne, G. Weinakor, and J. Farrell-Beck (1992) *The History of Costume* (New York: HarperCollins), pp. 190–203.

29. D. B. Van Dalen, E. D. Mitchell, and B. L. Bennett (1953) *A World History of Physical Education* (Englewood Cliffs, N.J.: Prentice-Hall), pp. 104–155.

30. J. Strutt (1876) *The Sports and Pastimes of the People of England* (London: Chatto and Windus); P. Cunnington and A. Mansfield (1969) *English Costume for Sport and Recreation* (New York: Barnes and Noble), p. 134.

31. M. Kraus (1959) *The United States to 1865* (Ann Arbor: University of Michigan Press), p. 327; F. R. Dulles (1965) *America Learns to Play: A History of Recreation* (New York: Appleton-Century), p. 137; L. W. Banner (1983) *American Beauty: A Social History Through Two Centuries of the American Idea, Ideal, and Image of the Beautiful Woman* (New York: Knopf), pp. 229–231; C. W. Griffin (1982) "Physical Fitness," in *Concise Histories of American Popular Culture,* ed. M. T. Inge (Westport, Conn.: Greenwood Press), pp. 262–269; Van Dalen, Mitchell, and Bennett, op. cit., pp. 366–369.

32. D. Riesman and R. Denney (1951), republished as "Football in America: A Study in Culture Diffusion," in *The Sporting Image,* ed. P. J. Zingg (New York: University Press of America), pp. 209–225.

33. Augustine (1972) *Concerning the City of God Against the Pagans*, book 14, trans. H. Bettenson, ed. D. Knowls (Harmondsworth: Penguin), chap. 16, p. 577.

34. L. White, Jr. (1970) *Medieval Technology and Social Change* (Oxford: Oxford University Press).

35. M. von Boehn (1932) *Modes and Manners*, vol. 1, trans. J. Joshua (New York: B. Blom), p. 280.

36. R. S. Wieck (1988) *Time Sanctified: The Book of Hours in Medieval Art and Life* (New York: George Braziller).

37. B. Castiglione (1959) *The Book of the Courtier*, trans. C. H. Singleton (Garden City, N.Y.: Doubleday/Anchor Books).

38. S. Thrupp (1948) *The Merchant Class of Medieval London* (Ann Arbor: University of Michigan Press), pp. 169–174. Similarly, W. Boulting (1910) reported that women in the fourteenth, fifteenth, and sixteenth centuries worked in occupations that varied from water carriers to painters to governesses. See W. Boulting, *Women in Italy* (London: Methuen), pp. 336–339. See also A. Abram (1916) "Women Traders in Medieval London," *Economic Journal* (26): 276–285.

39. J. Rossiaud (1985) "Prostitution, Sex and Society in French Towns in the Fifteenth Century, in *Western Sexuality: Practice and Precept in Past and Present Times*, ed. P. Aries and A. Bejin (New York: Basil Blackwell), pp. 76–113.

40. J. M. Vincent (1935) *Costume and Conduct in the Laws of Basel, Bern and Zurich 1370–1800* (Baltimore: Johns Hopkins University Press), pp. 44–45. Also T. Veblen (1953) *The Theory of the Leisure Class* (New York: Mentor), pp. 123–124. Originally published 1899. Also Q. Bell (1976) *On Human Finery* (New York: Schocken Books), pp. 139–141.

41. G. Chaucer (1952) *Canterbury Tales*, trans. N. Coghill (Baltimore: Penguin Books), pp. 29–30, 274–296.

42. Art historian Anne Hollander warned against interpreting a fashion in which the stomach is emphasized as suggesting pregnancy. Paintings representing the pregnant Virgin Mary visiting the pregnant Saint Elizabeth often show "the women with a hand placed on the other's belly but their bellies are no more enlarged then they would normally be." See A. Hollander (1978) *Seeing Through Clothes* (New York: Viking), pp. 109–110. However, over a two-hundred-year period the black plague decimated a large portion of Europe's population. Veneration of the Madonna and fear of death characterized the period. Women's power to nourish through breast-feeding acquired religious meaning in early Renaissance culture, as M. R. Miles (1985) pointed out in the "Virgin's One Bare Breast: Female Nudity and Religious Meaning in Tuscan Early Renaissance Art," in *The Female Body in Western Culture*, ed. S. R. Suleiman (Cambridge: Harvard University Press), p. 110. In Elizabethan England the queen's body figured as a political motherhood, concluded L. A. Montrose (1983) in "Shaping Fantasies Figurative of Gender and Power in Elizabethan Culture," *Representations* 1: 2. Queen Elizabeth's uncovered bosom signified her status as a maiden, but the shape of her breasts was that of a "selfless bountiful mother." The desired message was that the queen was the source of her subject's sustenance (p. 64). A. Marwick, moreover, noted that in the later Middle Ages sensuousness was considered beautiful. In the *Temptation of St. Anthony* by Henrick Met de Bles (known as Il Civetta), from the mid-sixteenth century, the breasts and stomachs are large and "highly tactile," suggesting physical intimacy. See A. Marwick (1988) *Beauty in History* (London: Thames and Hudson), pp. 68–69.

43. C. B. Milbank (1989) *New York Fashion: The Evolution of American Style* (New York: Harry N. Abrams), pp. 170–199.

44. M. and A. Batterberry (1977) *Fashion: The Mirror of History* (New York: Greenwich House), pp. 100–108; Hollander, op. cit., pp. 365–367, 383.

45. F. Boucher (1965) *Twenty Thousand Years of Fashion* (New York: Henry N. Abrams), pp. 223–225; M. and A. Batterberry, op. cit., pp. 124–127.

46. J. T. Molloy (1977) *The Women Dress for Success Book* (Chicago: Follett Publishing).

47. M. Warner (1982) *Joan of Arc: The Image of Female Heroism* (New York: Vintage), p. 149; P. Brown (1988) *The Body and Society* (New York: Columbia University Press), pp. 1–2, 156–159.

48. Warner, op. cit., p. 135.

49. Ibid., pp. 154–155, 169.

50. L. M. Guthrie (1984) "I Was a Yeomanette," in *Proceedings, U.S. Naval Institute* (Annapolis, Md.: U.S. Naval Institute); S. H. Godson (1984) "Women Power in World War I," in *Proceedings, U.S. Naval Institute* (Annapolis, Md.: U.S. Naval Institute).

51. L. W. Banner (1983) *American Beauty: A Social History … Through Two Centuries of the American Idea, Ideal, and Image of the Beautiful Woman* (New York: Knopf), p. 174.

52. *New York Times*, August 1, 1991.

53. R. Borker (1978) "To Honor Her Head: Hats as a Symbol of Women's Position in Three Evangelical Churches in Edinburgh, Scotland," in J. Hoch–Smith (1978) *Women in Ritual and Symbolic Roles* (New York: Plenum), pp. 55–72.

54. For the description of the various current styles, see D. Hoffman's article, "The Fashion in Getting Fit," *New York Times*, November 5, 1989.

55. *New York Times*, March 10, 1991.

56. *New York Times*, July 9, 1991.

Chapter 8

1. P. B. Gove, ed. (1967) *Webster's Third New Dictionary of the English Language* (Springfield, Mass.: G & C Merriam).

2. K. Myers (1988) "Fashion 'n' Passion: A Working Paper," in *Zoot Suits and Second-Hand Dresses: An Anthology of Fashion and Music*, ed. A. McRobbie (Boston: Unwin Hyman), pp. 189–197.

3. B. P. Prusak (1974) "Women: Seductive Siren and Source of Sin," in *Religion and Sexism: Images of Women in Jewish and Christian Traditions*, ed. R. R. Reuther (New York: Simon and Schuster), pp. 85–142.

4. S. M. Lyman (1989) *The Seven Deadly Sins: Society and Evil*, revised and expanded edition (Dix Hills, N.Y.: General Hall), pp. 54–56.

5. Prusak, op. cit., pp. 101, 105.

6. M. von Boehn (1932) *Modes and Manners*, vol. 1, trans. J. Joshua (New York: B. Blom), pp. 207–208, 280.

7. Ibid., p. 280.

8. Prusak, op. cit., p. 101.

9. Ibid., p. 99.

10. L. Langner (1959) *The Importance of Wearing Clothes* (New York: Hastings House), pp. 46–47.

11. *The Statutes at Large from the Magna Carta to the End of the Eleventh Parliament of Great Britain (1701)*, vol. 1 (1762), ed. D. Pickering (Cambridge: Cambridge University Press), p. 383.

12. L. Mahood (1990) *The Magdalenes: Prostitution in the Nineteenth Century* (New York: Routledge, Chapman and Hall), p. 42.

13. G. Simmel (1957) "Fashion," *American Journal of Sociology* 62: 541–558. Originally published 1904.

14. M. Baerwald and T. Mahony (1960) *The Story of Jewelry* (New York: Abelard-Schuman); also M. Wilson (1967) *Gems* (New York: Viking), p. 98.

15. M. and A. Batterberry (1977) *Fashion: The Mirror of History* (New York: Greenwich House), p. 107; also A. Hollander (1978) *Seeing Through Clothes* (New York: Viking), pp. 187–189.

16. M. Scott (1980) *The History of Dress Series, Late Gothic Europe, 1400–1500* (London: Mills and Boon).

17. J. Mayo (1984) *A History of Ecclesiastical Dress* (New York: Holmes and Meier), pp. 40, 61.

18. F. Boucher (1965) *Twenty Thousand Years of Fashion* (New York: Harry N. Abrams), p. 184.

19. Scott, op. cit., pp. 57, 63, 112, illus. 63; M. Davenport (1972) *The Book of Costume* (New York: Crown Publishing), pp. 307–308.

20. L. Lawner (1987) *Lives of the Courtesans* (New York: Rizzoli).

21. M. and A. Batterberry, op. cit., p. 283.

22. Ibid., pp. 326, 327.

23. The custom of kings' acquiring mistresses as feminine companions was common. The term "courtesan" surfaced in French in 1549. It was spelled "courtisan" and had no attached definition. By 1587 it designated "one attached to a prince." In the court language of 1601 in Italy, a "courtizan" was described as follows: "A whore is for every rascal, a courtizan is for the cortizen, individuals attached to the court." See *Oxford English Dictionary on Historical Principles* (1955), ed. C. T. Onions (Oxford: Clarendon Press), p. 1061. With Henry IV (1589–1610), courtesans became "status symbols" displayed in public to demonstrate and compare with those of other monarchs. See V. and B. Bullough (1978) *Prostitution: An Illustrated Social History* (New York: Crown Publishers), p. 147. A liaison with the king was "profitable." Many women gathered around the palace hoping to catch the king's eye.

24. M. and A. Batterberry, op. cit., p. 161.

25. A. Marwick (1988) *Beauty in History* (London: Thames and Hudson), p. 112.

26. M. and A. Batterberry, op. cit., p. 165.

27. G. L. Mosse (1978) *The Final Solution: A History of European Racism* (New York: Howard Fertig), pp. 8–9.

28. According to art historian Kenneth Clark (1956) in *The Nude: A Study in Ideal Art Form* (London: John Murray), the depiction of the nude in Greek art underwent changes that mirrored changes in desired social conduct. It went "from the physical to the moral sphere." Early sculptures presented proud naked men. They were rigid figures in repose. Later, the finely tuned muscles of athletes and soldiers in action inspired artists to focus on showing the movement in the body and supported the idea that the male body should be battle-ready. By the fifth century, when democracy became a political and social goal, a new ideal of beauty was evident. Harmonious proportions emphasized a balanced whole, communicating strength, grace, and gentleness and reflected the search for an orderly society.

29. Marwick, op. cit., p. 85.

30. M. Kates, "Do You Look Good in Purple and Puce? Pay $35 and Find Out: 'Personal Color Consultant' Offers Colorful Suggestions," *Wall Street Journal*, August 6, 1973.

31. S. Caygill (1980) *Color the Essence of You* (Millbrae, Calif.: Celestial Arts).

32. C. Jackson (1973) *Color Me Beautiful: Discover Your Natural Beauty Through the Colors that Make You Look Great and Feel Fabulous* (New York: Ballantine Books). Umberto Eco suggested that we communicate with color. Color in a society is categorized by codes and units of expression; members of a group recognize a limited number of them. To produce a more refined social consciousness of "our cultural way of defining contents," artistic activity often works against such social codes and collective categorization. See U. Eco (1986) "How Culture Conditions the Colors We See." In *On Signs,* ed. M. Blonsky (Baltimore: Johns Hopkins University Press), pp. 157–176.

33. *Webster's Third International Dictionary, Unabridged* (1967) (Springfield, Mass.: G & C Merriam), p. 962.

34. In the latter part of the nineteenth century, however, an "elitist" pattern of consumption emerged. Although courtly life was dead, Rosalind H. Williams observed, the ex-

ternal forms of courtly taste assumed new importance, outlasting the social order in which they originated. See R. H. Williams (1982) *Dream Worlds: Mass Consumption in Late Ninteenth-Century France* (Berkeley: University of California Press), pp. 56, 107–153.

35. J. Laver (1963) *Costume* (New York: Hawthorne Books), pp. 88–95; B. Payne, G. Weinakor, and J. Farrell-Beck (1992) *The History of Costume: From Ancient Mesopotamia Through the Twentieth Century* (New York: HarperCollins), pp. 486–488, 502–504; E. Saunders (1955) *The Age of Worth: Couturier to Empress Eugenie* (Bloomington: Indiana University Press), pp. 40, 49, 126–127.

36. J. Richardson (1966) *The Courtesan* (Cleveland: World Publishing), p. 1.

37. Marwick, op. cit., pp. 272–282.

38. Richardson, op. cit., pp. 209–210.

39. Ibid., pp. 227–230.

40. Models also became objects of envy, as the Ziegfeld girl had before. So esteemed had the model become by the mid-1920s that John Robert Powers, an out-of-work actor who organized the first modeling agency, was able to employ New York debutantes—women who normally considered work degrading. See L. W. Banner (1983) *American Beauty: A Social History Through Two Centuries of the American Idea, Ideal, and Image of the Beautiful Woman* (New York: Knopf), p. 263.

41. L. A. Erensberg (1981) *Steppin' Out: New York Nightlife and the Transformation of American Culture, 1890–1930* (Westport, Conn.: Greenwood Press).

42. C. F. Funnell (1983) *By the Beautiful Sea* (New Brunswick, N.J.: Rutgers University Press), pp. 148–149.

43. R. Wolf (1991) *Goya and the Satirical Print in England and on the Continent 1730–1850* (Boston: Boston College Museum of Art), pp. 1–4.

44. V. Steele (1991) *Women of Fashion: Twentieth Century Designers* (New York: Rizzoli), p. 108; also M. Turim (1984) "Designing Women," in *Fabrications: Costume and the Female Body*, ed. J. Gains and C. Herzog (New York: Routledge), p. 223.

45. B. Willoughby and R. Schickel (1974) *The Platinum Years* (New York: Random House), pp. 8–11, 245–258.

46. Elia Kazan's 1956 movie *Baby Doll* portrays a thumb-sucking child bride who sleeps in a crib.

47. C. R. Milbank (1989) *New York Fashion* (New York: Harry A. Abrams), pp. 210–216.

48. Wolf, op. cit., pp. 70, 84, 85; also see V. and B. Bullough, op. cit., p. 152.

Chapter 9

1. E. Goffman (1951) "Symbols of Class Status," *British Journal of Sociology* A (4): 294–303.

2. T. Veblen (1953) *The Theory of the Leisure Class* (New York: Mentor Books), p. 42. Originally published 1899.

3. Ibid., p. 199.

4. S. A. Ostrander (1984) *Women of the Upper Class* (Philadelphia: Temple University Press), p. 3.

5. D. McClelland (1961) *The Achieving Society* (Princeton: Van Nostrand).

6. Goffman, op. cit.; W. H. Form and G. P. Stone (1957) "Urbanism, Anonimity and Status Symbolism," *American Journal of Sociology* 62 (5): 504–514.

7. M. Mann (1986) *The Sources of Social Power*, vol. 1 (Cambridge: Cambridge University Press).

8. M. Bloch (1961) *Feudal Society*, vols. 1 and 2, trans. L. A. Manyon (Chicago: University of Chicago Press); F. L. Ganshof (1961) *Feudalism*, trans. P. Grierson (New York: Harper and Row).

9. Mann, op. cit., p. 399.

10. Ibid., p. 337.

11. Ibid., p. 409.

12. Ibid., p. 397.

13. Ibid., pp. 381–390; J. M. Vincent (1935) *Costume and Conduct in the Laws of Basel, Bern and Zurich 1370–1800* (Baltimore: Johns Hopkins University Press).

14. S. M. Lyman (1989) *The Seven Deadly Sins: Society and Evil*, revised and expanded ed. (Dix Hills, N.Y.: General Hall), pp. 136–137.

15. Ibid., 141–142.

16. C. Morris (1972) *The Discovery of the Individual 1050–1200* (New York: Harper Torchbooks), pp. 158–160.

17. Ibid., pp. 139–140.

18. Ibid., pp. 37–49; Mann, op. cit., 383–390.

19. M. Chambers et al. (1974) *The Western Experience* (New York: Knopf), pp. 306–307.

20. Morris, op. cit., p. 74.

21. M. and A. Batterberry (1977) *Fashion: The Mirror of History* (New York: Greenwich House), p. 86.

22. U. Eco (1986) *Art and Beauty in the Middle Ages* (New Haven: Yale University Press), p. 7.

23. Ibid., p. 6.

24. Ibid., p. 13.

25. Ibid., p. 15.

26. Mann, op. cit., p. 409.

27. M. and A. Batterberry, op. cit., p. 71.

28. F. Boucher (1965) *Twenty Thousand Years of Fashion* (New York: Harry N. Abrams), p. 164.

29. Ibid., p. 163.

30. Ibid., p. 164.

31. M. and A. Batterberry, op. cit., p. 71.

32. Ibid., p. 70.

33. *Encyclopedia Britannica* (1911), 11th ed., vol. 27 (Cambridge: Cambridge University Press); F. E. Baldwin (1928) *Sumptuous Legislation and Personal Regulation in England* (Baltimore: Johns Hopkins University Press), p. 45; Vincent, op. cit.; *The Statutes at Large from the Magna Carta to the End of the Eleventh Parliament of Great Britain (1701)*, vol. 1 (1762), ed. D. Pickering (Cambridge: Cambridge University Press), p. 466.

34. J. Schneider (1978) "Peacocks and Penguins: The Political Economy of European Cloth and Colors," *American Ethnologist* 5 (3): 413–447.

35. In Eco, op. cit., pp. 78, 99, 101.

36. J. Maritain (1924) *Art and Scholasticism*, trans. J. F. Scanlan (New York: Scribner's), pp. 46–55.

37. *Selected Writings of St. Thomas Aquinas* (1965), trans. R. P. Goodwin (New York: Bobbs-Merrill), pp. 111–112.

38. Maritain, op. cit., pp. 19–22.

39. Ibid., pp. 22–25, 40–53.

40. In Eco, op. cit., p. 99.

41. M. and A. Batterberry, op. cit., p. 86.

42. R. Pistolese and R. Horsting (1970) *History of Fashions* (New York: John Wiley and Sons), pp. 154–163.

43. R. S. Weick, ed. (1988) *Time Sanctified: The Book of Hours in Medieval Art and Life* (New York: George Braziller), pp. 27–30.

44. V. Reinburg (1988) "Prayers and the Book of Hours," in Weick, op. cit., p. 39.

45. L. R. Poos (1988) "Social History and the Book of Hours," in Weick, op. cit., p. 34.

46. Ibid., p. 37.

Chapter 10

1. The root of the word "leisure" is the Latin *licre*, which means "to be permitted," suggesting that leisure is about the opportunity to do nothing. It is different from recreation, which is an antidote to work and entails a refreshment of the spirit, body, or both and has always been a culturally legitimate activity. Warren I. Susman suggested that leisure as a cultural value emerged in the beginning of the twentieth century as the belief in abundance permeated public consciousness. See W. I. Susman (1984) *Culture as History: The Transformation of American Society in the Twentieth Century* (New York: Pantheon Books), pp. xxii–xxvii. The notion of abundance has characterized the perception of the United States abroad, at least since the beginning of the twentieth century, suggested Stuart and Elizabeth Ewen (1979) in *Channels of Desire: Mass Images and the Shaping of American Consciousness* (New York: McGraw-Hill), pp. 44–47.

2. T. Veblen (1953) *The Theory of the Leisure Class* (New York: Mentor), p. 42. Originally published 1899.

3. Ibid., p. 42.

4. P. Mack (1987) "Political Rhetoric and Poetic Meaning in Renaissance Culture: Clement Marot and the Field of the Cloth of Gold," in *Politics and Culture in Early Modern Europe,* ed. P. Mack and M. C. Jacobs, *Essays in Honor of H. G. Koenigsberger* (Cambridge: Cambridge University Press), p. 59.

5. Ibid., pp. 70–71.

6. J. H. Elliott (1987) "The Court of the Spanish Habsburgs: A Peculiar Institution?" in *Politics and Culture in Early Modern Europe,* ed. P. Mack and M. C. Jacobs, *Essays in Honor of H. G. Koenigsberger* (Cambridge: Cambridge University Press), pp. 1–24.

7. Ibid., pp. 19, 21.

8. Ibid., pp. 20, 23–24.

9. Veblen, op. cit., p. 48.

10. N. Elias (1978) *The Civilizing Process: The Development of Manners* (New York: Urizon), pp. 100–101, 216–217.

11. The Metropolitan Museum of Art (1982) *The Art of Chivalry: European Arms and Armor* (New York: The American Federation of Arts), pp. 11–14; Elias, op. cit., pp. 205–212.

12. The end came about after a series of battles around 1300. Armored mounted knights, surrounded by their retainers, were defeated by armies of infantry pikemen made up of well-to-do farmers and town inhabitants. This sudden shift in the fortunes of war weakened the autonomous lord, hastened the demise of classic feudalism, and eventually led to the death of knighthood and the role behavior and attire of the knight.

13. Elias, op. cit., pp. 102–116.

14. Ibid., p. xv.

15. Veblen, op. cit., pp. 46–49.

Chapter 11

1. J. H. Elliott (1987) "The Court of the Spanish Habsburgs: A Peculiar Institution?" in *Politics and Culture in Early Modern Europe,* ed. P. Mack and M. C. Jacobs (Cambridge: Cambridge University Press), pp. 5–24.

2. A. Hollander (1978) *Seeing Through Clothes* (New York: Viking), pp. 367–369; M. Scott (1980) *The History of Dress Series, Late Gothic Europe, 1400–1500* (London: Mills and Boon); M. and A. Batterberry (1977) *Fashion: The Mirror of History* (New York: Greenwich House), p. 89.

3. C. Mukerji (1983) *From Graven Images: Patterns of Modern Materialism* (New York: Columbia University Press), p. 31.

4. F. Boucher (1965) *Twenty Thousand Years of Fashion: The History of Costume and Personal Adornment* (New York: Harry N. Abrams), p. 210.

5. Mukerji, op. cit., pp. 166–167, 170–171.

6. Scott, op. cit., pp. 30, 32.

7. Hollander, op. cit., p. 367.

8. E. Saunders (1955) *The Age of Worth: Couturier to Empress Eugènie* (Bloomington: Indiana University Press), pp. 111–113.

9. Ibid., pp. 121–122.

10. G. Simmel (1957) "Fashion," *American Journal of Sociology,* 62: 541–558. Originally published 1904.

11. J. Nef (1958) *Cultural Foundation of Industrial Civilization* (New York: Harper and Row).

12. Mukerji, op. cit., pp. 190–228.

13. Simmel, op. cit., p. 549.

Chapter 12

1. N. Wolf (1991) *The Beauty Myth: How Images of Beauty Are Used Against Women* (New York: William Morrow), pp. 18, 102–103, 171–172.

2. S. de Beauvoir (1953) *The Second Sex,* trans. H. M. Parshley (New York: Knopf), pp. xxx, 336, 408–409, 411–412, 428–429; also in A. Marwick (1988) *Beauty in History* (London: Thames and Hudson), p. 29.

3. R. T. Lakoff and R. L. Scherr (1984) *Face Value: The Politics of Beauty* (Boston: Routledge), p. 56.

4. M. Webster, Jr., and J. E. Driskell, Jr. (1983) "Beauty as Status," *American Journal of Sociology* 89 (1): 140–165.

5. Marwick, op. cit., p. 393.

6. That physical attractiveness plays an important role in American society is made evident by the old cliché that "What is beautiful is good," observed G. L. Patzer (1985) in *The Physical Attractiveness Phenomena* (New York: Plenum Press), p. 1. Also see K. K. Dion (1986) "Stereotyping Based on Physical Attractiveness: Issues and Conceptual Perspectives," in *Appearance, Stigma and Social Behavior,* ed. C. P. Herman, M. P. Zanna, and E. T. Higgins, The Ontario Symposium on Personality and Social Psychology, vol. 3 (Hillsdale, N.J.: Erlbaum).

7. J. Ross and K. R. Ferris (1981) "Interpersonal Attraction and Organizational Outcome: A Field Experiment," *Administrative Science Quarterly* 26: 617–632.

8. D. Barthel (1988) *Gender and Advertising: Putting on Appearances* (Philadelphia: Temple University Press).

9. T. Veblen (1953) *The Theory of the Leisure Class* (New York: Mentor Books), p. 108. Originally published 1899.

10. Ibid., p. 107.

11. L. W. Banner (1983) *American Beauty: A Social History Through Two Centuries of the American Idea, Ideal, and Image of the Beautiful Woman* (New York: Knopf), p. 157.

12. D. H. Jacques (1859) *Hints Toward Physical Perfection* (New York: Fowler and Wells), pp. 44–49, 223.

13. D. G. Brinton and G. H. Nepheys (1870) *The Laws of Health in Relation to Human Form* (Springfield, Mass.: W. J. Holland), p. 48.

14. In J. B. Abrams (1983) "The Thinning of America: The Emergence of the Ideal of Slenderness in American Popular Culture, 1870–1930" (Thesis submitted to the Department of History in partial fulfillment of the requirements for the degree of bachelor of arts with honors, Harvard University), pp. 3–6.

15. T. S. Sozinskey (1877) *The Culture of Beauty* (Philadelphia: Allen, Lane and Scott), p. 63.

16. Banner, op. cit., p. 11.

17. Banner, op. cit., pp. 266–269.

18. Lakoff and Scherr, op. cit., pp. 78–79.

19. Ibid., p. 77.

20. C. R. Milbank (1989) *New York Fashion: The Evolution of American Style* (New York: Harry N. Abrams), pp. 206, 210, 226.

21. B. Payne, G. Weinakor, and J. Farrell-Beck (1992) *The History of Costume: From Ancient Mesopotamia Through the Twentieth Century* (New York: HarperCollins), pp. 614–615; M. and A. Batterberry (1977) *Fashion: The Mirror of History* (New York: Greenwich House), pp. 383–385.

22. M. and A. Batterberry, op. cit., pp. 282–283.

23. T. A. Bailey and D. M. Kennedy (1987) *The American Pageant* (Lexington, Mass.: D. C. Heath), pp. 589–590.

24. Lakoff and Scherr, op. cit., p. 103.

25. Veblen, op. cit., p. 125.

26. Ibid., pp. 94–97, 109.

27. Marwick, op. cit., pp. 414–415.

28. Ibid., p. 414.

29. A. R. Burns (1965) *The Pelican History of Greece* (New York: Penguin Books), pp. 73, 199.

30. K. Clark (1956) *The Nude: A Study of Ideal Art* (London: John Murray), p. 25.

31. Ibid., p. 48; also H. Hoover and J. Fleming (1982) *The Visual Arts: A History,* 3d ed. (Englewood Cliffs, N.J.: Prentice-Hall), pp. 148–149.

32. M. Chambers et al. (1974) *The Western Experience* (New York: Knopf), pp. 76–77.

33. In films, bad guys look bad. They are marked by various disfigurements and disabilities, such as missing limbs and eyes, as R. Bogdan pointed out in his study of freak shows. The beautiful queen in *Snow White and the Seven Dwarfs* was transformed into a wart-nosed hunchback before she set out to accomplish her hideous scheme. Another example is Captain Hook in *Peter Pan.* In horror films the association of evil with disability is even more common, Bogdan pointed out. "Monsters" are deformed, disproportionately built, exceptionally large, exceptionally small, or speech impaired, and in the film they are perpetrators of violence. See R. Bogdan (1988) *Freak Shows: Presenting Human Oddities for Amusement and Profit* (Chicago: University of Chicago Press), pp. vii–viii.

34. H. Sigall and N. Ostrove (1975) "Beautiful But Dangerous: Effects of Offender Attractiveness and Nature of the Crime on Juridic Judgement," *Journal of Personality and School Psychology* 31 (3) 410–414.

35. G. L. Mosse (1978) *The Final Solution: A History of European Racism* (New York: Howard Fertig), p. 94.

36. S. L. Gilman (1985) *Difference and Pathology: Stereotypes of Sexuality, Race and Madness* (Ithaca, N.Y.: Cornell University Press), pp. 15–31, 76–108.

37. In Marwick, op. cit., p. 247.

38. Ibid., p. 247.

39. Ibid., pp. 167–193.

40. J. Richardson (1967) *The Courtesan* (Cleveland: World Publishing); A. Latour (1958) *Kings of Fashion,* trans. M. Savill (London: Weidenfeld & Nicholson).

41. *New York Times,* September 16, 1991.

42. Marwick, op. cit., p. 289.

43. Richardson, op. cit., pp. 220–231.

44. Banner, op. cit., pp. 258–259.

45. Bogdan, op. cit., pp. 3–11.

46. W. Chapkis (1986) *Beauty Secrets: Women and the Politics of Appearance* (Boston: South End Press), pp. 1–2.

47. M. T. Gnudi and J. P. Webster (1950) *The Life and Times of Gaspare Tagliacozzi: Surgeon of Bologna 1545–1599* (New York: Herbert Reichner).

48. "Children's Height Linked to Test Scores," *New York Times,* October 2, 1986; "Two French Doctors Face Charges for Hormone Use," *New York Times,* July 22, 1993.

49. S. Cohen, "Nip and Tuck: To These Six Plastic Surgeons Beauty Is Not Skin-Deep. It's a Measure of Creativity," *New York Times,* August 9, 1992.

50. *New York Times,* September 24, 1991.

51. *New York Times,* September 25, 1991.

52. E. Rosenthal, "Revising Plastic Surgery to Preserve Ethnic Identity," *New York Times,* September 25, 1991.

53. H. C. Bredemeier and J. Toby (1960) *Social Problems in America* (New York: John Wiley and Sons), pp. 17–18.

54. J. Hansen and E. Reed (1986) *Cosmetics, Fashions and the Exploitation of Women* (New York: Pathfinder Press), pp. 48–50.

55. Ibid., p. 57.

56. Lakoff and Scherr, op. cit., p. 143.

57. Ibid., p. 142.

Chapter 13

1. *New York Times,* November 11, 1991.

2. L. W. Banner (1983) *American Beauty: A Social History Through Two Centuries of the American Idea, Ideal, and Image of the Beautiful Woman* (New York: Knopf), p. 219.

3. Ibid., p. 220.

4. Ibid., p. 221.

5. Ibid., pp. 207–208.

6. A. Marwick (1988) *Beauty in History* (London: Thames and Hudson), p. 225.

7. Banner, op. cit., p. 223.

8. Ibid., p. 224.

9. The term "stigma" is of Greek derivation and was originally a mark carved or burnt into the skin to identify undesirables. The ancient Greeks believed strongly that those who violated exisiting norms (traitors, criminals, slaves) needed to be identified so they could be avoided. Erving Goffman applied the concept to modern society. He argued that those with traits that differ from the normal or normative in society are treated as if they bear a mark of disgrace. The person is stigmatized as others withdraw their acceptance and distort the person's real identity to fit stereotypical expectations. See E. Goffman (1963b) *Stigma: Notes on the Management of a Spoiled Identity* (Englewood Cliffs, N.J.: Prentice-Hall).

10. U. Sinclair (1927) *Oil!* (New York: Albert Charles Boni), p. 332.

11. N. Wolf (1991) *The Beauty Myth: How Images of Beauty Are Used Against Women* (New York: William Morrow).

12. *New York Times,* May 28, 1991.

13. T. Brokaw, "Senior-Circuited," *New York Times Magazine,* January 6, 1991.

14. B. B. Hess (1976) *Growing Old in America* (New Brunswick, N.J.: Transaction Books), pp. 20–26.

15. Goffman, op. cit.

16. E. C. Hughes (1945) "Dilemmas and Contradictions of Status," *American Journal of Sociology* (50): 353–359.

17. Goffman, op. cit., p. 91.

18. *New York Times,* June 7, 1993.

19. A. Achenbaum (1978) *Old Age in the New Land* (Baltimore, Md.: Johns Hopkins University Press).

20. S. Ewen (1976) *Captains of Consciousness* (New York: McGraw-Hill).

21. C. Perati (1987) *Extraordinary Origins of Everyday Things* (New York: Harper and Row).

22. Ibid., pp. 24–27.

23. P. J. Zingg (1988) "Myth and Metaphor: Baseball in the History and Literature of American Sport," in *The Sporting Image: Readings in American Sport History*, ed. P. J. Zingg (Lanham, Md.: University Press of America), pp. 253–272; also "Progress and Flight: An Interpretation of the American Cycle Craze of the 1890s," *The Sporting Image: Readings in American Sport History*, ed. P. J. Zingg (Lanham, Md.: University Press of America), pp. 227–246; D. S. Eitzen and G. H. Sage (1988) *Sociology of American Sport* (Dubuque, Iowa: Wm. C. Brown), p. 28.

24. Ewen, op. cit., pp. 41–47.

25. Ibid., pp. 114–116, 162.

26. H. S. Canby (1947) *American Memoire* (Boston: Houghton Mifflin).

27. F. R. Dulles (1940) *America Learns to Play: A History of Popular Recreation 1607–1940* (New York: Appleton-Century); also P. J. Zingg, ed. (1988) *The Sporting Image: Readings in American Sport History* (Lanham, Md.: University Press of America).

28. L. A. Sussmann (1989) "The Women's Movement, the Women's Colleges and Modern Dance" (Paper delivered at the Meetings of the Eastern Sociological Society, March 16–19).

29. M. L. Rosenkrantz (1972) *Clothing Concepts: A Social Psychological Approach* (New York: Macmillan), p. 213.

30. *New York Times*, May 28, 1991.

31. *New York Times*, May 13, 1991.

32. T. Smeeding, B. Boyle Torrey, and M. Rein (1988) "Patterns of Income and Poverty: The Economic Status of Children and the Elderly in Eight Countries," in *The Vulnerable*, ed. J. L. Palmer, T. Smeeding, and B. Boyle Torrey (Washington, D.C.: Urban Institute Press), p. 115.

33. R. Reinhold, "New Population Trends Transforming U.S.," *New York Times*, January 6, 1977.

34. P. Kerr, *New York Times*, August 27, 1991.

35. J. Weed (1991) "The Life of a Marriage," in *Sociology*, 4th ed., ed. B. B. Hess, E. W. Markson, and P. J. Stein (New York: Macmillan), pp. 296, 297.

36. D. Riesman (1954) "Some Clinical and Cultural Aspects of the Aging Process," in *Individualism Reconsidered* (New York: Free Press), pp. 484–491.

37. R. Baker, *New York Times*, July 17, 1993.

38. Riesman, op. cit., pp. 486–489.

39. J. B. Kessler (1980) *Getting Even with Getting Old* (Chicago: Nelson-Hall), p. 121.

Chapter 14

1. J. R. Head, Sr. (1967) "Medicine from 1800 to 1850," in *The Growth of Modern Medicine*, ed. F. Stenn (Springfield, Ill.: Charles C. Thomas), pp. 107–123.

2. N. Poynter (1971) *Medicine and Man* (London: C. A. Watts), p. 23.

3. M. E. Lichtenstein (1967) "The Origins of Modern Surgery: 1850–1900," in *The Growth of Modern Medicine*, ed. F. Stenn (Springfield, Ill.: Charles C. Thomas), pp. 124–136.

4. S. E. Cayleff (1987) *Wash and Be Healed: The Water-Cure Movement and Women's Health* (Philadelphia: Temple University Press); also A. C. and M. Fellman (1981) *Making Sense of Self: Medical Advice Literature in Late Nineteenth-Century America* (Philadelphia: University of Pennsylvania Press).

5. Head, op. cit., p. 111.

6. Reader's Digest (1980) *Stories Behind Everyday Things* (Pleasantville, N.Y.: Reader's Digest Association), p. 34.

7. C. Perati (1987) *Extraordinary Origins of Everyday Things* (New York: Harper and Row).

8. Reader's Digest, op. cit.

9. Ibid.

10. Ibid., p. 35.

11. Cayleff, op. cit., pp. 110–112.

12. W. Root and R. de Rochemont (1976) *Eating in America: A History* (New York: Ecco Press); Cayleff, op. cit., p. 118.

13. C. J. Rooney, Jr. (1985) *Dreams and Visions: A Study of American Utopias 1865–1917* (Westport, Conn.: Greenwood Press), p. 159.

14. W. H. Wehrmacher (1967) "Medicine Since 1900," in *The Growth of Modern Medicine*, ed. F. Stenn (Springfield, Ill.: Charles C. Thomas), p. 139.

15. A. C. and M. Fellman, op. cit.

16. W. I. Susman (1984) *Culture as History: The Transformation of American Society in the Twentieth Century* (New York: Pantheon Books), p. 112.

17. R. and J. Dubos (1952) *The White Plague: Tuberculosis, Man and Society* (Boston: Little, Brown), pp. 33–43.

18. Ibid., pp. 169–172, 213–219.

19. H. Woods (1910) *The Conquest of Consumption* (New York: Houghton Mifflin).

20. *Los Angeles Evening Herald*, September 4, 1920.

21. F. M. Pottinger (1952) *The Fight Against Tuberculosis* (New York: Henry Schuman).

22. Susman, op. cit., p. 112.

23. J. J. Mulheron (1879) "Obesity—A Few Thoughts on Its Nature and Treatment," *New Preparations* 3 (11): 271.

24. I. L. Dublin (1930) "The Influence of Weight on Certain Causes of Death," *Human Biology* 2 (2): 160–184.

25. L. E. Axtell (1916) "Obesity: Its Related Pathology," *Journal of the Michigan State Medical Society* 15 (5): 226–231.

26. A. Kellerman (1918) *Physical Beauty* (New York: George H. Doran), pp. 15–26.

27. L. H. Peters (1918) *Diet and Health with Key to Calories* (Chicago: Reilly & Lee). This book was ranked sixth on the non-fiction best-seller list in 1923 and first in 1924 and 1925. Reported in A. P. Hackett and J. H. Burke (1977) *Eighty Years of Best Sellers, 1895–1975* (New York: Bowker).

28. E. H. Ackerknecht (1982) *A Short History of Medicine* (Baltimore, Md.: Johns Hopkins University Press), p. 231.

29. The Wellness Letters have also been turned into encyclopedias of health information. See, for example, the University of California, Berkeley (1991) *The Wellness Encyclopedia: The Comprehensive Family Resource for Safeguarding Health and Preventing Illness* (Boston: Houghton Mifflin).

30. *New York Times*, July 28, 1993.

31. W. G. Sumner (1925) *What Social Classes Owe to Each Other* (New Haven: Yale University Press), pp. 43–44.

32. *New York Times*, January 23, 1989.

33. U. Sinclair (1927) *Oil!* (New York: Albert Charles Boni), p. 294.

34. P. Nystrom (1928) *The Economics of Fashion* (New York: Roland Press), p. 9.

35. Pottinger, op. cit., pp. 205–208.

36. *New York Times*, February 10, 1991.

Chapter 15

1. E. Goffman (1971) *Relations in Public* (New York: Harper and Row), p. 202.

2. Ibid., pp. 195–237. Goffman (1963b) called clothing tie-signs "stigma symbols that are voluntarily employed" in *Stigma: Notes on the Management of Spoiled Identity* (Englewood Cliffs, N.J.: Prentice-Hall), pp. 46, 144–145.

3. The notion of a counterculture, a subculture whose values, norms, and lifestyle challenge the basic assumptions of the surrounding society, has been discussed by M. J. Yinger (1982) *Countercultures: The Promise and Peril of a World Turned Upside Down* (New York: Free Press).

4. C. R. Brooks (1989) *The Hare Krishna in India* (Princeton, N.J.: Princeton University Press).

5. S. J. Judah (1974) *The Hare Krishna and the Counterculture* (New York: John Wiley and Sons); B. E. Rockford (1985) *Hare Krishna in America* (New Brunswick, N.J.: Rutgers University Press).

6. B. Rowland (1981) *The Art and Architecture of India* (New York: Penguin Books), p. 53; D. D. Kosambi (1969) *Ancient India: A History of Its Culture and Civilization* (Cleveland: World Publishing Company), pp. 108–109.

7. G. S. Ghurye (1958) *Bharatanatya and Its Costume* (Bombay: Bindor), pp. 48–51; M. Stutley (1980) *Ancient Indian Magic and Folklore* (London: Routledge and Kegan Paul), pp. 41–48, 61–64.

8. Kosambi, op. cit., pp. 105, 134.

9. Ibid., pp. 82–102.

10. Ibid., pp. 106–108; R. C. Craven (n.d.) *A Concise History of Indian Art* (New York: Oxford University Press), p. 33.

11. Kosambi, op. cit., pp. 106–111; Craven, op. cit., p. 32; R. F. Willis (1986) *World Civilizations: From Ancient Times Through the Sixteenth Century*, 2d ed. (Lexington, Mass.: D. C. Heath), pp. 70–71.

12. W. M. Kephart (1982) *Extraordinary Groups: The Sociology of Unconventional Life-Styles* (New York: St. Martin's), pp. 48–90.

13. L. M. Gurel (1979) "Four Hundred Years of Custom and Tradition: The Dress of Gentle Folk," in *Dimensions of Dress and Adornment: A Book of Readings*, ed. L. M. Gurel and M. S. Beeson (Dubuque, Iowa: Kendall/Hunt Publishing), pp. 40–50.

14. C. Wright (1986) *Mass Communication: A Sociological Perspective*, 3d ed. (New York: Random House).

15. S. Poll (1962) *The Hasidic Community of Williamsburg* (New York: Free Press).

16. Poll, op. cit., p. 60.

17. A. Lurie (1981) *The Language of Clothes* (New York: Random House), pp. 85–86.

18. Juliet Ash considered the Rastafarians' clothing "pure." She noted that the Rastafarians' obsession with appearance reflects their music and social roots. See J. Ash (1988) "The Business of Couture," in *Zoot Suits and Second Hand Dresses*, ed. A. McRobbie (Winchester, Mass.: Unwin Hyman), pp. 208–214.

19. L. E. Barret (1977) *The Rastafarians: Sounds of Cultural Dissonance* (Boston: Beacon Press); R. M. Mulvaney (1990) *Rastafari and Reggae: A Dictionary and Source Book* (Westport, Conn.: Greenwood Press), p. 69.

20. S. Cosgrove (1984) "The Zoot Suit and Style Warfare," in *Zoot Suits and Second Hand Dresses*, ed. A. McRobbie (Winchester, Mass.: Unwin Hyman), pp. 3–22.

21. M. Mazon (1984) *The Zoot Suit Riots: The Psychology of Symbolic Annihilation* (Austin: The University of Texas Press), p. 7.

22. O. Paz (1961) *The Labyrinth of Solitude: Life and Thought in Mexico*, trans. L. Kemp (New York: Grove Press). Quoted in Mazon, op. cit., pp. 114–116.

23. Ibid., pp. 109–114.

24. Mazon, op. cit., pp. 85–89.

25. Cosgrove, op. cit., p. 19.

26. H. Thompson (1967) *Hell's Angels: The Strange and Terrible Saga of the Outlaw Motorcycle Gangs* (New York: Ballantine Books), p. 95.

27. Ibid., p. 75.

28. Ibid., p. 73.

29. Ibid., p. 90.

30. Ibid., p. 90.

31. Ibid., p. 12.

32. Ibid., p. 57.

33. Ibid., p. 102.

34. Ibid., p. 100.

35. Ibid., pp. 100–101.

36. Ibid., p. 96.

37. K. Schoemer, "How Many Angels Danced at the Benefit?" *New York Times*, October 23, 1991.

Chapter 16

1. *New York Times*, February 10, 1991.

2. *New York Times*, July 29, 1992.

3. *New York Times*, March 1, 1993.

4. *New York Times*, July 22, 1991.

5. H. H. Hyman (1942) "The Psychology of Status," *Archives of Psychology*, no. 269.

6. E. Hurlock (1949) *Adolescent Development* (New York: McGraw-Hill), p. 15.

7. M. L. Rosencranz (1972) *Clothing Concepts: A Social-Psychological Approach* (New York: Macmillan), pp. 104–105.

8. *New York Times*, July 30, 1992.

9. *New York Times*, December 8, 1991.

10. The quotes in the following paragraphs are taken from student papers on the development of personal style, specifically the students' clothing experiences from early childhood on. Fashion Institute of Techology, New York, 1980–1992.

11. *New York Times*, December 8, 1991.

12. *New York Times*, September 11, 1990.

13. Student paper, Fashion Institute of Technology, New York.

14. *Toby Reports* (Spring 1985): 88; G. Dullea, "Madonna's New Beat Is a Hit, But Song's Message Rankles," *New York Times*, September 18, 1986.

15. Madonna's look-alike contest took place in May 1985 (store communication).

16. R. Martin and H. Koda (1989) *Jocks and Nerds: Men's Style in the Twentieth Century* (New York: Rizzoli).

17. *New York Times Magazine*, November 10, 1991.

18. See S. B. Kaiser (1985) *The Social Psychology of Clothing* (New York: Macmillan), pp. 239–240.

19. *Outweek*, November 28, 1990.

20. R. B. Edgerton and H. F. Dingman (1963) "Tatooing and Identity," *International Journal of Social Psychiatry* (9): 143–153; also J. H. Burma (1965) "Self Tatooing Among Delinquents," in *Dress Adornment and the Social Order*, ed. M. E. Roach and J. B. Eicher (New York: John Wiley and Sons), pp. 271–276.

21. C. R. Saunders (1989) *Colonizing the Body: The Art and Culture of Tatooing* (Philadelphia: Temple University Press).

22. E. Goffman (1963b) *Stigma: Notes on the Management of Spoiled Identity* (Englewood Cliffs, N.J.: Prentice-Hall).

23. E. B. Hurlock (1965) "The Arbiters of Fashion," in *Dress Adornment and the Social Order*, ed. M. E. Roach and J. B. Eicher (New York: John Wiley and Sons), p. 354.

24. Ibid., p. 355.

25. *Women's Wear Daily* 119 (1969), pp. 4–5; Rosencranz, op. cit., p. 224.

26. *Newsweek*, February 1, 1982, p. 59; "Nancy Reagan's Preference for Red," *Harper's Bazaar* (February 1984): 164.

27. P. Mathur, "Kathryn Hamnett, an Interview," *Blitz* (London), November 1989, pp. 22–27.

28. *New York Times*, December 17, 1991.

29. "Benetton's True Colors," *Ad Week*, August 24, 1992, pp. 27–30; "Corporate Profile: Benetton Colorful and Color Blind," *PR* (September 1991): 35–36; G. Shafer, "Benetton's United Front for Casual Colorful Fashion," *California Apparel News*, June 14, 1985, pp. 30–31.

30. M. J. Horn and L. M. Gurel (1981) *The Second Skin: An Interdisciplinary Study of Clothing*, 3d ed. (Boston: Houghton Mifflin), p. 196.

31. D. L. Wieder and D. H. Zimmerman (1974) "Generational Experience and the Development of Freak Culture," *Journal of Social Issues* 30 (2): 137–161.

32. M. Brake (1985) *Comparative Youth Culture* (New York: Routledge), p. 91.

33. R. H. Bainton (1952) *The Reformation of the Sixteenth Century* (Boston: Beacon Press); M. Mann (1986) *The Social Sources of Power*, vol. 1 (Cambridge: Cambridge University Press), pp. 463–472.

34. M. and A. Batterberry (1977) *Fashion: The Mirror of History* (New York: Greenwich House), pp. 194–197; B. Payne, G. Weinakor, and J. Farrell-Beck (1992) *The History of Costume: From Ancient Mesopotamia Through the Twentieth Century* (New York: HarperCollins), p. 438.

35. "Ku Klux Klan (KKK)," in *Collins Encyclopedia* (New York: Macmillan), 1985, p. 193; D. M. Chalmers (1965) *Hooded Americanism: The First Century of the Ku Klux Klan* (Garden City, N.Y.: Doubleday).

36. Chalmers, op. cit., p. 194.

Chapter 17

1. R. Marin, "Grunge: A Success Story," *New York Times*, November 15, 1992.

2. J. Jeannine, "Fashion's Young and Downwardly Mobile Set," *The Sunday Record*, February 7, 1993.

3. "Faith and Fashion Cross Paths in the New Talisman Jewelry, Soul Chains," *Mademoiselle* (June 1993), p. 14.

4. M. and A. Batterberry (1977) *Fashion: The Mirror of History* (New York: Greenwich House), pp. 107–109.

5. V. Steele (1988) *Paris Fashion* (New York: Oxford University Press), p. 23.

6. M. and A. Batterberry, op. cit., p. 144; Steele, op. cit., p. 22; B. Payne, G. Weinakor, and J. Farrell-Beck (1992) *The History of Costume* (New York: HarperCollins), pp. 364, 398–399.

7. M. and A. Batterberry, op. cit., p. 143.

8. Ibid., pp. 140–142.

9. A. M. Earle (1903) *Two Centuries of Costume in America 1620–1820* (Rutland, Vt.: Charles E. Tuttle), pp. 323–348; W. E. Wyckopf and H. C. Pitz (1935) *Early American Dress* (New York: B. Blom), p. 165.

10. A. Hollander (1978) *Seeing Through Clothes* (New York: Viking), pp. 370–373.

11. R. E. Neustadt (1960) *Presidential Power* (New York: John Wiley and Sons); also P. Woll and S. E. Zimmerman (1992) *American Government: The Core* (New York: McGraw-Hill), pp. 197–200.

12. R. Baker (1982) *Growing Up* (New York: New American Library), pp. 88–89, 122–123.

13. R. J. Sickels (1980) *The Presidency: An Introduction* (Englewood Cliffs, N.J.: Prentice-Hall), p. 6.

14. M. J. Horn and L. M. Gurel (1981) *The Second Skin: An Interdisciplinary Study of Clothing*, 3d ed. (Boston: Houghton Mifflin), p. 59.

15. In a lecture on May 18, 1992, at the Fashion Institute of Technology in New York, American designer Oscar de la Renta explained why, despite the added expense, he showed his fall 1992 collection in Paris.

16. Parisian and Italian designer boutiques line Fifth and Madison Avenues in New York City and have displays in major department stores throughout the United States. In the *New York Times* on Sept. 25, 1990, Woody Hochswender noted the expansion of Christian Dior into the U. S. market. According to the article, French-made merchandise would be offered in new stores in Beverly Hills, San Francisco, and Costa Mesa, California, and in Chicago and New York. Plans included a proposal to transform the Bonwit Teller site in Manhasset, New York, "into a series of luxury shops."

17. J. D. Barber (1977) *The Presidential Character: Predicting Performance in the White House*, 2d ed. (Englewood Cliffs, N.J.: Prentice-Hall); also in J. D. Barber (1980) "The Presidential Character," in *Classics of the American Presidency*, ed. H. A. Bailey, Jr. (Oak Park, Ill.: More Publishing), pp. 41–49. Barber suggested that the personality characteristics of a president, particularly his level of activity and enjoyment of life, may be used to predict the quality of his presidency. Robert J. Sickels, evaluating historical data of presidents and their childhood experience, concluded that there was no "neat matching" between childhood experience and adult presidential performance. See Sickels, op. cit.

18. S. R. Weisman (1984) "Ronald Reagan's Magical Style," in *American Government Personalities and Politics*, ed. P. Woll (Boston: Little, Brown), pp. 175–190.

19. L. Cannon (1990) *President Reagan: The Role of a Lifetime* (New York: Simon and Schuster), p. 20.

20. K. P. Phillips (1990) *The Politics of Rich and Poor: Wealth and the American Electorate in the Reagan Aftermath* (New York: Random House).

21. W. Raspberry, *Washington Post National Weekly Edition*, October 24–30, 1988.

22. *New York Times*, January 14, 1989.

23. J. C. Flugel (1966) *The Psychology of Clothes* (London: Hogarth Press), p. 59.

24. S. M. Lyman (1978) *The Seven Deadly Sins: Society and Evil* (New York: St. Martin's), pp. 72–74.

25. T. Veblen (1953) *The Theory of the Leisure Class* (New York: Mentor Books). Originally published 1899.

26. L. W. Banner (1983) *American Beauty: A Social History Through Two Centuries of the American Idea, Ideal, and Image of the Beautiful Woman* (New York: Knopf), p. 13.

27. B. Barber and L. S. Lobel (1952) "Fashion in Women's Clothes and the American Social System," *Social Forces* 31: 124–131.

28. G. M. Boyd, "Bush Inaugural Will Signal Open, Accessible President," *New York Times*, January 21, 1989, p. 7.

29. *Christian Science Monitor*, November 11, 1990.

30. *New York Times*, December 9, 1990.

31. Ibid.

32. *New York Times*, September 7, 1991.

33. See fashion magazines' offerings for fall 1990.

34. W.E.A. Budge and W. Thompson (1961) *Amulets and Talismans* (New Hyde Park, N.Y.: University Books).

35. There are other examples in history where fashion became more feminine during war. The most obvious is seen in a 1991 exhibit of World War II fashion at the Metropolitan Museum of Art in New York.

36. H. Blumer (1969) "Fashion: From Class Differentiation to Collective Selection," *Sociological Quarterly* 10: 275–291.

37. In a news story reporting that Wal-Mart outdistanced Sears as top U.S. retailer, the reporter attributed Wal-Mart's success to its use of new technology and new distribution methods. These innovations made it possible for Wal-Mart to keep better track of what it sold and what it did not sell and reorder what did (The Associated Press, April 12, 1991).

A description of the change in marketing strategies can be found in news about moves made by business executives. On May 14, 1992, Stephanie Strom reported in *USA Today* that the head of Lee Jeans shifted careers to become a maker of youthwear. She stated that the executive was hired because he had worked at The Limited, a company that has been very successful at finding out what consumers want and giving it to them.

38. A. M. Schlesinger, Sr. (1980) "Our Presidents: A Rating by 74 Historians," in *Classics of the American Presidency,* ed. H. A. Bailey, Jr., op. cit., pp. 380–386; D. B. James (1988) "Values, Structure and Presidential Power," *Presidental Studies Quarterly* 18(4): 761–784; R. G. Hoxie (1980) "The Power to Command," *Classics of the American Presidency,* ed. H. A. Bailey, Jr., op. cit., pp. 91–98.

39. R. Pistolese and R. Horsting (1970) *History of Fashions* (New York: John Wiley and Sons), pp. 287–288; M. and A. Batterberry, op. cit., 294–303.

40. D. L. Moore (1949) *The Woman in Fashion* (London: B. T. Batsford), p. 174.

41. Pistolese and Horsting, op. cit., p. 287.

42. A. T. Bailey and D. M. Kennedy (1987) *The American Pageant* (Lexington, Mass.: D. C. Heath), pp. 722–732.

43. F. L. Allan (1931) *Only Yesterday* (New York: Harper Brothers).

44. B. J. Bernstein, ed. (1970) *Politics and Policies of the Truman Administration* (Chicago: Quadrangle Books).

45. C. R. Milbank (1989) *New York Fashion: The Evolution of American Style* (New York: Harry N. Abrams), p. 143; also Payne, Weinakor, and Farrell-Beck, op. cit., pp. 604–607.

46. R. J. Donovan (1977) *Conflict and Crisis: The Presidency of Harry S. Truman* (New York: Norton), p. 163; also G. W. Cobliner (1950) "Feminine Fashion as an Aspect of Group Psychology: Analysis of Written Replies Received by Means of Questionnaire," *Journal of Social Psychology* 31: 283–289.

47. Payne, Weinakor, and Farrell-Beck, op. cit., pp. 614–615; M. and A. Batterberry, op. cit., p. 383.

48. Bailey and Kennedy, op. cit., p. 842.

Chapter 18

1. Sociologists generally agree that socialization is the process by which one internalizes culture and develops a sense of self. The notion of the self as an individuated being apart from family and community has its roots in the medieval period. It was in the late nineteenth century that the *idea* of private, personal identity became common. With the work of Henry James, Charles Horton Cooley, and George Herbert Mead, the study of the self came to be established as an important scientific pursuit. These theorists regarded the self as a distinct "universe" that could advance knowledge on the human condition. They saw the self and society as mutually intertwined. Critical theory, in contrast, views the self as a hostage of social arrangements. Responding to the question of why capitalism survived despite Karl Marx's expectation of its demise, critical theorists have suggested that capitalism encouraged the deepening and redoubling of false consciousness. Through experiences in the early years, the self had been further "co-opted." It had become accustomed to processes of domination and reification, developing false needs.

2. E. R. Leach (1957) "Magical Hair," Curl Bequest Prize Essay, *Journal of Royal Anthropological Institute* 88 (Part 2): 147–164.

3. T. J. Flygare (1977) "Teachers' Private Lives and Legal Rights," *Educational Digest* 42 (6): 26–28.

4. J. Rangel, "Top State Court Allows Inmate to Shun Haircut," *New York Times,* November 12, 1986.

5. "Mustaches Are Issue for Police," *New York Times,* July 1, 1992.

6. W. Wilson and the Editors of *Esquire* Magazine (1985) *Man at His Best: Esquire Guide to Style* (Reading, Mass.: Addison-Wesley).

7. "Airline Removes Agent for Not Using Makeup," *New York Times,* May 11, 1991.

8. "Continental Retracts Its Makeup Mandate for Female Workers," *New York Times,* May 16, 1991.

9. "Judging a Book's Sales by the Cover's Color," *New York Times,* November 26, 1991.

10. L. McGill (1980) *Disco Dressing* (Englewood Cliffs, N.J.: Prentice-Hall), p. 5.

11. Ibid., p. 1.

12. Ibid., p. 4.

13. Ibid., p. 5.

14. K. Anspach (1967) *The Why of Fashion* (Ames: Iowa State University Press), p. 314.

15. T. Egan, "Northwest Noir: An Art of Seriously Goofy," *New York Times,* July 14, 1991.

16. Wilson and the Editors of *Esquire* Magazine, op. cit., p. 188.

17. Ibid., p. 147.

18. J. C. Flugel (1966) *The Psychology of Clothes* (London: Hogarth Press), pp. 76–77.

19. Wilson and the Editors of *Esquire* Magazine, op. cit., pp. 20–32, 67.

20. S. J. Sweat and M. A. Zentner (1985) "Attributions Toward Female Appearance Styles," in *The Psychology of Fashion,* ed. M. R. Solomon (Lexington, Mass.: Lexington Books), pp. 321–333.

21. Flugel, op. cit., p. 75.

22. Ibid., pp. 74–76.

23. Ibid., pp. 61–62.

24. Ibid., p. 64.

25. R. A. Yassin (1985) "Art in Motion: Wearable Art," Indianapolis Museum of Art Exhibit, March 2–31. In a story in *Women's Wear Daily* (April 3, 1992), a distinction was made between wearable art and fashion. The story reported that Robert Lee Morris, who had designed fashion jewelry for Donna Karan, was opening a new show in his Soho gallery, Artwear. The collection would consist of fantasy pieces that could be worn.

26. On exhibit at the galleries of the Fashion Institute of Technology, February 11 to April 19, 1986.

27. Reporting from Paris (*New York Times,* July 24, 1989), Carrie Donovan noted that although fashion trends used to start in Paris and in due time show up in New York, now trends go both ways. Since 1988 New Yorkers have been sporting biker shorts as street fashion; now (in 1989) Parisians have taken them up in a big way. The snug shorts are worn with well-cut jackets, flat pumps, and chic Chanel-type bags.

28. Wilson and the Editors of *Esquire* Magazine, op. cit., pp. 22–23.

29. Reported by Jerry Schwartz in the *New York Times,* February 8, 1992.

30. R. Martin and H. Koda (1989) *Jocks and Nerds: Men's Style in the Twentieth Century* (New York: Rizzoli).

31. Flugel, op. cit., pp. 79–84.

32. *New York Times,* July 11, 1991.

33. S. Inoue (1980) "Interactions and Interpretations in Everyday Life," in *Studies in Symbolic Interaction,* ed. N. K. Denzin (Greenwich, Conn.: JAI Press), p. 1; also, William Grimes reports on a new type of sunglasses, E-54, that are popular because they are flirty. Glasses are designed to cover up, and a woman who pushes this pair of glasses down her nose, ostensibly to get a better look, "throws out a provocative gesture." See W. Grimes, *New York Times,* May 31, 1992.

34. Flugel, op. cit., p. 79.

35. Ibid., p. 80.

36. Ibid., p. 81.

37. Ibid., p. 83.

38. *New York Times,* September 23, 1990.

39. *New York Times,* April 28, 1991.

40. J. Talamini (1982) *And Boys Will Be Girls* (Washington, D.C.: University Press of America); also A. Levin (1978) "Dressing Up in Limbo," *New Times* (August): 7.

41. D. H. Feinbloom (1976) *Transvestites and Transsexuals* (New York: Delacorte Press).

42. T. Veblen (1953) *The Theory of the Leisure Class* (New York: Mentor Books), pp. 111–140 (originally published 1899); also J. Books (1979) *Showing Off in America* (Boston: Little, Brown).

43. See B. B. Hess, E. W. Markson, and P. J. Stein (1991) *Sociology*, 4th ed. (New York: Macmillan), pp. 350, 543. In trying to predict what the 1990s would be like for executives, Dierdre Fanning observed, "Executive stress is in vogue for 1991, but only because the country has slipped into recession." Executives will have to work longer and harder just to keep pace economically. See D. Fanning, *New York Times*, August 31, 1992.

44. *New York Times*, January 30, 1992.

45. "Costume Jewelry Gaining New Luster in the Search for Marketable Collectibles," *Antiques Today* 1992.

46. N. and E. Calas (1971) *Icons and Images of the Sixties* (New York: Dutton).

47. A. Mitchell (1978) *Values and Life Styles* (Menlo Park, Calif.: Stanford Research Institute [SRI]).

48. *New York Times*, August 26, 1992.

49. H. Smith (1982) *Beyond the Post-Modern Mind* (New York: Crossroads).

50. *New York Times*, July 18, 1991.

Conclusion

1. "President's Tie Tells All: Trumpets Are for Glory," *New York Times*, September 14, 1993.

2. B. Malinowski (1948) *Magic Science and Religion and Other Essays* (Garden City, N.Y.: Doubleday/Anchor). Originally published 1925.

3. *New York Times*, August 29, 1993.

Bibliography

Achenbaum, A. 1978. *Old Age in the New Land.* Baltimore: Johns Hopkins University Press.

Ackerknecht, E. H. 1982. *A Short History of Medicine.* Baltimore: Johns Hopkins University Press.

Aguilar, L. E. 1984. *Latin America.* Washington, D.C.: Stryker-Post Publications.

Alexander, E. 1990. *The Venus Hottentot.* Charlottesville: University Press of Virginia.

Allan, F. L. 1931. *Only Yesterday.* New York: Harper Brothers.

"A Message of Importance for the Serious Reader," *Esquire,* December 1968, pp. 186–189.

Apolonio, U., ed. 1973. *Futurist Manifestos: Documents of Twentieth Century Art.* New York: Viking Press.

Arnold, E. 1978. *Flashback! The 50's.* New York: Knopf.

Bade, P. 1979. *Femme Fatale: Images of Evil and Fascinating Women.* New York: Mayflower Books.

Baerwald, M., and T. Mahoney. 1960. *The Story of Jewelry.* New York: Abelard-Schumer.

Bailey, H. A., Jr., ed. 1980. *Classics of the American Presidency.* Oak Park, Ill.: More Publishing.

Baker, R. 1982. *Growing Up.* New York: New American Library.

Banner, L. W. 1983. *American Beauty: A Social History Through Two Centuries of the American Idea, Ideal, and Image of the Beautiful Woman.* New York: Knopf.

Barber, B., and L. S. Lobel. 1952. "Fashion in Women's Clothes and the American Social System," *Social Forces* 31: 124–131.

Barber, J. D. 1977. *The Presidential Character: Predicting Performance in the White House.* 2d ed. Englewood Cliffs, N.J.: Prentice-Hall.

Barret, L. E. 1977. *The Rastafarians: Sounds of Cultural Dissonance.* Boston: Beacon Press.

Barthes, R. 1967. *Elements of Semiology.* Trans. A. Lavers and C. Smith. London: Jonathan Cape.

————. 1972. *Mythologies.* Trans. A. Lavers. New York: Hill and Wang.

————. 1977. *Image-Music-Text.* Trans. S. Heath. New York: Noonday Press.

————. 1983. *The Fashion System.* Trans. M. Ward and R. Howard. New York: Hill and Wang.

Batterberry, M. and A. 1977. *Fashion: The Mirror of History.* New York: Greenwich House.

Baudrillard, J. 1981. *Simulacres et Simulation.* Paris: Éditions Galilée.

Bell, Q. 1976. *On Human Finery.* New York: Schocken Books.

Bernstein, B. J., ed. 1970. *Politics and Policies of the Truman Administration.* Chicago: Quadrangle Books.

Bishop, K. 1992. "Schools Order Students to Dress for Safety Sake," *New York Times,* January 22.

Bloch, M. 1961. *Feudal Society.* Trans. L. A. Manyon. Chicago: University of Chicago Press.

Blumer, H. 1968. "Fashion." In *International Encyclopedia of the Social Sciences.* New York: Macmillan.

————. 1969. "Fashion: From Class Differentiation to Collective Selection," *Sociology Quarterly* 10: 275–291.

Boehn, M. von. 1927. *Modes and Manners of the Nineteenth Century 1843–1878.* Vol. 3. Trans. M. Edwards. London: Dent.

————. 1932. *Modes and Manners.* Vol. 1. Trans. J. Joshua. New York: B. Blom.

Bogdan, R. 1988. *Freak Shows: Presenting Human Oddities for Amusement and Profit.* Chicago: University of Chicago Press.

Boucher, F. 1965. *Twenty Thousand Years of Fashion: The History of Costume and Personal Adornment.* New York: Harry N. Abrams.

Brain, R. 1979. *The Decorated Body.* New York: Harper and Row.

Bredemeier, H. C., and J. Toby. 1960. *Social Problems in America.* New York: John Wiley and Sons.

Brenninkenmeyer, I. 1963. *The Sociology of Fashion.* Paris: Librairie du Recueil Sirey; Koln-Opladen: Westdeutscher-Verlag.

Brooks, C. R. 1989. *The Hare Krishna in India.* Princeton, N.J.: Princeton University Press.

Brown, P. 1988. *The Body and Society: Men, Women and Sexual Renunciation in Early Christianity.* New York: Columbia University Press.

Budge, W.E.A., and W. Thompson. 1961. *Amulets and Talismans.* New Hyde Park, N.Y.: University Books.

Bullough, V. and B. 1978. *Prostitution: An Illustrated Social History.* New York: Crown Publishers.

Bureau of Labor Statistics. 1988. Bulletin 2307. Washington, D.C.: U.S. Government Printing Office.

Carlyle, T. 1967. *Sartor Resartus.* New York: Dutton. (Originally published in 1838)

Carman, W. Y. 1957. *British Military Uniforms from Contemporary Pictures: Henry VII to the Present Day.* London: Leonard Hill.

Cassirer, E. 1961."Ideational Content of the Sign." In *Theories of Society: Foundations of Modern Sociology,* ed. T. Parsons et al. Vol. 2, pp. 1004–1008. New York: Free Press.

Chalmers, D. M. 1965. *Hooded Americanism: The First Century of the Ku Klux Klan, 1865–1965.* Garden City, N.Y.: Doubleday.

Chambers, M., R. Grew, T. Herlihy, T. Rabb, and I. Woloch. 1974. *The Western Experience.* New York: Knopf.

Child, H., and D. Colles. 1971. *Magic and Superstition: Ancient and Modern.* New York: Scribner's.

Clark, K. 1956. *The Nude: A Study in Ideal Art Form.* London: John Murray.

Clegg, R., and W. A. Thompson. 1979. *Modern Sports Officiating: A Practical Guide.* 2d. ed. Dubuque, Iowa: W. C. Brown.

Cobliner, G. W. 1950. "Feminine Fashion as an Aspect of Group Psychology: Analysis of Written Replies Received by Means of Questionnaire," *Journal of Social Psychology* 31: 283–289.

Coser, L. A. 1992. *Maurice Halbwachs on Collective Memory.* Chicago: University of Chicago Press.

Cosgrove, S. 1984. "The Zoot Suit and Style Warfare." In *Zoot Suits and Second Hand Dresses,* ed. A. McRobbie. Winchester, Mass.: Unwin Hyman.

Costumes of Religious Orders of the Middle Ages. 1983. West Orange, N.J.: Albert Saifer. (Originally published in 1718)

Craven, R. C. Undated. *A Concise History of Indian Art.* New York: Oxford University Press.

Creelan, P., and R. Granfield. 1989. "The Polish Peasant and Pilgrim's Progress Morality and Mythology in W. I. Thomas' Social Theory." Paper delivered at the Meeting of the American Sociological Association.

Cunnington, P., C. Lucas, and A. Mansfield. 1967. *Occupational Costume in England from the 11th Century to 1914.* London: Adam & Charles Black.

Davenport, M. 1972. *The Book of Costume.* New York: Crown Publishing.

Davis, F. 1986. "Gender, Fashion and the Dialectic of Identity." Paper prepared for the Society for the Study of Symbolic Interaction Symposium on Information, Communication, and Social Structure held at the University of Iowa, May 1–3, 1986.

———. 1992. *Fashion, Culture and Identity.* Chicago: University of Chicago Press.

de Certeau, M. 1985. *Heterologies: Discourse on the Other.* Trans. B. Massumi. Minneapolis: University of Minnesota Press.

Deruisseau, L. G. 1939. "Dress Fashions of the Italian Renaissance," *CIBA Review* (January).

Donovan, R. J. 1977. *Conflict and Crisis: The Presidency of Harry S. Truman.* New York: Norton.

Douglas, M. 1970. *Natural Symbols.* New York: Pantheon Books.

Dulles, F. R. 1940. *America Learns to Play: A History of Popular Recreation, 1607–1940.* New York: Appelton-Century.

Ebin, V. 1979. *The Body Decorated.* London: Thames and Hudson.

Eco, U. 1986. "How Culture Conditions the Colors We See." In *On Signs,* ed. M. Blonsky. Baltimore: Johns Hopkins University Press.

Eder, D., and S. Parker. 1985. "Cultural Reproduction of Gender Relations and Values: The Effect of Extracurricular Activities on Peer Group Culture." Paper delivered at the Meeting of the American Sociological Association.

Elliott, J. H. 1987. "The Court of the Spanish Habsburgs: A Peculiar Institution?" In *Politics and Culture in Modern Early Europe,* ed. P. Mack and M. C. Jacobs. Cambridge: Cambridge University Press.

Erman, A. 1971. *Life in Ancient Egypt.* New York: Dover Publications. (Originally published in 1894)

Fairlie, H. 1973. *The Kennedy Promise.* New York: Doubleday.

Faludi, S. 1991. *Backlash.* New York: Doubleday.

Faris, J. C. 1972. *Nuba Personal Art.* London: Duckworth.

Farren, M. 1985. *The Black Leather Jacket.* New York: Abbeville Press.

Fisk, J. 1989. *Understanding Popular Culture.* Boston: Unwin.

Flugel, J. C. 1966. *The Psychology of Clothes.* London: Hogarth Press. (Originally published in 1930)

Forbes, W. H. 1968. "Laboratory Field Studies: General Principles." In *The Physiology of Heat Regulation and the Science of Clothing,* pp. 320–329, ed. L. H. Newburgh. New York: Stretchet Haffner.

Form, W. H., and G. P. Stone. 1957. "Urbanism, Anonimity and Status Symbolism," *American Journal of Sociology* 62 (5): 504–514.

Foucault, M. 1972. *The Archeology of Knowledge.* New York: Harper and Row.

Gains, J., and C. Herzog. 1990. *Fabrications: Costume and the Female Body.* New York: Routledge.

Gallagher, C., and T. Lacquer, eds. 1987. *The Making of the Modern Body: Sexuality and Society in the Nineteenth Century.* Berkeley: University of California Press.

Gans, H. J. 1974. *Popular Culture and High Culture.* New York: Basic Books.

Gaster, T. H. 1959. *The New Golden Bough: A New Abridgment of Sir James George Frazer's Classic Work.* New York: Criterion Books.

Gelb, I. J., P. Steinkeller, and R. M. Whiting, Jr. 1991. *Earliest Land Tenure Systems in the Near East: Ancient Kudurrus.* The Oriental Institute: University of Chicago Publications, vol. 104.

Ghurye, G. S. 1958. *Bharatanatya and Its Costume.* Bombay: Bindor.

Godson, S. H. 1984. "Women Power in World War I." In *Proceedings, U.S. Naval Institute.* Annapolis, Md.: U.S. Naval Institute.

Goffman, E. 1951."Symbols of Class Status," *British Journal of Sociology.* A (4): 294–303.

———. 1959. *The Presentation of Self in Everyday Life.* Garden City, N.Y.: Doubleday.

———. 1963a. *Behavior in Public Places.* New York: Free Press.

———. 1963b. *Stigma: Notes on the Management of Spoiled Identity.* Englewood Cliffs, N.J.: Prentice-Hall.

———. 1967. *Interaction Ritual.* Garden City, N.Y.: Doubleday/Anchor Books.

———. 1971. *Relations in Public.* New York: Harper and Row.

Gombrich, E. 1979. *The Sense of Order: A Study in the Psychology of Decorative Arts.* Ithaca, N.Y.: Cornell University Press.

Gorman, T. 1979. *Three and Two* (as told to Jerom Holtzman). New York: Scribner's.

Gottdiener, M. 1977. "Unisex Fashions and Gender-Role Change," *Semiotic Scene* 1 (3): 13–37.

Gross, E., and G. P. Stone. 1964. "Embarrassment and the Analysis of Role Requirements," *American Journal of Sociology* 57 (July): 1–15.

Guthrie, L. M. 1984. "I Was a Yeomanette." In *Proceedings, U.S. Naval Institute*. Annapolis, Md.: U.S. Naval Institute.

Halbwachs, M. 1980. *The Collective Memory.* Trans. F. J. Ditter, Jr., and V. Y. Ditter. New York: Harper and Row.

Hansen, J., and E. Reed. 1986. *Cosmetics, Fashions, and the Exploitation of Women.* New York: Pathfinder Press.

Hargreaves-Mawdsley, W. N. 1963a. *A History of Academic Dress in Europe Until the End of the Eighteenth Century.* Oxford: Clarendon Press.

_____. 1963b. *A History of Legal Dress in Europe Until the End of the Eighteenth Century.* Oxford: Clarendon Press.

Hargrove, E. C. 1980. "Presidential Pesonality and Revisionist Views of the Presidency." In *Classics of the American Presidency,* ed. H. A. Bailey, Jr. Oak Park, Ill.: More Publishing.

Harris, M. 1985. *Bikers: Birth of a Modern-Day Outlaw.* London: Faber and Faber.

Hartmann, S. M. 1982. *The Home Front and Beyond: American Women in the 1940s.* Boston: Twayne Publishers.

Head, J. R., Sr. 1967. "Medicine from 1800 to 1850." In *The Growth of Modern Medicine,* ed. F. Stenn. Springfield, Ill.: Charles C. Thomas.

Hebdige, D. 1979. *Subculture: The Meaning of Style.* New York: Methuen.

Hess, B. B. 1976. *Growing Old in America.* New Brunswick, N.J.: Transaction Books.

Hill, D. A. 1968. *Magic and Superstition.* London: Feltham Hamlin.

Hoch-Smith, J. 1978. *Women in Ritual and Symbolic Roles.* New York: Plenum.

Hollander, A. 1978. *Seeing Through Clothes.* New York: Viking Press.

Hooper, W. 1915. "The Tudor Sumptuary Laws," *English Historical Review* 30: 444–449.

Hoxie, R. G. 1980. "The Power to Command." In *Classics of the American Presidency,* ed. H. A. Bailey, Jr. Oak Park, Ill.: More Publishing.

Hyman, H. H. 1942. "The Psychology of Status," *Archives of Psychology,* no. 269.

Inglis, B. 1965. *A History of Medicine.* New York: World Publishing Company.

Jacques, D. H. 1859. *Hints Toward Physical Perfection.* New York: Fowler and Wells.

James, D. B. 1988. "Values, Structure and Presidential Power," *Presidental Studies Quarterly* 18 (4): 761–784.

Johnson, H. 1990. *Sleepwalking Through History: America in the Reagan Years.* New York: Norton.

Johnson, J. D., and P. J. Xanthos. 1981. *Tennis.* 4th ed. Dubuque, Iowa: Wm. C. Brown.

Joseph, N. 1986. *Uniforms and Nonuniforms: Communication Through Clothing.* Westport, Conn.: Greenwood Press.

Kahlenberg, M. H., and A. Berlant. 1972. *The Navajo Blanket.* New York: Praeger.

Kaiser, S. B. 1985. *The Social Psychology of Clothing.* New York: Macmillan.

Kantrowicz, E. H. 1966. "Kingship Under the Impact of and Scientific Jurisprudence." In *Twelfth-Century Europe and the Foundations of Modern Society,* pp. 89–111, ed. M. Clagett, G. Post, and R. Reynolds. Westport, Conn.: Greenwood Press.

Kearns, D. 1977. "Lyndon Johnson's Political Personality." In *The Presidency Reappraised,* ed. E. T. Cronin and R. G. Tugwell. 2d ed. New York: Praeger.

Kellerman, A. 1918. *Physical Beauty.* New York: George H. Doran.

Kessler, J. B. 1980. *Getting Even with Getting Old.* Chicago: Nelson-Hall.

König, R. 1973. *A La Mode: On the Social Psychology of Fashion.* New York: Seabury Press.

Kosambi, D. D. 1969. *Ancient India: A History of Its Culture and Civilization.* Cleveland: World Publishing Company.

Kunz, G. F. 1915. *The Magic of Jewels and Charms.* Philadelphia: J. B. Lippincott.

Lamy, P., and J. Levin. 1984. "Punk and Middle-Class Values: A Content Analysis." Paper delivered at the Meeting of the American Sociological Association.

Langner, L. 1959. *The Importance of Wearing Clothes.* New York: Hastings House.

Laver, J. 1937. *Taste and Fashion: From the French Revolution to Today.* London: George G. Herrap.

————. 1963. *Costume.* New York: Hawthorne Books.

————. 1969. *Modesty in Dress.* Boston: Houghton Mifflin.

Lawner, L. 1987. *Lives of the Courtesans.* New York: Rizzoli.

Lawrence, C. F. 1981. *The German "Bauernkrieg" of 1525: Organization and Action of Peasant Revolt.* Ann Arbor, Mich.: University of Michigan Microfilm International.

Leach, E. R. 1957. "Magical Hair." Curl Bequest Prize Essay. *Journal of Royal Anthropological Institute* 88 (2): 147–164.

Leach, M., ed. 1971. *Dictionary of Folklore Mythology and Legend.* New York: Funk and Wagnals.

Levin, A. 1978. "Dressing Up in Limbo," *New Times* (August): 7.

Levin, D. B., with W. Hoffer. 1992. *Inside Out: A True Story of Greed, Scandal and Redemption.* New York: Berkley Books.

Lewis, P. 1978. *The Fifties.* Philadelphia: J. B. Lippincott.

Lichtenstein, M. E. 1967. "The Origins of Modern Surgery: 1850–1900." In *The Growth of Modern Medicine*, ed. F. Stenn. Springfield, Ill.: Charles C. Thomas.

Lobelle-Caluwe, H. Undated. *The Memlingmuseum in St. John Hospital.* Bruges, Belgium: Die Keure.

Lofland, L. H. 1973. *A World of Strangers. Order and Action in Urban Public Space.* New York: Basic Books.

Lurie, A. 1981. *The Language of Clothes.* New York: Random House.

Lurker, M. 1980. *The Gods and Symbols of Ancient Egypt.* London: Thames and Hudson.

Lyman, S. M. 1978. *The Seven Deadly Sins: Society and Evil.* New York: St. Martin's.

————. 1989. *The Seven Deadly Sins: Society and Evil.* Revised and expanded ed. Dix Hills, N.Y.: General Hall.

McClelland, D. 1961. *The Achieving Society.* Princeton: Van Nostrand.

McGill, L. 1980. *Disco Dressing.* Englewood Cliffs, N.J.: Prentice-Hall.

Mack, P., and M. C. Jacobs, eds. 1987. *Politics and Culture in Early Modern Europe.* Cambridge: Cambridge University Press.

Mahood, L. 1990. *The Magdalenes: Prostitution in the Nineteenth Century.* New York: Routledge, Chapman and Hall.

Malinowski, B. 1948. *Magic Science and Religion and Other Essays.* Garden City, N.Y.: Doubleday/Anchor Books. (Originally published in 1925.)

Malvano, L. 1988. *Fascismo e politica dell'immagine.* Torino: Bollati Boringhieri.

Mannheim, K. 1952. *Essays on the Sociology of Knowledge*, ed. S. Kecskemeti. London: Routledge and Kegan Paul.

Maritain, J. 1924. *Art and Scholasticism.* Trans. J. F. Scanlan. New York: Scribner's.

Martin, R., and H. Koda. 1989. *Jocks and Nerds: Men's Style in the Twentieth Century.* New York: Rizzoli.

Marwick, A. 1988. *Beauty in History.* London: Thames and Hudson.

Mayer-Thurman, C. C. 1975. *Raiment for the Lord's Service: A Thousand Years of Western Vestments.* Chicago: The Art Institute of Chicago.

Mayo, J. 1984. *A History of Ecclesiastical Dress.* New York: Holmes and Meier.

Mazon, M. 1984. *The Zoot Suit Riots: The Psychology of Symbolic Annihilation.* Austin: University of Texas Press.

Miles, M. R. 1985. "The Virgin's One Bare Breast: Female Nudity and Religious Meaning in Tuscan Early Renaissance Art." In *The Female Body in Western Culture*, ed. S. R. Suleiman. Cambridge: Harvard University Press.

Millman, M. 1980. *Such a Pretty Face: Being Fat in America.* New York: Norton.

————. 1977. *The Women Dress for Success Book.* Chicago: Follett Publishing.

Molloy, J. T. 1978. *Dress for Success.* New York: Warner Books.

Montrose, L. A. 1983. "Shaping Fantasies Figurative of Gender and Power in Elizabethan Culture," *Representations* 1: 2.

Moore, D. L. 1949. *The Woman in Fashion.* London: B. T. Batsford.

Morgan, T. E., ed. 1990. *Victorian Sages and Cultural Discourse.* New Brunswick, N.J.: Rutgers University Press.

Morris, C. 1972. *The Discovery of the Individual 1050–1200.* New York: Harper Torchbooks.

Mosse, G. L. 1978. *The Final Solution: A History of European Racism.* New York: Howard Fertig.

Mukerji, C. 1983. *From Graven Images: Patterns of Modern Materialism.* New York: Columbia University Press.

Mulvaney, R. M. 1990. *Rastafari and Reggae: A Dictionary and Source Book.* Westport, Conn.: Greenwood Press.

Murray, H. A., ed. 1960. *Myth and Mythmaking.* Boston: Beacon Press.

Myers, R. J. 1972. *Celebrations: The Complete Book of American Holidays.* Garden City, N.Y.: Doubleday.

Nef, J. 1958. *Cultural Foundation of Industrial Civilization.* New York: Harper and Row.

Neustadt, R. E. 1960. *Presidential Power.* New York: John Wiley and Sons.

Newburgh, L. H., ed. 1968. *The Physiology of Heat Regulation and the Science of Clothing.* New York: Stretchet Haffner.

Nickel, H., H. W. Pyhrr, and L. Tarassuk. 1982. *The Art of Chivalry.* New York: The Metropolitan Museum of Art.

Nystrom, P. 1928. *The Economics of Fashion.* New York: Roland Press.

Olsen, M. E., and M. N. Martin, eds. 1993. *Power in Modern Societies.* Boulder: Westview Press.

Ostrander, S. A. 1984. *Women of the Upper Class.* Philadelphia: Temple University Press.

Payne, B., G. Weinakor, and J. Farrell-Beck. 1992. *The History of Costume: From Ancient Mesopotamia Through the Twentieth Century.* New York: HarperCollins.

Perati, C. 1987. *Extraordinary Origins of Everyday Things.* New York: Harper and Row.

Perinbanayagam, R. S. 1987. "Drama in Everyday Life." In *Studies in Symbolic Interaction,* ed. N. K. Denzin. Vol. 8. Greenwich, Conn.: JAI Press.

Peters, L. H. 1918. *Diet and Health with Key to Calories.* Chicago: Reilly & Lee.

Pickering, D., ed. 1762. *The Statutes at Large from the Magna Carta to the End of the Eleventh Parliament of Great Britain (1701).* Vol. 1. Cambridge: Cambridge University Press.

Poll, S. 1962. *The Hasidic Community of Williamsburg.* New York: Free Press.

Pottinger, F. M. 1952. *The Fight Against Tuberculosis.* New York: Henry Schuman.

Powell, P., and L. Peel. 1988. *'50s & '60s Style.* New York: Chartwell Books.

Poynter, N. 1971. *Medicine and Man.* London: C. A. Watts.

Pritchet, H. C. 1977. "The President's Constitutional Position." In *The Presidency Reappraised,* ed. T. E. Cronin and R. G. Tugwell. New York: Praeger.

Proceedings, U.S. Naval Institute. Annapolis, Md.: U.S. Naval Institute.

Rabinow, P. 1975. *Symbolic Domination: Cultural Form and Historical Change.* Chicago: University of Chicago Press.

Reagan, R. 1990. *An American Life: The Autobiography.* New York: Simon and Schuster.

Rechy, J. 1977. *The Sexual Outlaw: A Documentary.* New York: Grove Press.

Reuther, R. R., ed. 1974. *Religion and Sexism: Images of Women in Jewish and Christian Traditions.* New York: Simon and Schuster.

Richardson, J. 1966. *The Courtesan.* Cleveland: World Publishing.

Riesman, D. 1954. *Individualism Reconsidered.* New York: Free Press.

Roach, M. E., and J. B. Eicher, eds. 1985. *Dress Adornment and the Social Order.* New York: John Wiley and Sons.

Rockford, B. E., and E. Burke. 1985. *Hare Krishna in America.* New Brunswick, N.J.: Rutgers University Press.

Root, W., and R. de Rochemont. 1976. *Eating in America: A History.* New York: Ecco Press.

Rose, P. I. 1972. *Seeing Ourselves, Readings in Sociology and Society.* New York: Knopf.

Rowland, B. 1981. *The Art and Architecture of India.* New York: Penguin Books.

Rucker, M., D. Taber, and A. Harrison. 1981. "The Effect of Clothing Variation on First Impressions of Female Job Applicants: What to Wear When?" *Social Behavior and Personality* 9 (1): 53–64.

Rudofsky, B. 1971. *The Unfashionable Human Body.* Garden City, N.Y.: Doubleday.

Safire, W. 1990. "Keep Your Shirt On," *New York Times Magazine,* May 13.

Salmon, E., ed. 1977. *Bernhardt and the Theater of Her Time.* Westport, Conn.: Greenwood Press.

Saunders, E. 1955. *The Age of Worth: Couturier to Empress Eugènie.* Bloomington: Indiana University Press.

Schlenker, B. 1980. *Impression Management: The Self Concept, Social Identity, and Interpersonal Relations.* Monterey, Calif.: Brooks-Cole.

Schlesinger, A. M., Sr. 1980. "Our Presidents: A Rating by 74 Historians." In *Classics of the American Presidency,* pp. 380–386, ed. H. A. Bailey, Jr. Oak Park, Ill.: More Publishing.

Schneider, J. 1978. "Peacocks and Penguins: The Political Economy of European Cloth and Colors," *American Ethnologist* 5 (3): 413–447.

Scott, M. 1980. *The History of Dress Series, Late Gothic Europe, 1400–1500.* London: Mills and Boon.

Selected Writings of St. Thomas Aquinas. 1965. Trans. R. P. Goodwin. New York: Bobbs-Merrill.

Sennett, R. 1974. *The Fall of Public Man.* New York: Knopf.

Severin, T. 1973. *Vanishing Primitive Man.* New York: American Heritage.

Sickels, R. J. 1980. *The Presidency: An Introduction.* Englewood Cliffs, N.J.: Prentice-Hall.

Sigall, H., and N. Ostrove. 1975. "Beautiful But Dangerous: Effects of Offender Attractiveness and Nature of the Crime on Juridic Judgement," *Journal of Personality and Social Psychology* 31 (3).

Simmel, G. 1957. "Fashion," *American Journal of Sociology* 62: 541–558. (Originally published in 1904)

Sinclair, U. 1927. *Oil!* New York: Albert Charles Boni.

Smeeding, T., B. Boyle Torrey, and M. Rein. 1988. "Patterns of Income and Poverty: The Economic Status of Children and the Elderly in Eight Countries." In *The Vulnerable,* ed. J. L. Palmer, T. Smeeding, and B. B. Torrey. Washington, D.C.: Urban Institute Press.

Smith, G., and B. J. Smith, eds. 1972. *The Police Gazette.* New York: Simon and Schuster.

Sorensen, T. C. 1965. *Kennedy.* New York: Harper and Row.

Sozinskey, T. S. 1877. *The Culture of Beauty.* Philadelphia: Allen, Lane and Scott.

Spencer, H. 1969. *The Principles of Sociology,* ed. S. Andreski. Hamden, Conn.: Archon Books.

Steele, V. 1985. *Fashion and Eroticism.* New York: Oxford University Press.

———. 1988. *Paris Fashion.* New York: Oxford University Press.

———. 1991. *Women of Fashion: Twentieth-Century Designers.* New York: Rizzoli.

Stern, J. 1986. "Literary Images of Women in Work Force: Colonial Times to Present," *F.I.T. Review* 3 (1).

Stone, G. P. 1959. *Clothing and Social Relations: A Study of Appearance in the Context of Community Life.* Ph.D. diss. submitted to the Dept. of Sociology, University of Chicago, July 1959.

_____. 1962. "Appearance and the Self." In *Dress Adornment and the Social Order,* ed. M. E. Roach and J. B. Eicher. New York: John Wiley and Sons.

Stone, L. 1965. *The Crisis of the Aristocracy.* London: Oxford University Press.

Strommenger, E. Undated. *500 Years of the Art of Mesopotamia.* New York: Harry N. Abrams.

Stutley, M. 1980. *Ancient Indian Magic and Folklore.* London: Routledge and Kegan Paul.

Suleiman, S. R., ed. 1985. *The Female Body in Western Culture.* Cambridge: Harvard University Press.

Sumner, W. G. 1925. *What Social Classes Owe to Each Other.* New Haven: Yale University Press.

Susman, W. I. 1984. *Culture as History: The Transformation of American Society in the Twentieth Century.* New York: Pantheon Books.

Taylor, F. 1911. *The Principles of Scientific Management.* New York: Harper Brothers.

Thompson, H. 1967. *Hell's Angels: The Strange and Terrible Saga of the Outlaw Motorcycle Gangs.* New York: Ballantine Books.

Thompson, J., ed. 1983. *Image Impact for Men.* New York: A & W Publishers.

Thompson, J. B. 1990. *Ideology and Modern Culture.* Stanford: Stanford University Press.

Tolmach, R. L., and L. R. Scherr. 1984. *Face Value: The Politics of Beauty.* Boston: Routledge.

Turner, V. W. 1969. *The Ritual Process.* New York: Aldine.

U.S. Bureau of Labor Statistics. 1988. *Labor Force Statistics Derived from the Current Population Survey.* Bulletin 2307. Washington, D.C.: U.S. Department of Labor, Bureau of Labor, Statistics.

Uzane, L. O. 1898. *Fashions in Paris. The Various Phases of Feminine Taste and Esthetics from 1797 to 1897.* London: William Heinemann.

Van Dalen, D. B., E. D. Mitchell, and B. L. Bennett. 1953. *A World History of Physical Education.* Englewood Cliffs, N.J.: Prentice-Hall.

Veblen, T. 1953. *The Theory of the Leisure Class.* New York: Mentor Books. (Originally published in 1899.)

Vicary, G. Q. 1989. "Visual Art as Social Data: The Renaissance Codpiece," *Cultural Anthropology* 4 (1): 3–25.

Wagner, R. 1986. *Symbols That Stand for Themselves.* Chicago: University of Chicago Press.

Walch, M. 1985. "American Sportswear Colors," *American Fabrics and Fashion* 133: 4–5.

Walkowitz, J. R. 1980. *Prostitution and Victorian Society.* Cambridge: Cambridge University Press.

Wax, M. 1957. "Themes in Cosmetics and Grooming," *American Journal of Sociology* 62: 588–593.

Williams, R. H. 1982. *Dream Worlds: Mass Consumption in Late Nineteenth-Century France.* Berkeley: University of California Press.

Williams, Robin M., Jr. 1970. *American Society: A Sociological Interpretation.* 3d ed. New York: Knopf.

Willoughby, B., and R. Schickel. 1974. *The Platinum Years.* New York: Random House.

Wilson, M. 1967. *Gems.* New York: Viking.

Wilson, W., and the Editors of *Esquire* Magazine. 1985. *Man at His Best: The Esquire Guide to Style.* Reading, Mass.: Addison-Wesley.

Witherspoon, G. 1977. *Language and Art in the Navajo Universe.* Ann Arbor: University of Michigan Press.

Wolf, N. 1991. *The Beauty Myth: How Images of Beauty Are Used Against Women.* New York: William Morrow.

Wolf, R. 1991. *Goya and the Satirical Print in England and on the Continent 1730–1850.* Boston: Boston College Museum of Art.

Woll, P., and S. E. Zimmerman. 1992. *American Government: The Core.* New York: McGraw-Hill.

Wood, M. 1990. "Consumer Behavior: Impression Management by Professional Servers."
    Paper prepared for presentation at the 85th Annual Meeting of the American Sociologi-
    cal Association, Washington, D.C., August 11–15.

Wulsin, F. R. 1968. "Adaptations to Climate Among Non-European Peoples." In *The Physiol-
    ogy of Heat Regulation and the Science of Clothing,* ed. L. H. Newburgh. New York:
    Stretchet Haffner.

Zanker, P. 1990. *The Power of Images in the Age of Augustus.* Trans. P. Shapiro. Ann Arbor:
    University of Michigan Press.

About the Book and Author

Rich with illustrations, *Dress Codes* systematically analyzes the meaning and relevance of clothing in American culture. Presented here in one book for the first time are theories of clothing and an up-to-date analysis of images of power and authority, gender, seduction (the sexy look, the alluring look, the glamorous look, the vulnerable look), wealth and beauty, youth and health, and leisure and political hierarchy. Taken together, the chapters offer to the student and the general reader a complete "semiotics of clothing" in a form that is highly readable, very entertaining, and thoroughly informative. The illustrations provide fascinating glimpses into the history of American fashion and clothing—along with their antecedents in Europe—as well as a fine collection of images from the more familiar world of contemporary America.

After ten years of teaching and research, Rubinstein has identified six distinct categories of dress in American society, upon which *Dress Codes* is based. "Clothing signs" have only one meaning and are instituted by those in authority as required attire (police uniform, nun's attire); "clothing symbols," which have several meanings and involve individual choice (designer clothing, jewelry); "clothing tie-signs," which are specific types of clothing that indicate membership in a community outside mainstream culture (Hasidic, Amish, or Hare Krishna attire); "clothing tie-symbols," which act as a means of broader social affiliation emanating especially from fears, hopes, and dreams (Save the Earth clothing, Pro-Choice T-shirts, Madonna's crosses); "personal dress," which refers to the "I" component we bring in when dressing the public self (bowtie, dramatic, or artistic attire); and "contemporary fashion," which is the interaction between political and economic events and consumer sentiments, involving public memory.

Written in a lively and entertaining style, *Dress Codes* will fascinate both general readers and students interested in the history of fashion and costume, fashion design, human development, and gender studies.

Ruth P. Rubinstein is professor of sociology at the Fashion Institute of Technology, State University of New York.

Index